LEADING LADIES

22 Visionary Women Share Their Journeys, Insights, & Secrets To Network Marketing Leadership

"This is a no-holds-barred, genuine collection of personal lessons from twenty-two women who have faced the good, the bad, and the ugly of personal and professional life, turning challenges into triumphs and becoming the heroines of their own stories."

— Donna Johnson

LEADING LADIES

22 Visionary Women Share Their Journeys, Insights, & Secrets To Network Marketing Leadership

ntwrkr PUBLISHING
ntwrkr.com

LEADING LADIES

22 Visionary Women Share Their Journeys, Insights, & Secrets To Network Marketing Leadership

Copyright © 2024 · ntwrkr Publishing LLC

All rights reserved. No portion of this book may be reproduced, stored in a retrieval system, or transmitted in any form or by any means - electronic, mechanical, photocopy, recording, scanning, or other - except for brief quotations in critical reviews or articles, without the prior written permission of the publisher.

ISBN 979-8-9860322-4-5 eBook
ISBN 979-8-9860322-5-2 Paperback

ntwrkr PUBLISHING
ntwrkr.com

DEDICATION

To My Family

I do everything for you.

I do nothing without you.

Alisa Hussey

Dylan Hussey

Brielle Hussey

Emerson Hussey

Finley Hussey

CONTENTS

Dedication   *vi*

Foreword   *xi*

Acknowledgements   *xvii*

Introduction   *xix*

1. Sarah Zolecki - The 'BE' Attributes   **1**
How Cultivating Relationships Transforms Your Life & Business

2. Kathleen Vicenzotti - Mastering Self-Leadership   **17**
The 3 Core Traits That Will Inspire The World To Follow You

3. Aspen Emry - Becoming Brave   **31**
Foundational Moments When Unrelenting Courage Shapes Your Life

4. Heather Cain Wisenbaker - Do It Messy, Do It Scared, Do It Now   **49**
Why Doing It Messy Is The Key To Success

5. Johanna Gil-Bala - The Power Of A Single Day   **67**
The 10 Superpowers I Use Everyday To Create My Ultimate Life

6. Misty Lavertu - If It's To Be...   **83**
The Network Marketing 'Personals' That Shape Your Path To Success

CONTENTS

7. Deni Robinson - The Art Of Seeing — **101**
How To Cast Your Personal Vision & Create A Legacy That Inspires Generations

8. Heidi Black - Alignments Before Assignments — **119**
How The People You Align Yourself With Dictate Your Life & Business Success

9. Diane Hochman - Life's Leverage — **137**
Unleashing Life's Hidden Leverage Points for Maximized Living

10. Alisha Lindsey - Be A Gold Digger — **153**
5 Ways To Excavate Greatness From The Women In Your Tribe

11. Michelle Barnes - You Are What You Think — **173**
The Path From Thought, To Feelings, To Action, To Results

12. Brittany Beck - Building Unbreakable Bonds — **191**
The Roadmap That Transforms Your Team Into A Sisterhood

13. Alyssa Favreau - The Time Is Now — **209**
7 Reasons To Start Chasing Your Dreams This Second

14. Danielle Singh - From Surviving To Thriving — **231**
Turning Your Traumatic Past Into An Empowered Future For Yourself & Others

15. Amalia Sorhent - It's All About Discipline — **251**
7 Daily Practices That Create The Foundation For Success

CONTENTS

16. Rene Terry - Don't Drop The Glass Balls   **271**
How To Identify & Prioritize The Most Important Things In Your Life

17. Julie Glass - Just Do The Thing   **287**
How To Take Action, Get Results, & Build Confidence Each Step of Your Journey

18. Barb Pitcock - The Wheel Of Success   **305**
The 4-Step Cycle That Creates Unlimited Success

19. Rebecca Ferris - Knowing Is Growing   **321**
The 3 Pillars For Every Leader To Grow Herself & Her Team

20. Lori Hart - You Can Have It All   **335**
Motherhood, Career, And Success In The Network Marketing Profession

21. Ursula Myers - Not Everyone's Going To Make It   **351**
The 5 Survival Skills Every Network Marketer Needs To Know

22. Jennifer Piper - Never Ever Quit   **371**
Why Grit & Determination Are The True Keys To Success

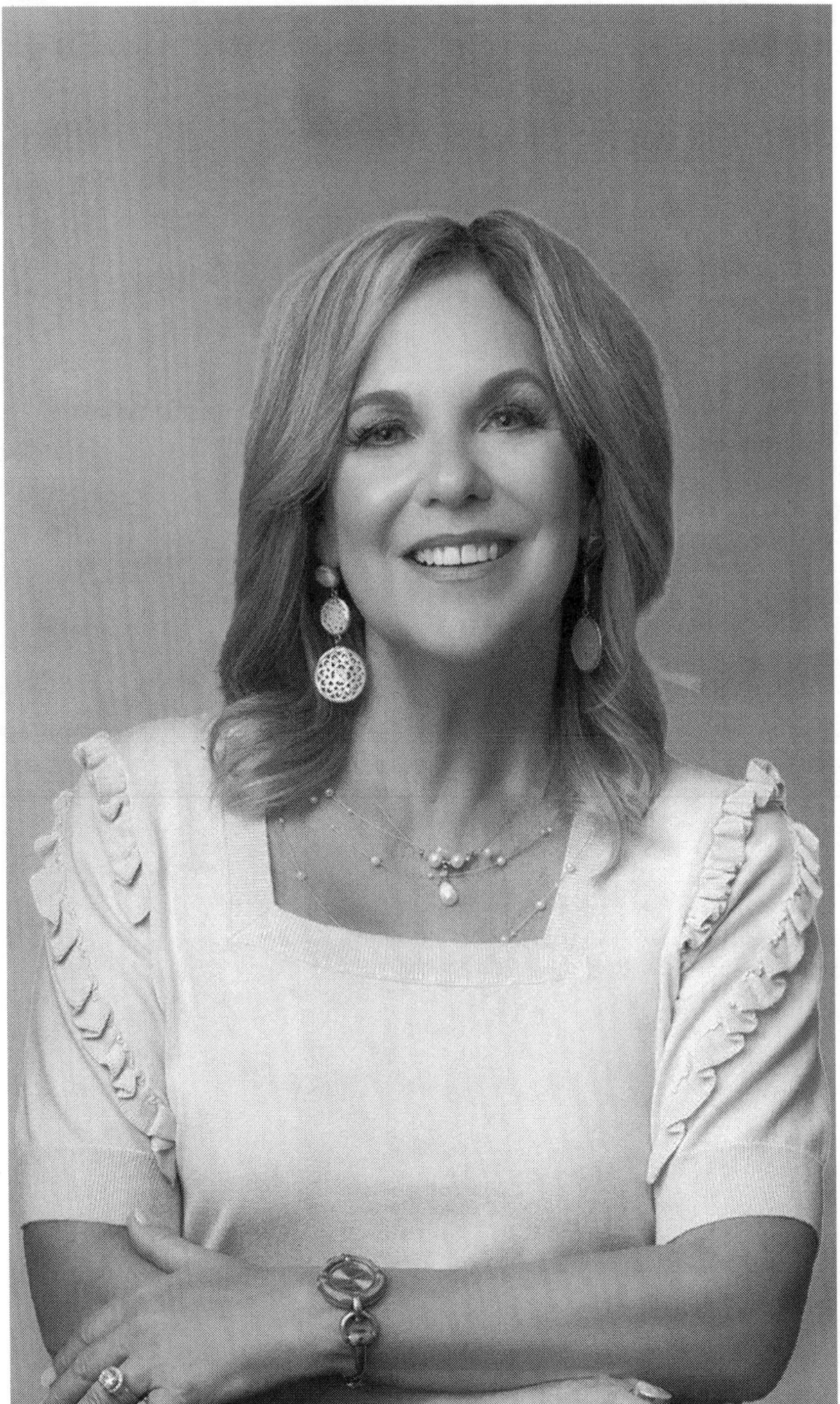

FOREWORD

"This is a no-holds-barred, genuine collection of personal lessons from twenty-two women who have faced the good, the bad, and the ugly of personal and professional life, turning challenges into triumphs and becoming the heroines of their own stories."

Donna Johnson

🌐 MentorDonnaJohnson.com
󰈌 Facebook.com/mentordonnajohnson
󰀵 Instagram.com/mentordonnajohnson

FOREWORD

Hello, ntwrkrs! I'm absolutely thrilled to introduce you to this collection of extraordinary journeys written by the *Leading Ladies* in the Network Marketing profession. With nearly half a century in this field—yes, I started before some of you were even born—I've seen this profession flourish and grow from the pre-computer, meeting-in-living-room days to the social-media-fueled online arena it is today. I joined my first company as a teenager, left after a decade, and have been with my current company for thirty-seven years.

In that time, I've built one of the largest sustainable global businesses in the organization—all while raising a family, gaining substantial personal and professional growth, and traveling the world. Based on my experience, and the experiences of so many other women I know in the field, I firmly believe that the Network Marketing profession is the ultimate career path for women who want to balance life's priorities. Any woman, anywhere, can optimize her career for family, finances, and freedom.

What makes this career path so unique for women is its equitable playing field—there are no glass ceilings here! Compensation plans are impartial: you meet the criteria, you reap the rewards. This profession is a *meritocracy*—it's a system designed to deliver success based on *what you do* rather than your race, gender, or educational background.

Before I entered the profession, my career confidence suffered. I had only minimal experience as a swim coach and a secretary. I didn't have a college degree. But as soon as I transitioned into Network Marketing, I became determined never to confine myself to a desk or let others determine my worth again. I reveled in the entrepreneurial spirit, and loudly declared myself "unemployable" by traditional standards!

I've fallen in love with knowing exactly what I need to do to be successful, and earning in direct proportion to my efforts—and I believe you will, too, once you truly understand your company's compensation plan and income disclosures. This is a profession where you can choose your own pace: you get to decide whether you walk, jog, or run, and whether you're looking for some extra pocket money, or substantial career income. The possibilities are truly limitless.

And, despite what the uninformed public may think, it's important to point out that Network Marketing isn't a get-rich-quick scheme. It's a platform for genuine enterprise, complete with all the risks and rewards of entrepreneurship, and it comes with something extraordinary: relationships. This profession is about building hope, not hype. Women, in particular, excel here due to our innate strengths in relationship-building, networking, and fostering community—skills that align perfectly with the ethos of the Network Marketing profession.

When Christopher approached me to write this foreword, I was overjoyed at the opportunity to support a project that promises to transform lives through its honest and vulnerable storytelling. This isn't just another social media facade of perfect women with perfect makeup and perfect lives. It's a no-holds-barred, genuine collection of personal lessons from twenty-two women who have faced the good, the bad, and the ugly of personal and professional life, turning challenges into triumphs and becoming the heroines of their own stories.

So, dive into these pages, arm yourself with a pen and paper for notes, and prepare to build your own legacy through the Network Marketing profession. I hope that one day, I get to read *your* story—the one about how you read this book, did the work, and became a fellow *Leading Lady* in this amazing field.

— Donna Johnson

Watch Donna's Video Now!
LeadingLadiesCourse.com

ACKNOWLEDGEMENTS

As I reflect on the journey of bringing this book to life, I am filled with immense gratitude and admiration for the incredible individuals who have played pivotal roles in its creation.

First and foremost, I extend my deepest appreciation to women everywhere. As the mothers of all people, your contributions are immeasurable. Your strength, wisdom, and nurturing spirits have profoundly impacted me and countless others. Your influence is woven into the fabric of this book, and for that, I am eternally grateful.

To Mary Knight, my Chief Operations Officer and the brilliant editor of this book, I offer my heartfelt thanks. Mary, without your tireless dedication, keen eye, and unwavering commitment, this book would not have been possible. Your exceptional work has elevated it to heights I could only dream of, and I am profoundly grateful for your partnership.

I also wish to acknowledge the extraordinary women leaders within the Network Marketing Profession. Though there are too many to name here, your contributions are deeply felt and appreciated. You have set the pace and the standard for excellence, demonstrating day in and day out what true leadership looks like. Your personal input, encouragement, and inspiration have been instrumental in my journey to create this book and stay the course to bring this vision to life. Your legacy is one of greatness, and I am honored to be influenced by you.

Finally, to my beloved wife, Alisa Hussey. Alisa, you have always been there for me, providing unwavering support and endless inspiration. Your light is a beacon that I constantly strive to achieve, and your presence in my life is a blessing beyond words. Thank you for being my rock, my muse, and my greatest cheerleader.

To all who read these words, may you find in this book the same inspiration, motivation, and encouragement that I have received from these remarkable women. Their impact is profound, and I am privileged to share their influence with you.

With deepest gratitude and respect,

Christopher Hussey

ntwrkr

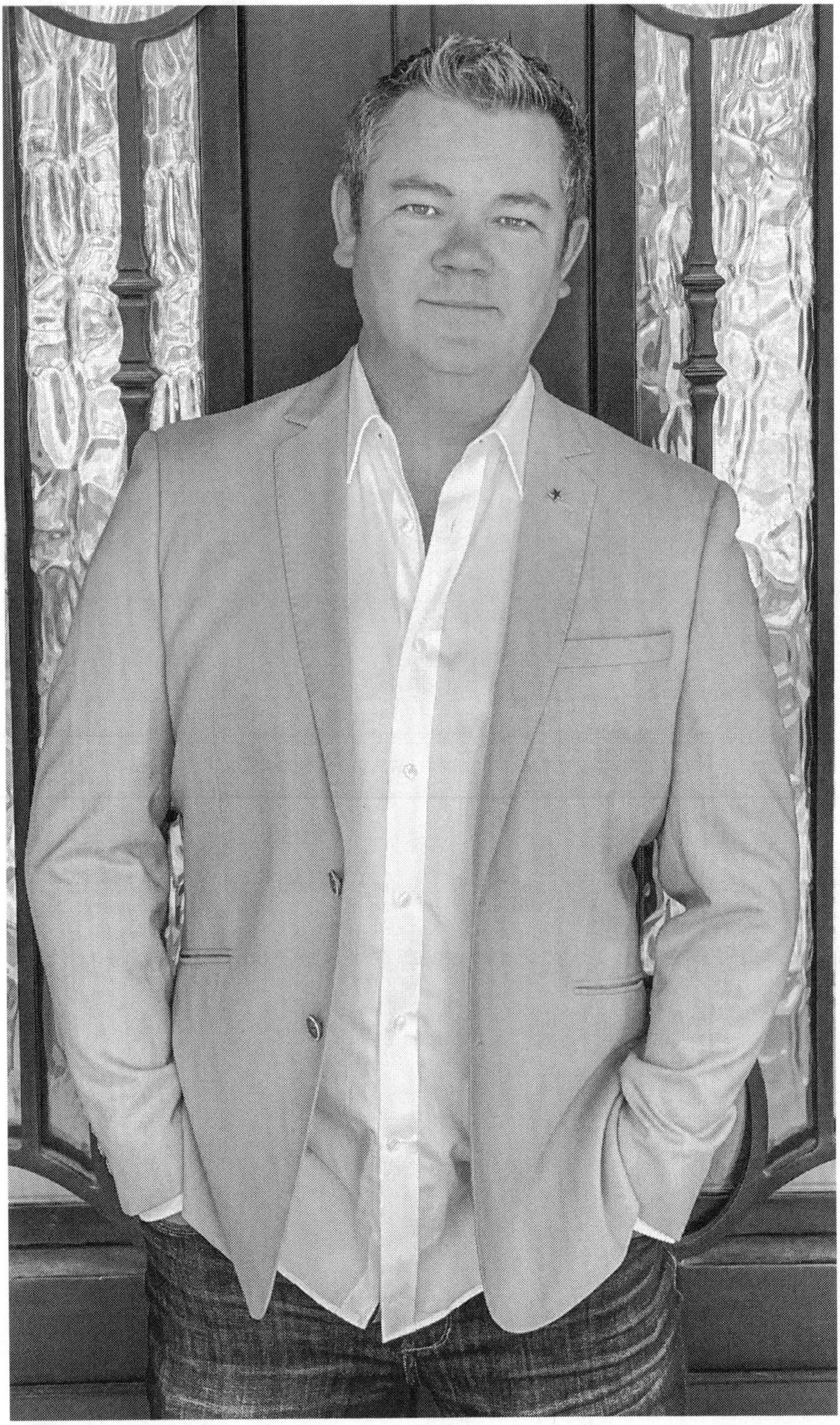

INTRODUCTION

"So whether you're just starting out, growing your career, or well-established in the Network Marketing Profession, this book is ready to transform your life."

Christopher Hussey

🌐 ChristopherHussey.com
f Facebook.com/TheOfficialHussey
📷 Instagram.com/TheOfficialHussey
♪ TikTok.com/@TheOfficialHussey

INTRODUCTION

Hello, ntwrkrs! I'm beyond excited to finally put this amazing collection of insights, wisdom, and lessons from twenty-two incredible women out into the world. Creating *Leading Ladies* has been one of the most rewarding experiences of my life—marked by unexpected plot twists, the full range of human emotions, and many profound realizations that have altered the way I see the Network Marketing profession.

After we chose the topic and name for this book, we started with a simple question to the top women leaders in the space: "As a successful Network Marketing professional, what one lesson or piece of knowledge would you make sure your daughter knew to be successful in this profession?" Little did we know the incredible journey this question would take us on.

Inside this book and the accompanying videos, you'll find the hard-won wisdom of 22 remarkable women, plus a foreword by the incomparable Donna Johnson. These women, who are both powerful leaders and accomplished Network Marketers, have achieved greatness in both their personal and professional lives. They've faced hardships, disappointment, and triumphs. They have shown resilience, a willingness to learn, and a determination to reach the top. Getting to know them through discovery and the interview process was both eye-opening and humbling.

But bringing this book together was more challenging and fulfilling than I ever imagined. We laughed, cried, and I learned so much about these incredible women. Their experiences, captured within these pages, are a testament to their unparalleled expertise and heartfelt journeys in Network Marketing. They have poured their hearts and emotions into these chapters, presenting their knowledge in a way that can immediately impact your business and life, helping you achieve the greatness you deserve.

So whether you're just starting out, growing your career, or well-established in the Network Marketing profession, this book is ready to transform your life. I firmly believe that Network Marketing is the greatest profession in the world. And if you're reading this book or watching the accompanying videos, then you're part of its constant evolution.

Along with this book, each author has recorded a video training on their chapter's subject matter. Between the written words and these videos, nothing is stopping you from reaching your highest potential in both business and in life!

Thank you for investing in *Leading Ladies*. I encourage you to read every single page, as each one holds actionable steps and valuable insights that can become the catalyst for your transformation. Take the knowledge, passion, and skills these *Leading Ladies* have shared and apply them with intention and determination.

Your future is in your hands—and I can't wait to see the life you create for yourself! Welcome to *Leading Ladies*.

LEADING LADIES

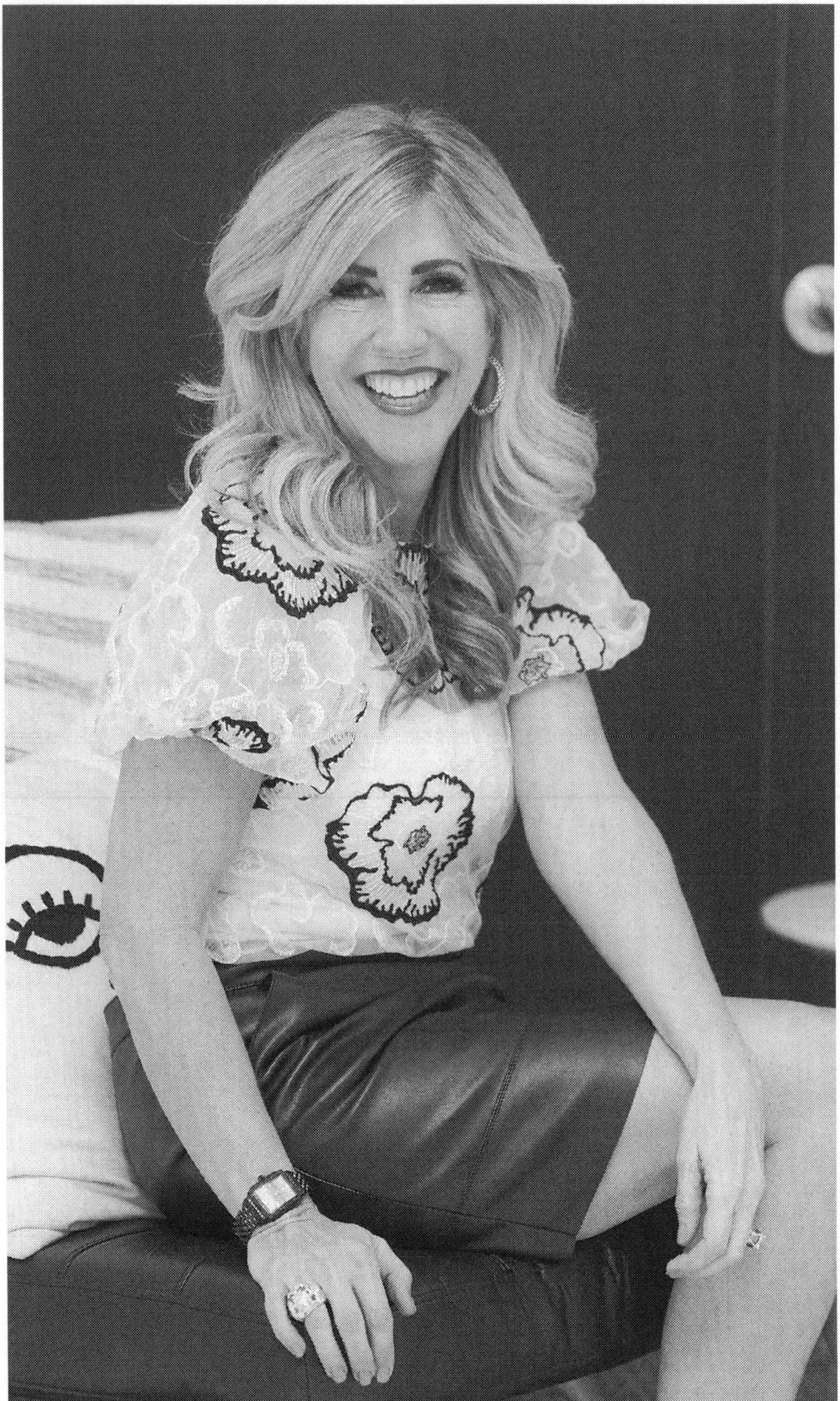

1

The 'BE' Attributes

How Cultivating Relationships Transforms Your Life & Business

Sarah Zolecki

🌐 SarahAndTony.com
🅕 Facebook.com/sarahzolecki
📷 Instagram.com/sarahzolecki
♪ Tiktok.com/@sarahzolecki

The 'BE' Attributes

Sarah Zolecki

Hello, fellow ntwrkrs, and congratulations on picking up this book! It feels like just yesterday when I finished my chapter in the last ntwrkr Publishing title, *Create Community,* but time certainly flies as life gets more exciting. I'm pumped to be teamed up with all these other talented and successful women, and It's a privilege to share my insights and experiences in Network Marketing with you.

I'm writing this chapter from my home in Minneapolis, Minnesota, where I juggle life as a mom to two wonderful soon-to-be tweens and as the wife of my amazing husband, Tony. We've been on this incredible adventure together, building our business side by side for the past nineteen years. What a ride it's been!

My career in Network Marketing began when I was just twenty-one, and over the years, I've navigated the waters of this profession in various stages of my life—as a single woman, a wife, and a mother. Each phase has offered unique challenges and opportunities, contributing to a well-rounded perspective I'm thrilled to share with you.

Despite a rocky start in my career (I didn't recruit a single person in my first three years!) I've seen my business grow to astonishing heights with the company I've been with for over a decade. We're doing almost one-hundred-fifty million in sales every year now, and I tell you that with both great excitement and great humility. It's almost surreal to think about it, considering where I started twenty-five years ago, but here we are, with a thriving business that spans the globe. Tony and I are infinitely grateful for the prosperity we've been able to create for ourselves and others.

In my opinion, the secret to my success is the emphasis I've placed on cultivating genuine relationships. This chapter, which I fondly call 'The 'BE' Attributes,' focuses on this important aspect of Network Marketing. And in it, I'll guide you through five key strategies that have not only transformed my business but my life as well.

So, what makes these strategies special, anyway? Well, they are simple yet profound. Often, we overlook the basics, thinking, "Oh, I know that already." But *knowing* and *doing* are two different things, and I've learned this the hard way. Early in my career, I was engaging in plenty of conversations, but I wasn't truly connecting with anyone. I was focusing on transactions, but I wasn't getting any traction. There was a huge disconnect between me and my prospects, and I could feel that something just wasn't working.

So, I decided to take a step back, slow down, and figure out what was missing from the way I interacted with people. Talking to them and inviting them to events just wasn't enough—I needed to find out how to cultivate and maintain genuine relationships. And what I found out was that there really is a science behind it! Now, I'm going to share that science with you on these pages, and take you through my personal experiences to illustrate the following steps I believe are key to building relationships.

First, we'll learn about how to *be loving*. Next, we'll talk about how to show up and *be human* with other humans. We'll then jump into strategies on how to *be creative,* and then follow that with insight on how to *be valuable.* Finally, we'll discuss the reasons why it's critical to *be a rock*. These might sound straightforward, but their power lies in their application. So, as we delve into each of these, I encourage you to not just read but to act! The goal is to embed these attributes into your daily practice. If you're ready to reframe the ways you build relationships in your life and your business, let's go!

Be Loving

What does it truly mean to be loving in the realm of both business and personal relationships? It's about genuine care, putting others' well-being and happiness at the forefront, and expressing this through our actions and words, every single day. The story I'm going to share with you throughout each section in this chapter is about an incredible woman named Amee, and how she became my best friend through my practice of The 'BE' Attributes.

I met Amee about fourteen years ago. Although we were both in the Network Marketing profession, we weren't in the same company or downline. Our paths just crossed one day, and there was an instant connection. Have you ever experienced that instant recognition of love upon meeting someone? Well, that's precisely what happened between Amee and me.

I made a conscious decision to celebrate Amee's successes within her own company, without ulterior motives, purely driven by love and admiration. Whether it was applauding her achievements as she reached new ranks at her company or simply checking in on her well-being, I made it a priority to show her love and support whenever I could. If she needed guidance, I was there. If I wanted to pay her a compliment, I didn't hesitate. I went out of my way to make her feel good and important, solely for being her authentic self.

This approach to relationships—meeting people where they are and making them feel valued without any hidden agendas—is the essence of being loving. It's about nurturing genuine connections that can lead to long-lasting relationships and a robust network. If you can find ways to be loving, it will turn into your superpower, and be the "stickiness" that brings people into your life or business and makes them want to stay.

You may have already picked up on this by now, but the action step here is to commit to having incredible relationships *and then do the work to make it happen.* Resist the temptation to merely transact with people, and instead, look for ways to make others feel cared for and appreciated.

Be Human

The next essential element in cultivating lasting relationships in Network Marketing is to be human. This might sound obvious, but let's dig deeper into what it truly means. Being human in our interactions is about authenticity, embracing the imperfections we all have, and understanding that everything we experience, from joyous moments to challenging crises, are just a part of this amazing thing called human life.

Take my friendship with Amee, for instance. As our relationship evolved beyond surface interactions, we discovered that our connection went deeper than simply being really fond of each other. We shared our successes and failures, our aspirations, and fears in conversations that veered in and out of our business and personal lives. Everything was on the table—from what excited us about our businesses to the family concerns that kept us awake all night. Our relationship was about understanding each other's essence, or as I like to call it, 'peeling back the layers of the onion' to reveal our true selves.

This level of honesty and openness is what being human is all about. It's the willingness to present your authentic self, warts and all! In the early days of my career, I struggled to recruit anyone because I wasn't being authentic. I was trying to emulate others, thinking that was the key to success. But this only created a barrier, preventing genuine connections.

Things began to change only when I started asking myself, "Am I okay with being me?" This is a crucial question for all of us. Are you comfortable with who you are, in all your imperfect glory? If not, it's a journey you need to embark on. For me, accepting myself was a turning point. Suddenly, people who resonated with the real Sarah found me, drawn to my authenticity. So, here are the action steps I'd like you to take to become more human:

1. Start by presenting your true self. Embrace the messy and imperfect parts of your life. Remember, it's not about creating an ideal image; it's about being genuine.

2. Adopt a mindset of giving, not taking. Part of being human is about leaving a positive impact on everyone you meet. I always strive to ensure that people are better off for having met me!

Being human means being vulnerable, open, and real. It's about showing up as you are, and in doing so, attracting those who appreciate and resonate with your authenticity. This is how lasting, meaningful connections are formed, and these connections will go beyond business transactions to become the foundation of a happy life.

Be Creative

The third indispensable aspect of relationship-building in our profession lies in embracing creativity. As Network Marketers, the importance of staying connected with people cannot be overstated. Our lives are a whirlwind of responsibilities, from parenting to careers, and managing personal relationships. When we add business into this mix, it becomes a balancing act of keeping all these plates spinning!

Being creative in Network Marketing means proactively seeking innovative ways to connect and stay engaged with people, regardless of whether they join your business or become a customer. It's about nurturing connections for their own sake.

You might be wondering how I maintained my relationship with Amee despite my growing business and my growing family, right? The answer is, I made an effort to remember and celebrate significant events in her life—birthdays, anniversaries, professional achievements. These gestures weren't about business; they were about genuine care and celebration, and they didn't take a lot of time. A simple call to check in, a message to say, 'I'm thinking of you,' or small, thoughtful gifts can make a world of difference.

We often receive intuitive nudges to reach out to someone. I encourage you to act on these. Believe me, a timely message or call can have a profound impact! It's astounding how often people have told me, "I was just thinking about you," or how a simple call can bring comfort and joy at just the right moment. These are the threads that weave strong, lasting connections. Now, let's talk about action steps.

1. Take a moment to connect online. Living in the digital age gives us plenty of opportunities to reach out to those we want to remember! Social media tags or DMs, emails, and texts can remind people that you're thinking of them.

2. Get to a networking event. I know, events can be daunting for some! But if you can step out of your comfort zone and attend, then they can be incredibly rewarding. It's in these moments, when we stretch ourselves, that we often forge the most meaningful connections and discover new opportunities.

So, challenge yourself to be the initiator. Don't wait for others to reach out; take the first step. Be the one who brings energy and innovation into your interactions. Remember, the effort you put into creatively

ntwrkr.com

building and maintaining relationships is an investment in your personal and professional growth!

Be Valuable

The fourth key element in fostering meaningful relationships in Network Marketing is to be valuable. This concept revolves around the previously mentioned idea of being a giver rather than being a taker. We've all encountered people who constantly take without giving back, and we know how draining that can be, right? It's important to ask yourself: How can I add value? How can I serve and support others?

Reflecting on my interactions with Amee, I often asked her, "How can I support you? What do you need from me?" This approach wasn't about expecting something in return; it was about genuinely wanting to contribute to her success. Whether it was peer-to-peer support, mentorship, or brainstorming sessions, the focus was on being a helpful and empowering presence in her life.

However, being valuable isn't just about what you can offer; it's also about being open to learning from others. Every relationship has the potential to be mutually enriching. Acknowledge that others have valuable insights and experiences from which you can learn, creating a symbiotic and dynamic relationship.

Here are some actionable steps to embody the trait of being valuable:

1. Identify your skills. Consider the skills and knowledge you've developed. How can you use these to positively impact someone else's life?

2. Share your knowledge. Think of three topics you're passionate about that others can benefit from. Start sharing your insights and expertise on these subjects with people and gauge their interest, delivering more knowledge as they become more engaged.

3. Seek mutual growth. Approach every relationship with the mindset of both contributing and learning. Recognize that every individual you meet can teach you something valuable.

Being valuable in Network Marketing isn't just about business transactions. It's about enriching the lives of others, helping them grow, and being a source of encouragement and empowerment. This approach not only helps others but also fosters your own personal and professional growth. It's about creating a network where everyone feels valued and supported.

Be A Rock

The final, yet crucial, element in cultivating relationships in Network Marketing is to be a rock. This metaphor encompasses being steady, solid, and dependable. It's about being that constant presence in people's lives, through the highs and lows, and through the good times and the tough times. Being a rock means that others know they can lean on you, trust you, and count on your unwavering support.

When I think back to my long relationship with Amee, the key to our lasting friendship was consistency. Over the years, I made sure to remain a steady presence in her life. It wasn't about being flashy or overbearing; it was about being there, consistently and reliably. This consistency was reflected in how I presented myself both offline and online. Everyone knew that what they saw was what they got with me—a transparent and genuine connection.

In a world where flakiness and unreliability are all too common, standing out as someone dependable is invaluable. The simple act of showing up, especially showing up when you said you will, can set you apart. Consistency creates certainty, and certainty builds trust. People are drawn to those they can rely on, those who are their champions in both personal and professional spheres!

Some actionable steps to embody this trait include:

1. Always follow through. Make it a point to show up and do what you say you will. Let your actions consistently reflect your words.

2. Create a feeling of certainty. Your consistency in action and attitude creates a sense of certainty for others. They know what to expect from you and that they can count on you.

3. Be supportive. Ensure that you're there for people, not just in business, but in life. Be their cheerleader, their confidant, and their rock!

As you become a rock for others, you also become a beacon of light, so to speak. In times of uncertainty, your steady presence can be a source of comfort and inspiration. By embodying these qualities, you become someone others aspire to emulate in their personal and professional growth.

So now that we've explored the five 'BE' Attributes, let's circle back to Amee's story. After a decade of nurturing our relationship, a moment came when she expressed interest in discussing business possibilities. This wasn't an overnight success; rather, it was the fruit of ten years of genuine relationship-building. This is a testament to the power of patience and authenticity in Network Marketing. It's not about putting a timeline on relationships but about genuinely caring and investing in them.

Each leader in my team has their own unique story, but one common thread is the absence of a timeline. I approached each relationship with the intent to support, understand, and grow together. This mindset of long-term relationship-building, not just for business but for personal growth, is what makes Network Marketing so unique and rewarding.

In this profession, we often focus on the immediate results. However, the true essence of success in this field is building long-lasting relationships that transcend business transactions. It's about being a loving, human, creative, and dependable presence in the lives of those around you. When you approach relationships from this place of authenticity and care, you will grow your business and also enrich your life and the lives of others.

As we wrap up our chapter on the art of relationship building in Network Marketing, let's reflect on The 'BE' Attributes we've discussed: Being Loving, Being Human, Being Creative, Being Valuable, and Being A Rock. Each of these attributes is a vital component in

ntwrkr.com

creating a successful, fulfilling career in this dynamic field.

Embracing these attributes isn't just about enhancing your business; it's about transforming the way you interact with the world. By coming from a place of genuine care, authenticity, creativity, contribution, and reliability, you'll find that your network expands not just in size but in depth and quality! You'll attract more leads, engage in more meaningful conversations, and build a business that's not just profitable but also deeply rewarding.

However, before you take these strategies out into the world, I want to remind you that this will require patience. This approach demands what I like to call a 'slowing down' in your business strategy. It's about taking the time to build real friendships, to cultivate relationships that go beyond mere transactions. People should see you as a real friend—someone who's there for them in more ways than just business. If you've been engaging in transactional conversations by the dozen, like I was early on, this might feel a little uncomfortable. But I promise, it's worth it!

I encourage you to focus on these five 'BE' Attributes and the action steps I've outlined. Implement them in your daily interactions and watch how they transform not only your business but also your personal growth. The true essence of Network Marketing lies in these human connections—in other words, the bonds we forge and the lives we touch.

Remember: the path to success in Network Marketing is paved with patience, empathy, and a willingness to be more than just a businessperson. You're a friend, a mentor, a confidant, and a source of inspiration to those around you.

I look forward to hearing your success stories that stem from these principles! Let's cultivate not just a network, but a community of amazing friendships and lasting connections. Here's to your success in Network Marketing, grounded in the powerful 'BE' Attributes. Let's make a difference, one relationship at a time! See you out there, ntwrkrs!

Watch Sarah's Video Now!
LeadingLadiesCourse.com

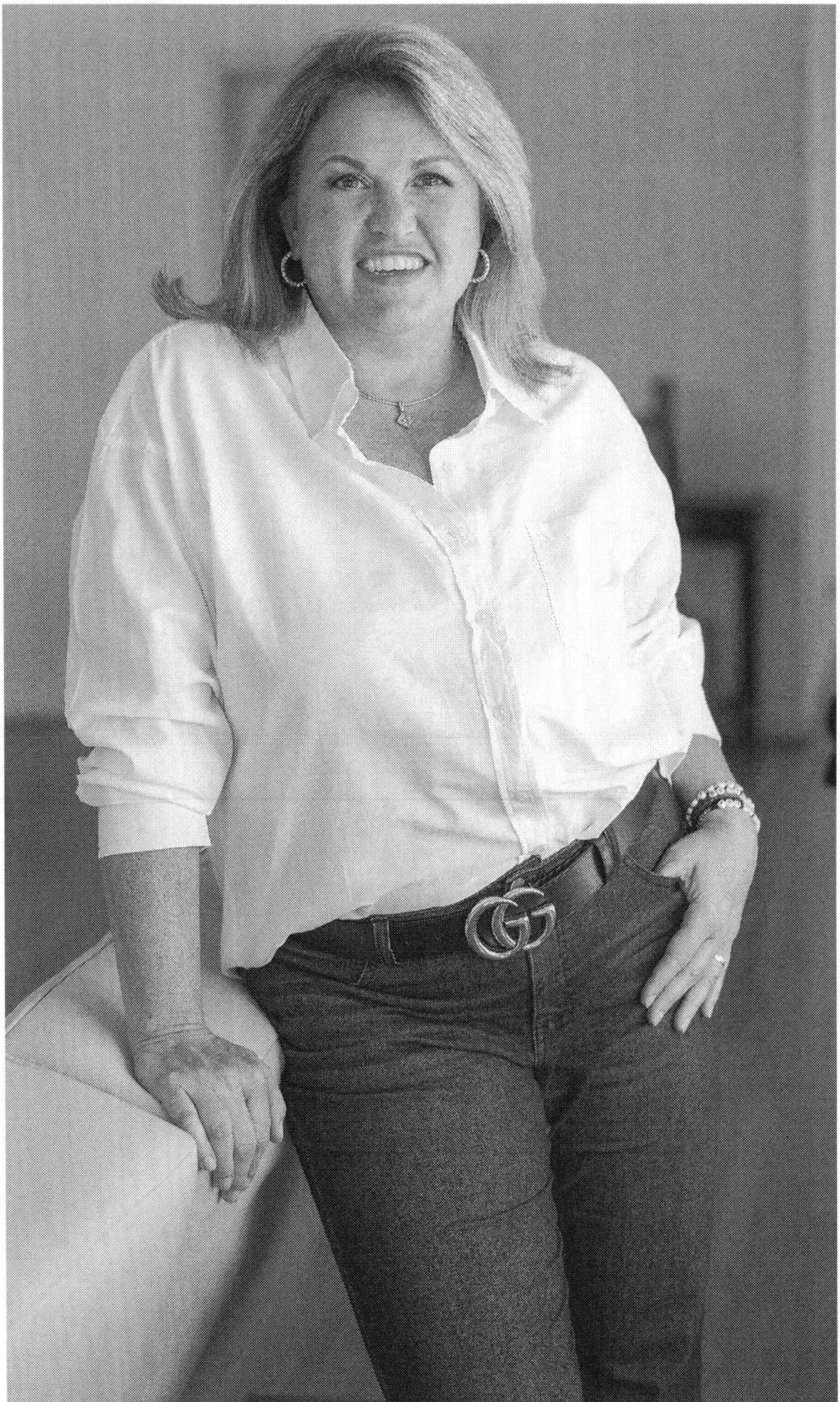

2

Mastering Self-Leadership

The 3 Core Traits That Will Inspire
The World To Follow You

Kathleen Vicenzotti

KathleenVicenzotti.com
Facebook.com/kathleen.vicenzotti
Instagram.com/kvicenzotti
Tiktok.com/@kvicenzotti

Mastering Self-Leadership

Kathleen Vicenzotti

Hello, fellow ntwrkrs! I'm absolutely thrilled to have you here with me on these pages as I dive into a topic I've been passionate about for decades—the art of self-leadership. Specifically, I'll be discussing three pivotal traits that will inspire others to follow your lead. As a seasoned sales trainer and coach, I've dedicated my career to helping Network Marketers, small business owners, solo entrepreneurs, and corporate teams make a significant impact and generate income from their passions. I'm grateful for the opportunity to be a part of this book and share my knowledge and personal experiences with you! As you read the following pages, I hope you are inspired to discover the art of self-leadership.

With thirty-five years of experience in the direct selling and Network Marketing profession, I've learned how to navigate this field, and now I have the privilege of helping others do the same. It wasn't always easy, and there were definitely times I had to learn the hard way, but once I was on the other side, I was able to design a career and a lifestyle that I love. And along the way, I've built multimillion-dollar teams, replaced my corporate income multiple times over, and earned monthly personal income that surpassed the *annual salaries* of many traditional 9-to-5 J.O.B.S.

I've coached thousands of independent consultants to replicate this success, and in doing so, I attracted the attention of the C-Suite at multiple companies, landing me executive-level positions within the industry. I've been able to work in the Network Marketing profession at every level—from the field to the corporate office to the boardroom. It's been quite the journey!

With all of that experience, I'm honored now to be able to share with you my knowledge about leadership—*self-leadership,* to be precise—because the path to leading others starts with the ability to lead oneself. As someone who has been in your shoes, hungry for growth and a richer life, I'm ready to share three traits that will make you not just an admirable leader but an inspirational one!

In this chapter, I'll discuss what I call the 3 Cs: *Clarity, Confidence*, and *Courage*. My goal is to help you become not just a decision-maker but a beacon to your team, encouraging others to make choices that align with their values and embark on a path that benefits everyone involved. I'll tell you how to be a clear example for others to follow and give you ways to show others what's possible when they believe in themselves. Because leadership is not about power and control—it's about inspiration. So, as you read, I'd like you to keep the following question at the top of your mind: what transformations might occur within your team, your community, and your career when you apply these principles of self-leadership in your life?

In the upcoming sections, we'll take a look at each of the 3 Cs through the lens of leadership. Are you ready to step up, take charge, and lead? If the answer is yes, then let's jump right in!

Clarity

Clarity, at its simplest, is about transparency and understanding—being able to tell your team what you're doing, and where you're going. But in the realm of self-leadership, it goes deeper than that. It becomes more about discovering, owning, and committing to an internal compass that aligns your values, passions, strengths, and weaknesses with your aspirations and desires.

With internal clarity comes enhanced self-awareness and decisiveness. When you understand yourself and your ambitions, you'll make choices on a daily, monthly, and yearly basis that align with your deeper goals. Clarity will help you craft a vision of success that's uniquely yours, and it will put you in the driver's seat to bring that vision to reality.

I remember being a new mother. It was a wonderful but taxing time when I was learning what it meant to raise a family. I still wanted and needed to work, but as I considered my options, I couldn't imagine giving up the freedom and flexibility to be with my child. This understanding led me to embrace the Network Marketing profession, because it offered so many things that a high-pressure corporate job couldn't. The journey to clarity wasn't instantaneous, but once I figured it out, everything changed.

Like many, I had followed the linear path of high school, college, and a good, corporate job. I wasn't quite sure at that age what I wanted to do, but I followed that path anyway, and delayed joining the working world even further by staying in school to get my MBA! Yet afterward, even with a master's degree, a coveted position at Ford Motor Company, and all the trappings of corporate success, there came a point when I realized that my job—while fun, exciting, and full of perks—was just funding a life I didn't want to be living. That's when I sought clarity on what I truly desired, leading me to integrate my career with my desire to spend more time with my family, exploring all that life had to offer.

Finding clarity showed me paths and opportunities that had previously been hidden. In fact, my direct sales career started because I half-heartedly agreed to host a jewelry party for a friend who was trying to earn an all-inclusive trip! However, I found myself surrounded by women who were working on their own schedules, making great money, and enjoying lots of time with their children and families. Once I had a clear idea of what I wanted my life to look like, I finally noticed that the answer was right in front of me.

This kind of internal clarity has been a cornerstone of my success, providing me with direction, motivation, and resilience. I urge you to seek your own clarity. Once you do that, the path will reveal itself. Here are a few tips that will be helpful in getting started:

1. Define your non-negotiables. Ask yourself what you want your life to look like, and then be honest with the answers! What excites you? What brings you joy? What are the must-haves? Don't stay stuck in a life that isn't aligned with who you want to be.

2. Be open to new possibilities. Take those blinders off and look around—there are people out there living their lives the way you want to live yours! See how they're doing it, and then embrace the fact that you don't know it all.

3. Get buy-in from your stakeholders. Do your spouse, your children, or other family members need to be included in this conversation? If they're not on the same page as you, things can get really messy. If your clarity and your new path forward will affect them, they need to be part of the discovery process.

4. Start taking action. Now that you know what you want, leverage your clarity to make informed decisions and take actions toward it. When you do this, you'll find that procrastination and indecision disappear completely, and focus and drive will take their place.

Confidence

Now that you're clear about your goals and you are finally taking action, it's important to develop the next critical trait: confidence. This means more than just feeling self-assured; rather, it's about trusting in your beliefs and skills. Confidence is using your abilities to achieve your goals with certainty. And if you're unsure of what confidence looks like, just think about some of the world's most successful people—they all share strong belief in themselves, take risks, and listen to their inner voice saying, "You can do this—I trust you."

I didn't grasp the power of this concept until my early career mentor, Mary, offered to "lend me her confidence" until I found my own. She was always saying, "If I can do it, so can you." That was a game-changer! She guided me to build my confidence through bite-sized actions and celebrating each small victory.

As I write this chapter, I'm reminded of a vivid experience I had this past summer—an adventure course where I found myself perched fifty or sixty feet above the ground. I was faced with swinging blocks, each suspended by ropes at precarious angles. I was absolutely frozen in terror as I stared out, filled with doubt and fear, my inner voice protesting loudly, "You *cannot* do this!"

But during those moments of temporary paralysis, another participant caught up to me. I stepped aside to let her pass, secretly hoping to glean confidence from her success. As she navigated those swaying planks with trust and precision, I realized something crucial: observing her path illuminated mine!

This epiphany was similar to my realization that I could transition from the security of a corporate job at Ford Motor Company to the uncertainties of a commission-based Network Marketing career. I needed to push beyond my comfort zone to forge a new life for myself and for my family. And the confidence to embark on this new journey was bolstered by clarity and vision.

In Network Marketing, just like on that adventure course, I sought out leaders to emulate. Some allowed me to shadow them, while others didn't. Regardless, I learned how to take the ingredients from their success and map out my own course. By watching how they did it, deconstructing the steps, and replicating them, I was confident that I, too, would find success. So, my challenge to you is to take the following steps to actively build your confidence:

1. Make a list of what it's going to take to do this. Can you see others achieving what you aspire to? What are they doing that you can do? Deconstruct their steps and map out your game plan to align with your unique strengths. Believe in and trust in yourself!

2. Seek out a mentor. This person can lend you their confidence when you have none and help you devise a strategy to start stacking up those wins on your way to your best life.

3. Recognize that seeing even a portion of the path can make the first step less daunting. Just as headlights only light a short stretch of road on a highway at night, you only need to see what's just in front of you on your map to success. As you progress, the rest will unveil itself!

Courage

At this stage, you already have the clarity you need to define the life you want, as well as the confidence to take the action to get there. You are equipped to realize your ambitions and listen to that inner voice that tells you, "You can do this." And this is where the final piece comes into play: courage, which is the strength to act—and keep acting—despite fear.

Remember, courage isn't the absence of fear, it's the resolve to face that fear in service of something greater. Remember that adventure course I wrote about? Yes, taking that first step onto the swinging plank was terrifying, but because I gained confidence by watching the woman before me do it, I could muster the courage to take the first step, then the next to keep going and complete it.

The 3 Cs actually build on themselves. Clarity gives you the desire to find confidence. And when you possess confidence, you naturally want to show up with the courage required to take bold steps. This interconnection is crucial, as every courageous act, each risk embraced, and every challenge conquered bolsters your confidence, which then promotes courage. It's a continuous cycle that will fuel growth and success for both you and your team!

Reflecting on my own journey, I think about the fear and anxiety I felt when I left a secure job to pursue Network Marketing full-time. I knew I had a mortgage payment coming up in a couple of weeks, but I had no income. My family was expecting me to pull something off, and quickly! And there I was, staring at a blank calendar, devoid of any bookings or leads. Despite knowing the doors this opportunity would open for me, I began to doubt myself, and my own insecurities got in the way of my future success.

I knew I needed a major dose of courage to confront the fears and mental barriers that were hindering me. And eventually, I found that embracing a 'no turning back' approach was what ultimately made way for my progress. When I severed ties with my previous job at Ford Motor Company, the need to succeed became non-negotiable. I was forced to embrace activities that previously intimidated me, as I knew that team building and duplication were critical in the Network Marketing profession.

Despite fear and the nagging whispers of unrealistic expectations, I pressed forward. I chose to face challenges head-on, *even if it meant being uncomfortable.* This is the mindset shift required of those who want success!

Consider this: What is one fear that is currently holding you back? You may possess clarity and confidence but find yourself frozen at the starting line. If that's you, it's going to be vital to identify your limiting beliefs and muster the courage to proceed. Does it sound too easy? Well, it's not easy—but it *is* simple. Courage is a two-step process: Feel the fear, and then do it anyway.

And courage does more than facilitate action! It's what will cement your leadership, both in life and in your professional pursuits, because it qualifies you to guide others through similar struggles. Where someone who hadn't had to dig deep for courage might give shallow platitudes to team members who were facing challenges like, "Don't worry, it'll be okay," or "Just push through," you'll be able to offer relatable stories of how you overcame the near-impossible.

So, what are the practical steps to develop courage?

1. Execute your well-crafted plan from step 2. Do this with conviction and dismiss any self-sabotaging narratives by replacing them with success stories you've heard from others. Just the execution of the plan itself will remind you that *you can do hard things,* which is the foundation of courage.

2. Enlist real-time support from your mentor, coach, or colleague. This person won't just be helping you plan, they'll be there in the trenches, encouraging you to push forward through difficult terrain. You might hate them during the process, but you'll love them later—trust me! I've been through it before, and together, you'll get there.

3. Celebrate every small victory. These tiny triumphs chip away at the monolith of fear. Remember, courage isn't always a lion's roar. Sometimes, it's the quiet affirmation at day's end that you did your best, and a promise to try again tomorrow.

The crux of true leadership lies in the following mantra: *before you can inspire or guide others, you must do so for yourself.* If I hadn't been so conflicted that I was forced to find clarity on the life I wanted, I wouldn't be here telling my story. If I hadn't ventured into the unknown and built my confidence up until I replaced and then exceeded my previous corporate incomes, I couldn't tell you to do the same. And if I hadn't stayed on the course, even when the obstacles were coming at me from all directions, I'd have a hard time looking my team in the eyes and challenging them to do the same.

This journey, as winding as the road has been, is what molded me into someone who has the life they wanted. Yes, my life and my priorities have evolved along the way, but each time I had to forge a new path to support those shifts, I turned to the principles of the 3 Cs, and I urge you to do the same:

Clarity: Know what you want, your values, desires, and intended outcome.

Confidence: Listen to that voice inside you that trusts your capabilities.

Courage: Embrace this remarkable force that will propel you far beyond your doubts and fears.

Are you willing to take the necessary steps today to build a fulfilling life, one that reflects your values, passions, and desires, and in turn, lead others by example?

The world is in dire need of leaders, and that leadership can be found within each and every one of you. Rise to the occasion and steer toward your destiny, because the finest leader you can aspire to be is the one that resides within! Thank you for sharing your time and attention with me. I hope my chapter emboldens you to author your own story and embrace the life you've envisioned. Remember, today is the first day of the rest of your life. So go out there and live it with clarity, confidence, and courage. Your future self will be grateful! Take care!

Watch Kathleen's Video Now!
LeadingLadiesCourse.com

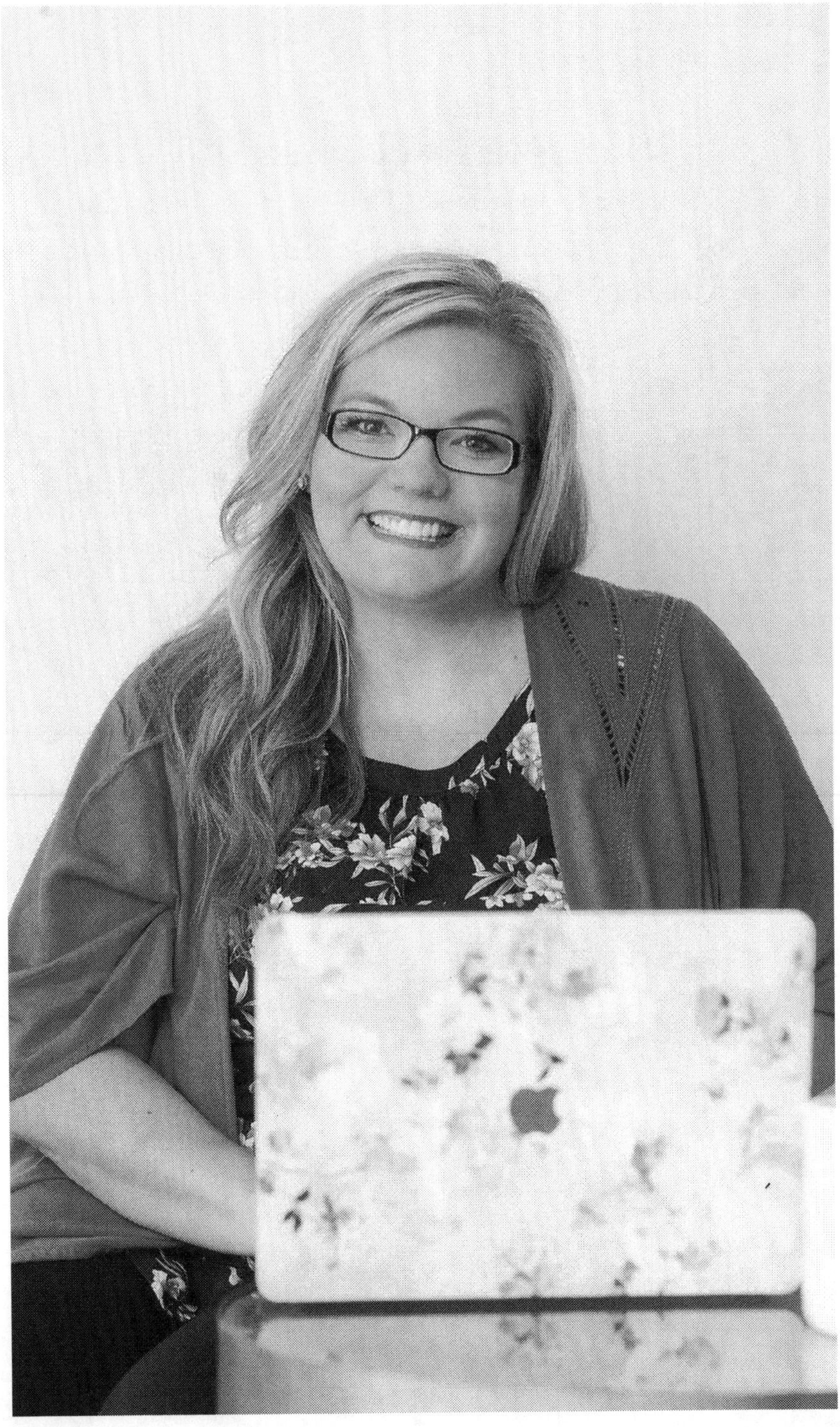

3

Becoming Brave

Foundational Moments When Unrelenting Courage Shapes Your Life

Aspen Emry

Facebook.com/aspen.emry
Instagram.com/aspenemry
Tiktok.com/@aspen_emry

Becoming Brave

Aspen Emry

Hi there, ntwrkrs! I'm excited that you've chosen to pick up this book and have found your way to my chapter! I'm so eager to share my extensive experience in this profession with you. I've had the incredible privilege of being a part of the Network Marketing world for over eighteen years. During this time, I've been through it all—from building in the field, to working in corporate positions, and even having the chance to be an owner. So, when I say I know what it takes to survive and succeed in this profession, it comes from firsthand experience!

Within the following pages, I'm going to delve deep into the subject of "Becoming Brave." While Network Marketing is my passion, it hasn't always been smooth sailing. I've encountered my fair share of challenges and had to muster the courage to overcome them! Together, we'll explore what it truly means to become brave, to make decisions that require unrelenting courage, and how these pivotal moments will shape your journey if you embrace them.

We'll start with brave beginnings. Then, we'll get into brave commitment and what that looks like day in and day out. We'll talk about brave relationships and how they differ from regular relationships, explore the concept of brave faith and the importance of believing before seeing results, and finally, we'll tackle the topic of brave perseverance, where we'll walk through the ways we can weather the storms of pain and discomfort.

So, are you ready to go on this journey with me? Let's jump in!

Brave Beginnings

Choosing a brave beginning is about more than just summoning the courage to take that first step. It's about taking one bold step after the other that can lead you into new and often intimidating territories! These are the kinds of beginnings that require sustained courage—the kind that makes your heart race and your palms sweat but also leads to amazing change and growth.

Brave beginnings are about saying 'yes' to opportunities that push you beyond your comfort zone to the very edge of your fears. But be prepared—it's not simply saying 'yes' to "Can you put away the dishes?" or "Should we have pizza tonight for dinner?" This is the yes that reshapes your life—the yes that stands between you and your dreams.

I faced this challenge in my Network Marketing career, after years of being a distributor in the field. I had the opportunity to move into a corporate position in field development, which was an entirely new side of the profession for me, but there was one catch: I'd have to fly all over the country over a dozen times per month.

Now, this may not sound like a huge demand for some of you, but for me, it meant staring my greatest fear in the face! This was not merely a little phobia, a bit of nervousness, or simply just not liking it. This was a real issue for me. I missed my sister's wedding because of it, as I was living in Nebraska with four small children and the event was in California. It just wasn't feasible to drive there with the kids. In another situation, at seven months pregnant, I drove twenty-four hours to attend an eight-hour meeting just so I didn't have to fly. As you can see, I wasn't just avoiding mere discomfort: my fear of flying was truly debilitating.

So, when I was presented with this opportunity to move into a corporate position, I had a big decision to make. Either I would have to let my dream job and the chance to advance in my career slip away, or I'd have to face my biggest fear.

Brave beginnings often involve confronting your own personal 'fear-of-flying' moments. These are the moments that define us, that shape our futures, and that prove to ourselves what we're truly capable of achieving. My journey from a high school teacher to a Network Marketer who flies all over the country was filled with anxiety, but it was also exhilarating and transformative.

Your brave beginning might look different from mine, but the essence is the same. It's about identifying what you truly want, acknowledging the fears and obstacles that stand in your way, and deciding to face them head-on. It's about taking inventory of your goals and aspirations, and then consciously choosing paths that lead you closer to them, even when those paths are lined with fear. To discover your brave beginning, here are three action steps:

ntwrkr.com

1. Define your dream. If you're going to face your fears, you'll want to have an amazing dream that makes the challenge worthwhile! Understanding what your biggest goals are, and why you have them in the first place, is the first and most critical step in your brave beginning.

2. Identify the fears that keep you stuck. Reflect on what stands in the way of you taking that leap toward your dream. Can you see it clearly? It's important to know exactly what you're afraid of so that you can practice facing it in the next step.

3. Practice the 'yes' and boldly take action. Bravery isn't the absence of fear, it's the decision to move forward despite the fear. So, practice saying 'yes' to your dream, and sit with the fear that comes with that. Do this until you can say 'yes' for real!

Brave beginnings are your moments of truth, where you decide whether to stay in the comfort of the known or venture into the vast potential of the unknown. Each brave 'yes' is a step towards a more empowered and fulfilling life. They are the moments where you truly start to live, grow, and thrive.

So, as you turn the pages of your life and your career, look for those moments that call for bravery. Lean into them, embrace them, and let them transform you. These brave beginnings are not just steps toward achieving your goals; they are defining milestones of your journey.

Brave Commitments

Brave commitment is a fundamental ingredient in the recipe for success, not only in the world of Network Marketing but in any endeavor. It's all about unwavering dedication to your goals, regardless of the sacrifices required or obstacles you face. This kind of commitment isn't just about showing up; it's about showing up with purpose, resilience, and a determination to succeed.

I remember when Network Marketing was a different ball game. Eighteen years ago, we didn't have social media at our fingertips—we relied on sheer grit and face-to-face interactions! I once drove through a blizzard from Nebraska to Colorado for a home event, only to sell a single lipstick. My earnings from that effort didn't even cover the gas money! I felt so defeated. On that long drive back home, with my thoughts and the radio as my companions, I grappled with doubts and fears. Was this path truly meant for me? Was it worth it?

However, this turned out to be a pivotal moment in my career. In that whirlwind of uncertainty, a realization dawned on me: true success isn't measured by the outcome of one event or one sale! It's measured by the courage to stay committed to your vision, regardless of the immediate results. That long drive back home wasn't just a physical journey; rather, it was a mental and emotional journey toward understanding the essence of brave commitment.

Brave commitment involves adjusting your expectations when it comes to efforts and results. It's recognizing that sometimes, the most time-consuming activities might not yield immediate results, while a casual conversation could open doors to incredible opportunities. It's about learning to detach from the highs and lows of the business, to fall in love with the process rather than the potential or the setbacks. Here are some practical ways to cultivate brave commitment in your life and business:

1. Detach from immediate outcomes and manage expectations. Understand that not every effort will lead to immediate success. Appreciate the journey, and trust that consistent effort will eventually pay off! Learning to navigate the ups and downs of this field without letting them dictate your self-worth or commitment will help you remain steadfast.

2. Embrace consistent effort and find joy in the process. Recognize that consistency is key, and wholeheartedly engage into those daily activities! Whether it's a good day or a challenging one, your commitment to keep going is what will, ultimately, lead to success. With this understanding, you will find joy, even in the mundane tasks.

Remember, brave commitment doesn't mean avoiding doubts or challenges; it means choosing to persevere despite them. It's about making the conscious decision to stay the course, even when the path is unclear or fraught with obstacles. It's this kind of bravery and commitment that transforms aspirations into achievements and dreams into realities.

Brave Relationships

Brave relationships are the lifeblood of success in Network Marketing. This profession is fundamentally about connecting with people on a deeper level and prioritizing their well-being and personal lives over sales figures. It's about building genuine, honest connections that go beyond the transactional nature of business. As we often say, 'people buy *people,* not products.' And once they buy, they stay for relationships built on authentic care and mutual respect.

Early in my Network Marketing career, brave relationships were everything. This was the time before social media, where building strong connections with people meant phone calls and in-person meetings. One of the most memorable interactions I had was with a woman I met at the gym, who I now lovingly refer to as the 'pink heart rate monitor girl.' I wore a similar heart rate monitor, and I figured our matching accessories were a sign that I should start a conversation with her. This casual conversation led to her joining my team!

After she joined, I asked her, "Who do you know who might also be interested in this business?" She thought for a moment and said, "There's a woman at the hospital I used to work with, she might want to join." So, we went and talked to her. And she signed up, too! Then, I asked this new woman from the hospital, "Who do you know who might be interested in this business?" And she said she had a neighbor who ran a daycare in her home, so we went and talked to her. And—you guessed it—she signed up as well!

So now we had the 'pink heart rate monitor girl,' the hospital co-worker, and the neighbor with the daycare, all from one conversation at the gym! I kept asking my "who do you know" question, this time to the neighbor with the daycare. She admitted that she didn't know anyone in Nebraska, where we lived, but she mentioned a friend in New York who would get on a call with us.

Little did I know, the friend in New York had been part of a Network Marketing business in the past, and it hadn't gone well. She was incredibly skeptical about our opportunity, and she wrote in big letters at the top of her notebook "RED FLAGS." She planned to capture all the negative parts of my story and company overview and then tell her friend how silly she was being, how too-good-to-be-true it all was. However, once I connected with her and really got to know her, she set aside those feelings and signed up right then and there! She could tell right away that we were different from the people she had worked with before.

What happened next was truly magical. When I asked her, "Who do you know?" she mentioned that she had family in Michigan who she thought might be interested. And before she had even made a single sale, I showed up for her in the best way I could: I set up an in-home party for her family members and drove eleven hours with my kids to Michigan.

I continued to pour into her after that, and we became the best of friends. This is a relationship that genuinely changed both our lives. She went on to find incredible success in the profession and change the lives of others who joined our organization. And to think, if I hadn't asked, "Who do you know" so many times after I'd met the woman in the gym, I wouldn't have known her!

It's remarkable what can happen when you genuinely care for people. Whether it's showing up for them, coaching them, praying for them, or going out of your way to do something special for them, this level of care will bring you an abundance of amazing relationships. Here are some ways you can build brave relationships in your Network

Marketing journey:

1. Give the gift of your time. Invest time in getting to know your team members. Go beyond business discussions and show genuine interest in their lives. Showing that you value their stories, dreams, and challenges by actively listening is a key component of building trust and understanding.

2. Celebrate them in small ways. Whether it's finding a few minutes at a conference to take them aside and congratulate them, or sending a handwritten note telling them you were thinking of them, these small gestures let people know that you care about them.

As you continue on your Network Marketing journey, remember the power of brave relationships. Invest in them, cherish them, and watch as they transform not just your business, but also the lives of those around you. Brave relationships are your truest asset in this journey, one that yields immeasurable rewards, both professionally and personally.

Brave Faith

Brave faith is a profound concept, especially in the world of Network Marketing. It's about trusting that we are on the right path, even when the destination is not fully visible or when the journey seems uncertain. As highlighted in the Bible, faith is likened to a lamp unto our feet, not a spotlight revealing every twist and turn of the path ahead! This metaphor beautifully encapsulates the essence of brave faith—it's about illuminating the next step, not the entire journey.

I've experienced the power of brave faith myself on a journey that intertwined my professional and personal life. Several years ago, my husband and I, along with our five children, faced a life-changing decision: whether or not to move from Nebraska to Florida, a place we had only ever vacationed in, for a new professional opportunity. This move was more than a geographical change; it was a leap of faith into the unknown, driven by a deep-seated belief that there was something greater waiting for us there. Ultimately, we took that leap.

However, in the initial period following our move, the challenges were tangible. We walked away from the business opportunity that had been the original catalyst for the move. The joy of living in a vacation destination was peppered with struggles, including missing family, watching our children adapt to their new environment, and realizing that the easy thing to do would be to leave and go back to the life we knew. Yet, amidst these challenges, a quiet voice of faith whispered reassurance to us that this move was part of a larger plan—a plan that wasn't fully revealed to us yet.

It would have been easy during those challenging times to shrug and say, "Well, we tried." There were plenty of moments when moving back to Nebraska felt like the right and obvious thing to do. But we trusted God and held tight to our faith. And because we weathered the storms of uncertainty and doubt, we experienced tremendous growth in every aspect of our lives.

Our children blossomed as they found new opportunities to learn, develop, deepen their faith, serve in ministry, and meet new people. Our marriage thrived on a new foundation of steadfastness and with even more quality time to be together unconsumed with the things that demanded our attention back home. We then started a new business that continues to soar to new heights day after day and year after year—a business where we are truly making the impact we have always dreamed of.

Brave faith is about surrendering to this process, not in a passive way but with an active trust. It's about believing that each step, even when shrouded in uncertainty, is leading you to where you need to be. This type of faith requires bravery because it often means walking through doors without knowing what lies on the other side and trusting that the journey itself has a purpose.

Here are some ways to cultivate brave faith in your Network Marketing journey and life:

1. Listen to your instincts. Pay attention to that inner voice or gut feeling guiding you. It often holds more wisdom than we give it credit for!

2. Trust the process and embrace flexibility. Even when discomfort arises or things don't immediately make sense to you, believe that each step is part of your growth and journey. Understand that this new path may not look exactly as you envisioned, so stay open to detours and new directions.

3. Find strength in the challenges and learn patience. Use difficult moments as opportunities to reinforce your faith and commitment to your goals. This commitment often requires patience, as it entails trusting that the results you seek are forming even when they're not yet visible.

ntwrkr.com

Our journey in Florida, filled with its trials and triumphs, became a testament to brave faith. It transformed our lives, our children's lives, and the very essence of our marriage and business. The decision to stay, fueled by this unwavering faith, led to incredible growth and opportunities that we couldn't have foreseen.

Brave Perseverance

Brave perseverance is the culmination of all the elements of bravery we've discussed. It's the inner strength and resolve to stay the course, even in the face of the most challenging circumstances. In Network Marketing, as in life, we often encounter situations that put us to the test—losing a significant part of our business, facing doubts and skepticism from others, or embarking on new ventures in seemingly impossible conditions. Brave perseverance is about unwaveringly holding onto our vision and purpose, even when the path ahead is rocky.

In the last section on brave faith, I mentioned that our move to Florida resulted in my husband and I starting a new business, which is now wildly successful. Starting a new venture is always challenging, even in favorable economic times. However, we faced enormous uncertainty because we were launching a business during the pandemic.

Our closest friends and family expressed concern—not because they didn't believe in us but because the timing seemed not just wrong, but foolish! Yet, we moved forward on the foundation of everything we'd done up to that point. After all, we had embodied brave beginnings by moving in the first place, we stayed committed when the opportunity that brought us there was no longer an option, we fostered brave relationships far from everyone we knew, and above all, we relied on brave faith to guide us through the challenging times. However, what truly anchored us through this tumultuous period was our brave perseverance.

I often say, "Perseverance is commitment on steroids." It represents a whole different level of commitment, and it allowed us to stand in our conviction that, even if everyone who said they would support us in the business walked away all at once, we would *still* keep going. Perseverance is what will set you apart. It will make you a difference-maker and a world-changer. Whether you apply it in your marriage, your business, or your health journey, it is *the* thing that will make or break all the action you've taken so far. Here are some key ways to cultivate brave perseverance in your life's journey.

1. Get clear on your calling. This is your life's purpose—the passion that ignites you. Knowing this will give you the strength to persevere through even the greatest challenges.

2. Find strength in your story. Your journey, including the struggles, is what makes your story compelling, relatable, and inspirational. It's the fuel for your growth and influence in this life, so embrace the challenging points and remind yourself that you're a survivor!

3. Know that God isn't finished with you yet. No matter where you are in your journey, there's always room for growth. You are a work in progress, continually evolving and reaching new heights.

Brave perseverance is about understanding that your dreams, your vision, and your 'why' are worth every effort. It's recognizing that you're not at the end of your journey—there's much more ahead! Yes, there will be trials. Yes, you'll have to dig deep and find your grit, and you must remove from yourself the option to quit. Brave perseverance will ultimately lead you to success.

As our time on these pages comes to an end, I want to challenge you to ask yourself where your next brave beginning lies. Say 'yes' to it, and then stick with it through brave commitment. Find your community, your inner circle, the people who are going to go on this journey with you, and foster brave relationships with them. When the storms come (and yes, they're coming), stay the course by relying on your brave faith. And when the path is at its highest, rockiest, most narrow point, keep going with brave perseverance.

If you're wondering if you can be this brave, if you can find it in yourself to take these actions and change your life, well, it's clear to me that you can. You've taken the first step to great success and great leadership *just by picking up this book*. Start small, flex the 'bravery muscle' each day, and soon, the woman staring back at you in the mirror will be the courageous and fierce leader who was there all along, just waiting to emerge!

I hope this chapter has inspired you to take action, and I can't wait to see you out there on social media, changing your life. Here's to your newfound bravery, ntwrkrs!

Watch Aspen's Video Now!
LeadingLadiesCourse.com

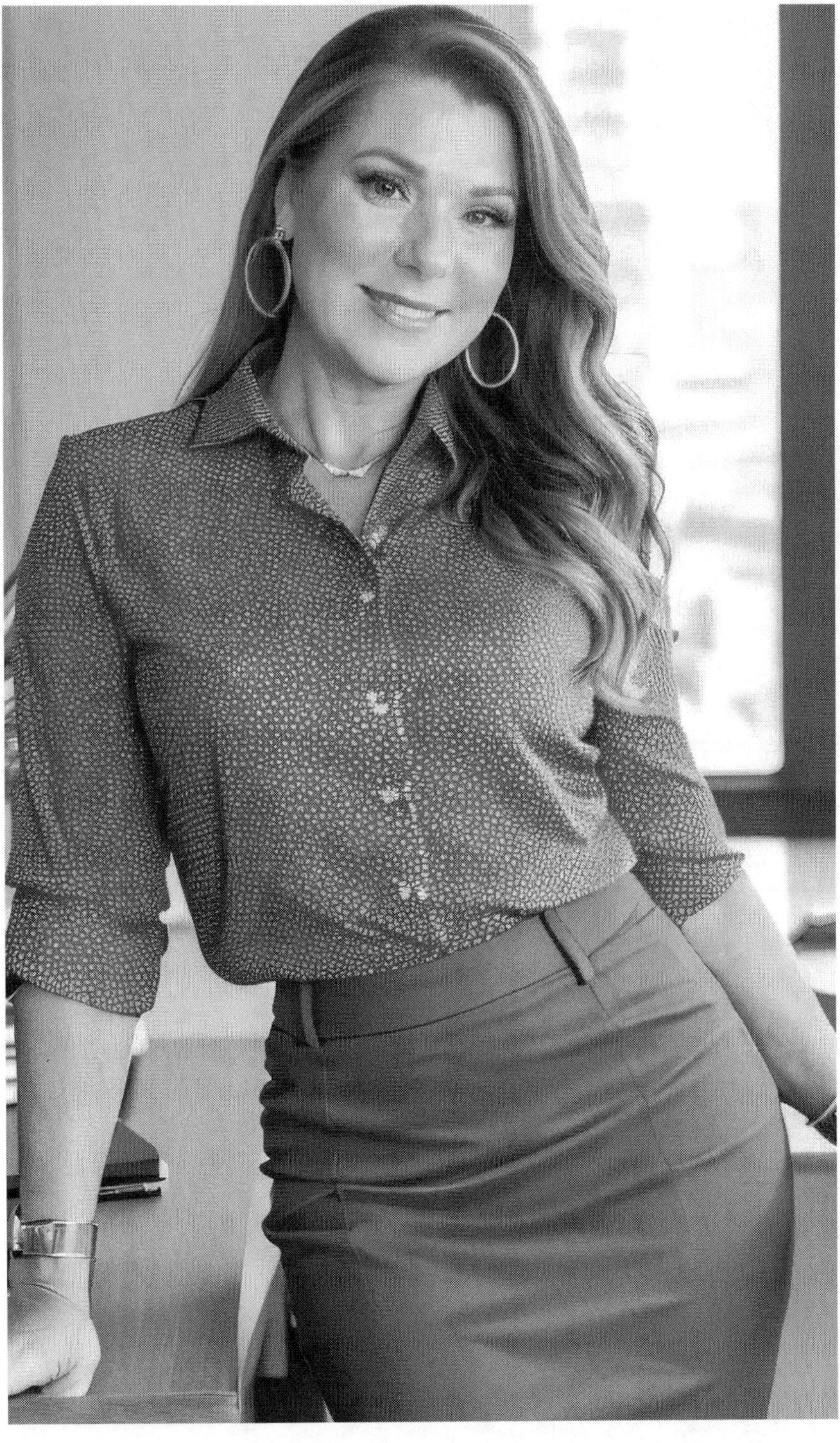

4

Do It Messy, Do It Scared, Do It Now

Why Doing It Messy Is The Key To Success

Heather Cain Wisenbaker

Facebook.com/heather.cain.18
Instagram.com/heathercainwisenbaker
Tiktok.com/@thecamifairy

Do It Messy, Do It Scared, Do It Now

Heather Cain Wisenbaker

Hi, ntwrkrs! I'm thrilled to be here and sharing my experiences on these pages with you! Before we dive in, let me give you a glimpse into my journey: I've been part of Direct Sales for over fourteen years, starting as what you might call a 'kitnapper' in the business, simply signing up to get discounts and free items on products I already loved. However, once I stepped behind the scenes, I dove in headfirst, finding it incredibly enjoyable work with no red tape—Network Marketing was refreshingly different from my previous professional life in the military. As a proud retired veteran of the United States Air Force, transitioning into direct sales was both an exciting and transformative experience!

This new path not only provided a platform for me to utilize my leadership skills and grow as an entrepreneur, but it also came at a time when I was embracing motherhood for the first time. My son was barely a year old when I retired, and since then, the opportunities and adventures in this field have been nothing short of a thrilling roller coaster ride that I'm eager to share.

In this chapter, I want to dive into a concept that I passionately believe in: *Do it messy, do it scared, do it now*. Embracing the 'messy' approach is crucial because all too often we become perfectionists, and this perfectionism becomes our biggest hurdle, obstructing our growth. My goal is to open your eyes to your potential; to demonstrate that perfectionism isn't necessary for success.

Yes, I'll admit, I've strived to be flawless in the past. But it's important to realize that the key to growth is to break free from that mindset. It's about taking action, not letting fear of judgment or the pursuit of perfection hold you back. It's about getting out there, sharing your story, and just doing it! This mindset has been a game-changer for me and a central lesson I impart to my team and other women in entrepreneurship. We often stand in our own way, but the mantra I live by and encourage others to adopt is straightforward: get out of your own way, and just do it!

So, are you ready to go on this mission with me?

We're about to explore five key areas that will revolutionize your approach to business. We'll delve into the ways that 'doing it messy' in products, systems, social media, leadership, and, crucially, authenticity—the glue that binds all these elements together—will lead you to success in Network Marketing!

Products

First off, let's tackle the topic of products. Do you believe that you need to master every product detail right away to share it with your team, your customers, or your social media following? Well, think again! You don't need to be an expert on every product detail right away. That knowledge will come naturally as you engage more with clients and your business. Trust in your company, your upline, and your mentors to guide your learning process.

Transitioning from a skincare company to one centered on fashion was a significant shift for me. Coming from a military police background, where I needed to know everything about anything, I was incredibly uncomfortable not having learned the entire catalog before getting out in the field. Initially, I was obsessed with perfection, meticulously detailing every product feature, its uses, and benefits. But after watching myself on video and being shocked at how robotic I sounded, I realized it was more about sharing my *enthusiasm*. "Hey, everyone, I'm loving what I'm doing. Check out this fantastic product," became my new approach. Getting too hung up on perfection hindered the potential for a genuine connection with others.

Embrace the messiness of the process: stumble, fumble, and fall. That's what makes you relatable. Authenticity resonates with people; they're drawn to someone who's real and imperfect just like themselves. Witnessing your journey, your growth—that's engaging. And not knowing everything is perfectly okay! I remember telling my troops during my service in the military, "If you don't know the answer, it's fine to say, 'I'm not sure, but I'll find out and get back to you.'" This genuine effort to engage opens the door to meaningful interactions.

The key point here is embracing your imperfections and showcasing your passion. There's always that one reason that draws you into what you're doing. Lean into that! The more you share why you fell in love with your venture, the more people are drawn to your story. It's your unique energy and passion that captivate them. So, the action steps for 'doing it messy' in this section are:

1. Make sure you're having fun! Let go of the need for flawlessness. Being overly structured and robotic can alienate people—they're looking for content they can connect with, not a step-by-step instruction manual.

2. Remember why you first joined and share that passion. This will help you to authentically draw your audience in. After all, they joined for a reason, too, and you can help remind them of that.

3. Let your expertise evolve gradually and share it with your team. Take the time to learn and understand your products, and watch as you become a relaxed, genuine expert. Then, you can continue to provide value to your team via the *learn, do, teach* process, consistently giving them new content to lean into.

Systems

Once I grasped the importance of delivering product knowledge in a relatable way, I realized the necessity of having a streamlined system—especially as a stay-at-home mom who transitioned into the role of a special needs homeschooling parent to my autistic son during COVID and beyond! Balancing my business alongside this new responsibility was challenging, to say the least, and I found myself drowning in notebooks—six or seven of them—for tracking different aspects of my business. Managing follow-ups, keeping track of conversations, and directing my energy became chaotic.

Everyone's life circumstances are unique, and mine required a streamlined follow-up system—something that would allow me to set tasks and then focus on other priorities. This approach made my interactions with clients more meaningful and encouraged more genuine connection. However, I faced a hurdle with my system implementation.

The perfectionist in me wanted everything lined up exactly how I thought it should be before I began using it. I sat on a texting system for eighteen months, hesitant to embrace it. This reluctance nearly led to shutting down, which was terrifying, considering the effort I'd put into building my brand and network! Eventually, I realized the importance of just diving in, learning in bits, and actively using the tools at my disposal. The key was *to start,* messy or not.

My day-to-day life as a mom, teacher, and therapist to my autistic son was already demanding. During the period of lockdown, I became everything for my son, which led to me losing touch with myself and the focus needed for my business. Adding professional responsibilities meant I had to be efficient and adaptable, making the most of the tools available to manage my time and tasks effectively.

So, the lesson here is to find a system that fits into your life seamlessly. Once you've chosen a system, commit to it and give it a fair chance. I was distracted by newer, seemingly better options, constantly switching from one shiny new system to another instead of dedicating myself to one and mastering it. I'll admit, I invested in over a dozen different systems, spending countless hours transferring my client information. I would try one, find it lacking in some areas, and then hop to another. This cycle of jumping between systems wasted weeks, if not months!

Finally, I returned to the very first system I had chosen, and it's the one I still use and love. It allows me to manage my client follow-ups automatically, freeing me to focus on deepening my relationships with more meaningful interactions beyond just sales. So, here's what I recommend:

1. Define what you need from a system. Is it more engagement with your community? Or more reach so you can find more customers? What's the purpose behind it? Make sure it's cost-effective, user-friendly, and scalable for team growth.

2. Look for tools that automate processes. Once you find them, start using them, even if they don't seem perfect! Even if they aren't your 'forever tools,' you'll gain valuable insight into what you want long-term by diving in and experimenting.

3. Fine-tune the system as you go. Check in with yourself periodically and assess how your system is working for you. It's ok to adapt and change your systems as your business grows!

Social Media

Now, let's shift gears to a crucial aspect of our business today: social media. When I first started in this profession, social media was just taking off. Facebook had only been around for a year or two, and the concept of online parties or a significant online presence was still novel. I was fortunate to be part of a company that was pioneering these online initiatives, guiding us on how to navigate this new terrain. However, even today, for anyone just starting out, I understand that the world of social media can be incredibly daunting and, honestly, quite intimidating. My advice? Look to your mentors, the resources your company offers, and lean into those. Utilize the tools at your disposal.

For many newcomers, and perhaps even for you, this online realm can feel foreign. Recording and sharing videos, for instance, doesn't come naturally for everyone! I witness it all the time with my new team members—it's a real culture shock for them, even if they've been posting personal pictures or funny videos for years.

When I first started out, I again let my military background lead, the result being that I approached social media with too much structure. But quickly, I reviewed my early live sessions to see how I'd done. And guess what? As you might guess, I found them almost unbearable to watch! Something had to be done, but I didn't know how to tweak my delivery just yet.

Then, on a quiet evening at home, with everyone else asleep and a bottle of wine for courage, I decided to let loose. I played around with all the filters, including one that was a face-distorting one to talk about 'spooktacular deals' in a mixed-up Irish-British accent. This was totally out of character for me! Still, it was also fun and refreshing, and I remembered that it didn't matter if it wasn't perfect, only that I was having fun doing it.

That moment marked a turning point for me. Even to this day, I look back and laugh because in my mind, a star was born—a bold, zany, off-beat, open book of a messy star, that is! It had dawned on me that if I wasn't enjoying myself, my audience probably wasn't either. Embracing the 'messy' became essential. I remember instances during my live sessions when my toddler, in the midst of potty training, would barge into the bathroom while in the camera's view. I'd have to pause my training, saying, "Excuse me a moment!" while attending to him. You could hear his little celebrations, and mine too, in the background—plus, my followers were cheering both him and me on. This was my a-ha moment. It was messy, and real, and authentically me. And as a result, I had finally connected with my tribe!

Sharing these slices of my life with my viewers became the real magic. It was about letting people into my world, just as you would with close friends. This approach resonated with me deeply, and I knew it was the direction I wanted to take my business in. By opening up and sharing my life, I was able to connect with my audience on a much more personal and authentic level. Now, let's focus on some practical steps for your social media strategy:

1. Start by jotting down all your fears about showing up as your imperfect self. They might be logical or completely irrational, but just identify what exactly is making you feel scared. Be honest—what are you truly afraid of?

2. Make short videos and then throw them away. Create a video, then simply discard it. There's no need to review it. In fact, I recommend not watching it at all! Repeat this process a few times. By the third or fourth attempt, you might feel ready to watch and evaluate your progress. This exercise is like a workout for your confidence! It's about strengthening your mindset and realizing that making videos isn't as daunting as it seems.

3. Share videos with your VIP group and ask for input. Take the leap and broadcast these videos in a space where you feel safe and supported. This group should be full of your cheerleaders, offering encouragement and love. Then, let your guard down, ask for their honest feedback, and use that feedback to improve your videos.

4. Share videos with the world. After you've completed steps one through three, you'll find that the fears you initially listed aren't as overwhelming as they seemed! Real-life moments, like your son running around or your husband interrupting with dinner, make your content relatable and authentic. *These are the moments that will encourage a connection with your audience.*

Leadership

Navigating leadership can indeed be a complex challenge, particularly when embracing the ethos of 'doing it messy.' It's important to recognize that while your business and company offer fantastic resources and tools, the challenge often lies in avoiding the trap of feeling compelled to mimic what you observe. When I began, I admired many leaders, incredible women who were achieving remarkable things. I'd catch myself thinking, "I wish I could be like that," yet deep down, I knew I wasn't the same.

I vividly remember seeing them walk across the stage and I was like, Oh my gosh, they're so gorgeous. I'm far from being a *fashionista*. I'm a country girl at heart, often in a jeep with my hair a mess, a stay-at-home mom covered in baby spit-up! That glamorous image just wasn't me. However, I realized that's not why people were drawn to me. They connected with the real, unpolished me. This realization led me to stop the self-comparisons and embrace my own light.

It took a leap of courage for me to step aside from trying to replicate others and embrace my uniqueness. Doing it messy, doing it scared—that was my mantra as I refined my leadership style. I realized that I had something distinct to offer, a different approach to leadership, a unique journey to share. And that's what you need to embrace.

Being an entrepreneur grants you the freedom to carve out your path. You're at the helm of your venture, steering it in the direction you choose. Draw inspiration from your leaders but focus on what brings you joy and where you envision your business heading! Forge your path, aligning it with your personal life and circumstances. Each of us brings our own wisdom to the table, and it's about leveraging that to craft a unique entrepreneurial journey. So, I want you to take the following crucial initial step: *Stop comparing yourself to others.*

Let your unique light shine through. When I understood that I didn't need to emulate others, my diverse background has shaped me and helps me connect with like-minded individuals.

I often hear from my team members, "I can't go live like you do." In the world of women's intimate fashion that I'm now part of, there's an element of boldness involved. Sometimes it almost feels like I'm wearing just my bathing suit! Initially, I had reservations, considering my background in the military and my male followers. I even wondered what my husband might think. But then I discovered how to present this tastefully and with grace, showcasing the empowering aspects of what I offer.

If I wasn't out there sharing this, who would? It was a call to action for me, and it spurred me to move forward. I tell my team, "You don't have to follow my path. Create your own journey, share it your way." It's about using the mentorship and tools provided by your company and tailoring them to fit your vision and goals. When you step out of the shadows and stop trying to be a replica of others, you'll reach your zenith.

You'll also gain the genuine respect of the people you help! I once had a client approach me in tears, thanking me for being brave enough to talk about women's issues and making her feel seen. If I hadn't had the courage to go live and share, I would have missed the ultimate reason most of us are in Network Marketing in the first place: we want to help people live better lives! So, here are some action steps to achieve your own unique brand of leadership:

1. Let your leaders guide you, not mold you. You're not supposed to be a carbon copy of your upline! Be inspired by your leaders, absorb all of their knowledge and wisdom, and then make it uniquely yours.

2. Use company resources as a springboard. Take the processes and tools given to you by your company and build an operational foundation for your business, and then add in your own systems. Remember, these resources were developed to maximize your success!

3. Promote unique leadership styles in your team. Once you have a

ntwrkr.com

team underneath you, it's quite possible that certain members will try to emulate your style because they don't yet understand how valuable their unique brand is. It's so important to encourage them and show them how to be authentic and celebrate their individual successes!

Authenticity

As I've emphasized throughout this chapter, my journey into the Network Marketing profession followed a lengthy career in the military. And in the years between retiring from the military and running my business full-time, I tried to blend a corporate civilian job, first-time motherhood, and a direct sales side hustle. However, I underestimated the immense challenge of navigating all three simultaneously. On top of the constant context-switching, my son was diagnosed with autism, which introduced new hurdles.

I knew that I couldn't be in all three places at once—the corporate world, the side hustle, and the world of full-time motherhood. So, I left the corporate job to pursue Network Marketing and motherhood. And I dived into this profession with everything I had! But all those years in the military began showing up in my interactions with my team. I'd been trained to maintain a strong front professionally; to never display weakness or vulnerability in front of my team. And I kept that strong front up, at least for a while.

However, trying to navigate the new territory autism was creating cracks in the dam, so to speak. I knew what autism was, of course, but this close personal connection to it brought a new level of anxiety, confusion, and a feeling of helplessness into my life. And one particularly rough day, during a live session, everything changed. I was conducting a tutorial for my clients when the emotional weight of my situation overwhelmed me.

Suddenly, I couldn't continue. I stopped and said, "I can't do this anymore. I just need to talk!" Tears flowed as I opened up about everything weighing on my heart. And in that revealing moment, I was shown the power of our platform—not just for promoting products but for connecting deeply with others who might be experiencing similar challenges.

That day, I became more than just a business owner; I became a voice for other parents navigating similar paths. Just as surprising, perhaps, was the realization that I, Heather, the former military police officer who didn't need anyone, *really needed that support network.* The outreach from people saying, "Heather, we're here for you, keep us updated," was more comforting than I could have imagined. And over time, I've built what I call my tribe—a group of people who are constantly there for support and encouragement. Whether it's celebrating good days or sharing the struggles of the bad ones, this community has become an integral part of my life. So, when it comes to authenticity, here are your action steps:

1. Open yourself up and be vulnerable. It's not about always being the one in tears, of course, but it's about sharing the full range of your experiences, from the falls and the triumphs.

2. Tell your stories, especially about the times you failed. Your story could be a beacon of hope for someone else who's facing similar challenges. They might see how you rise from difficult situations, shine

ntwrkr.com

even brighter, and find inspiration in your journey.

3. Boldly commit to bringing that authenticity into everything you do. Show that vulnerability, share your growth, and let others see how you navigate and learn from life's ups and downs.

Friends, I hope I've imparted to you through this chapter that authenticity (do it messy), vulnerability (do it scared), and imperfection (do it now) are essential to achieving success in the Network Marketing profession. I can't imagine where I'd be if I hadn't embraced these three qualities, but I know for certain that I wouldn't have the thriving, supportive business that I have today.

So, I encourage you: step into your authenticity, vulnerability, and imperfection! Be real in every aspect of your journey. Whether it's confronting your fears, navigating through the messiness, or simply forging ahead into the unknown, the key is to just get started and be genuine in every step you take. Take that leap, however daunting it may seem, and let your true self shine through in all you do. I'm rooting for you!

Watch Heather's Video Now!
LeadingLadiesCourse.com

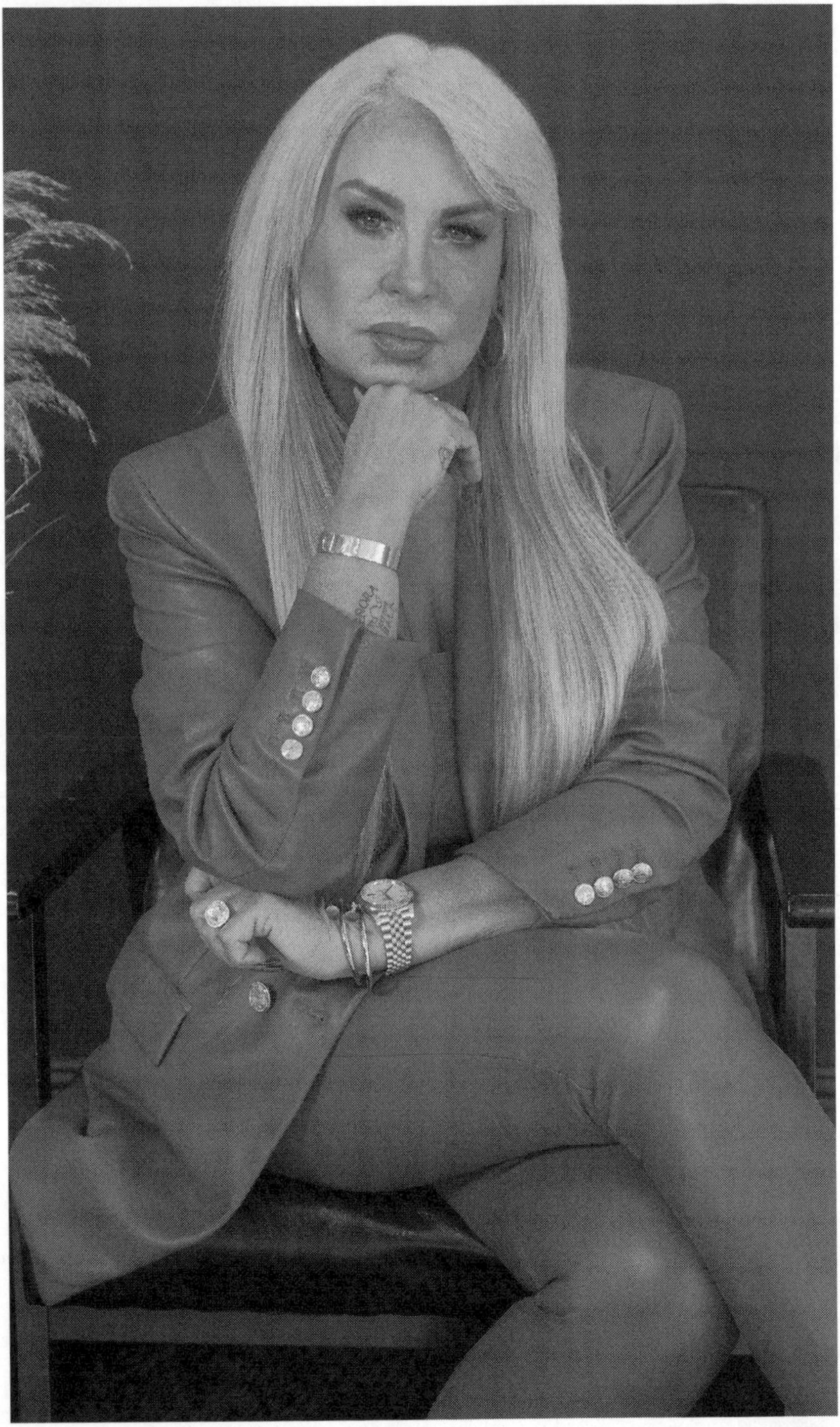

5

The Power Of A Single Day

The 10 Superpowers I Use Everyday To Create My Ultimate Life

Johanna Gil-Bala

Facebook.com/johanna.gil3
Facebook.com/johannagilbala
Instagram.com/senorabalaofficial
Tiktok.com/@johannagilbala

The Power Of A Single Day

Johanna Gil-Bala

Hello, beautiful ladies! I congratulate you for being here and for making the decision to become a professional in the amazing world of Network Marketing. I'm overjoyed to have you join me in this chapter and to share this special moment in your life with you! It fills me with happiness to be part of this grand project called *Leading Ladies*, where I'll provide you with tools to build your dream life and achieve all of your biggest dreams.

My name is Johanna Gil-Bala, but most people who know me call me *Mamasita*, or *Mrs. Bala-Bala: The Queen of Impact!* My passion is to help women who are searching for something: the mothers who are going through difficulties and want to feel valuable by providing for their children and themselves, or the woman who isn't yet able to spend more time with her children because she works outside the home. And what makes me qualified to do so, you might be wondering? Well, I used to be that woman! And to all of you who resonate with the woman I just described, I want to tell you that I'm here for you, and I can help.

I've been in this profession for about twenty-eight years, and I have a global business in more than seventeen different countries, in different languages, and in different cultures. I achieved all of this after arriving in the United States as an immigrant and being declared destitute after a few months. I had no home, no country, no family to support me, and I experienced worsening physical health every day. On top of that, I had three children that I struggled to care for.

One day, someone was kind enough to give me $100, and with those meager finances sustaining me and my kids, I began to develop what I call my "superpowers," which refer to the ten forces I access every day to propel my life forward. In this chapter, I'm going to share these superpowers with you, in hopes that you will turn your life into something incredible through the power of daily habit, just like I did.

My passion for Network Marketing extends to the women who can change their own lives and the world through this profession, so I'm determined to inspire, influence, and impact your life, helping you reach your potential and see your life and dreams transformed. So, are you ready to dive in?

1. Faith

I define faith as believing in something greater than ourselves—certainty in what we hope for and conviction in what we cannot see. To me, this is my trust in God, the one I know is my Creator. That's why I start each day with a moment of reflection, prayer, and meditation, connecting with God.

After all, if I prioritize making appointments with doctors, lawyers, friends, families, and partners, why shouldn't I start by making a daily appointment with God? This is the core of my relationship with Him. In

God's presence, extraordinary things happen that don't occur anywhere else. I bring all my fears, doubts, tears, joys, and greatest achievements to Him before I do anything else.

I cherish this time with Him, and I cherish our relationship. Additionally, I keep a gratitude journal and practice gratitude on a daily basis. Gratitude is the seed that makes many things possible—it truly is the seed of joy. Grateful people are happier, more satisfied, and are more appreciative of everyday-situations, like breathing, walking, eating, or simply waking up alive!

A grateful woman gives thanks for their friendships, family, communities, and much more, including all the things she loves about herself. She experiences more hope, optimism, and above all, self-esteem, which promotes introspection and self-knowledge, improving our learning capacity and ability to make intelligent decisions. So, start the morning with faith and gratitude to set the tone for your entire day!

2. Belief

Our beliefs shape our reality; they're the lens through which we view the world. The mind is powerful, and it responds to whatever you say to it. That's why words are so important! I make it a point never to say anything I don't want to manifest in my life.

Every day, I use at least five to ten positive affirmations to reinforce my empowered beliefs about myself and my potential. I write them down, read them, and listen to them recorded multiple times throughout the day. For example, I affirm that I am the creator of my future. I affirm that I finish what I start. And I affirm that I have the ability to make money.

In fact, I've crafted my unique personal affirmation statement that I read and listen to daily, and it goes like this:

My name is Johanna Gil-Bala. I listen to the voice of God within me. I am a guide and a leader, not a follower. Today, I will create, not destroy. I am a force for good. I set new standards. I challenge the possibilities. I am the head, not the tail. I am above, not below. I am one who lends, not one who borrows.

I am loved by God. I am blessed by God. I am chosen by God. I am elected by God. I am protected by God. No weapon formed against me shall prosper. Every tongue that speaks judgment against me shall be condemned.

Everything I touch turns to gold. I have the variability and the ability to create wealth. It is my season. It is my turn. I am healthy. I am rich. I am humble. I am strong. I am a champion. I will win.

I will never be broke for another day in my life because I am committed to a grand vision, bigger than myself, where nothing and no one can stand in my way. My goal is to liberate many women from their physical, mental, spiritual, emotional, or financial prisons. That's why I am filled with happiness and gratitude today.

As my entire organization ascends to the next level, with all my partners and friends becoming leaders and my organization becoming autonomous, I know I have the mental capacity to achieve everything I set out to do.

LEADING LADIES

Therefore, I demand persistence, determination, and continuous action from myself to achieve my goal. And here and now, I promise to execute that action.

So be it, so be it.

I invite you to craft your own affirmation statement like this one. Then, watch as reciting it daily not only strengthens your beliefs about yourself and what you can do but also manifests a new reality.

3. Dreams

Dreams are the burning desires for a material thing or an experience that, by offering us visions of what we want, shape our future. They motivate us to take action and see the possibilities of our future achievements and circumstances. Remember, you won't leave your current state until you decide where you prefer to be! Your dream is shaped by three choices:

1. *The voices you listen to, such as mentors or friends who influence you;*

2. *The amount time and resources you are willing to invest in your dream; and*

3. *Your faith and beliefs, which become the master of your life.*

I work on my dream every day, as it's easy to get absorbed by the world and fall back into old patterns. I also make sure that I have visual representations of my dream everywhere I look. For example, I have dream boards on the walls, I keep my dreams on my phone for quick access, and I place photos and statements related to my dream around my house—even in my bathroom!

I recommend writing down five to ten of your dreams in a journal every day, reading them aloud, and visualizing them. Imagine the sensation of achieving your dream. Visualization aligns your mind with your desired reality and helps you manifest it. It's essential to have visible reminders of your dreams, but remember that connecting them with emotion and action is key to propelling you toward achieving them.

4. Mindset

Your mindset lays the foundation for your perspective. Treat your thoughts like a garden that needs constant nurturing and care—the soil is your mindset, and it determines the quality of the plants and flowers that grow! So, cultivating a *growth mindset* allows you to embrace life's challenges, learn from experiences, and overcome obstacles. Not only that, but your mindset directs your mental programming; in other words, the thoughts and beliefs that shape your behavior and outcomes.

Investing in the development of a growth mindset will lead to healthy habits and new skills! I read and listen to personal growth and mindset content for 30 minutes daily, and I take notes. Afterward, I use these notes to reinforce what I learn and also to train my team or share on social media.

And, as I found out early on, it's easier to combine mindset development with routines I've already created. For instance, I learn while bathing, which I now consider a time for cleansing and a time for inspiration and motivation! Dressing and makeup are also intentional and related to my profession, keeping me motivated and relevant. In fact, I refer to my bathroom as my 'success university.' You can choose the best time for you and combine established habits with new ones you want to develop—called stacking habits—in order to get the most out of your time every day.

5. Discipline

Discipline is the ability to stay committed to your goals and take consistent action, even if you don't feel like doing it. It's about setting habits and prioritizing repetition so that taking these actions will eventually get much easier. Remember, your *commitment* to your goal is just as important as the goal itself! Discipline is what makes commitment stick.

In our profession, there are two main tasks: acquiring new associates and training them, and bringing in new partners while providing excellent customer service. For me, maintaining a daily agenda is crucial. I list all my personal and professional tasks, treating my business as if I were my own strictest boss! I prioritize my tasks and have pre-established time blocks with alarms to keep me focused and eliminate distractions. This approach helps me complete my work efficiently.

Discipline means focusing on priorities, and nothing else. One piece of advice I received is to dedicate myself to my profession with discipline for six months in order to then see most of my problems disappear. I also give myself a 90-day challenge at least once a year to maintain discipline and set an example for others. This is essential not only for personal growth but also for leading by example in my business.

6. Persistence

Persistence is the strength, energy, and determination to overcome obstacles and setbacks. It's what drives us, fortifies us, and enables us to achieve our goals—despite the challenges that arise—on the path to success. The key is to keep going, even when things get tough. This is where the *law of eventuality* comes into play, which states that consistent effort will eventually yield results. If you're not willing to commit to persistence and consistency, then you're choosing to accept disappointment and regret!

Persistence means doing what you must because you've decided to, regardless of whether you feel like it or not. For me, it's so important to develop a never-give-up attitude. I focus on my dreams and the life I'll have when I achieve them, working on overcoming my fears and doubts. This mindset helps me develop frustration tolerance.

To bolster my persistence, I've built an emotional support system because, as the saying goes, 'if you want to go fast, go alone; if you want to go far, go together.' The world's great achievers have support teams like personal trainers, coaches, and mentors to keep them motivated and persistent.

In my experience, surrounding myself with people who have achieved what I aspire to achieve is essential! Investing in a mentor or coach is part of my commitment to professional growth. Based on my goals, I have different individuals guiding me toward success. In our organization, we believe that finishing what you start is more important than starting. So, finish what you start, persist, involve others, and realize your dream!

7. Skill Development

The quality of your preparation for any endeavor directly impacts your performance and results! Skill development is the process of improving your abilities to perform better and achieve desired outcomes over time. Skills are the tools that enable us to reach our goals and build our lives and businesses, and they can be developed with time and effort.

This applies to absolutely everyone: success is attainable for anyone who commits to learning. All skills can be learned, and they foster the development of personal aptitudes essential for business growth. As Malcolm Gladwell tells us, mastery is not innate; it's created through practice and execution, requiring about 10,000 hours of guided practice to achieve.

Invest in your future by learning from those who have the knowledge you seek. True success comes from learning from those who are more experienced and applying that knowledge effectively. My daily mantra is to learn something new and teach something new. I choose skills that benefit my business and dedicate time each day to learning and mastering them.

For example, I aimed to become proficient in social media, so I took various classes to develop the necessary skills. While I continue to learn, I can confidently say that I know what I'm doing and can teach it to others. Studying and mastering the skills of this profession will propel you to the top and help you achieve your desired results!

8. Transformation

Transformation is not just about change; it's about evolving into our best selves. It involves altering our beliefs, perspectives, and behaviors for a more authentic and meaningful life. This transformation can be driven by various factors, such as the pursuit of a greater purpose or the desire to grow as a person. In our profession, where the focus is on people, embracing transformation is crucial!

Every day, I ask myself if I'm being the best version of myself and what I can do to transform into the leader I aspire to be for my global business. I analyze my beliefs and values to identify what motivates me and what holds me back, and I work on changing these to become a leader who inspires transformation in others. Setting clear goals and action plans is essential for progressing in this transformative journey.

This is not something that can be rushed, though. Transformation is a long-term process that requires patience and compassion toward oneself and others. It's about tuning into love to manifest our dreams more easily. Witnessing someone transform their life and become their best version, reaching heights they never imagined, brings me immense joy. It's a reminder that we are all capable of becoming new beings!

9. Unity

Unity is the cornerstone of my life and business, as it embodies the strength derived from collaboration and mutual support. I believe in the intrinsic value each individual brings, and I strive to appreciate and amplify that value. To encourage unity in my community, I implement a system where every client or associate who joins my organization fills out a Google form, providing me with comprehensive information such as their name, personal details, preferences, sizes, favorite colors, and more. This approach allows me to establish deeper connections and cater to their unique needs effectively.

And, as part of my commitment to continuously nurture the unity we've cultivated, I make it a daily practice to select five people from my community to connect with. Whether it's reaching out to say hello, taking a moment to react to their social media, or recognizing and celebrating their birthdays or those of their children, this small gesture not only strengthens our bonds but also cultivates a culture of appreciation and togetherness.

10. Love

Love is the most potent force that connects us to each other, and it drives us to make beautiful changes. For me, love is everything. True love is more than just a feeling; it's an action that shows favor towards oneself and others. Love is the essence of God. Love is the action that demonstrates empathy, support, and the desire for the good of others.

In our profession, we have the opportunity to express love in diverse ways, whether by helping, serving, supporting, or helping others achieve their dreams. By taking those actions, we're already showing love! My mentor and friend, Jesse Lee Ward, always said, "People hate for no reason, so I choose to love for no reason." I decided many years ago to love people for no reason, hoping my legacy would be that of a woman who served and loved unconditionally.

Every day, I start with self-love, affirming my worth and value in the mirror, and intentionally creating moments to express love, kindness, and generosity to my family, friends, and followers. I view each of my relationships as beautiful flowers in a garden that needs care, and I strive to make people feel better after being with me. Remember: to be unforgettable to others, we must do unforgettable things for them!

So, now that you understand the ten superpowers that I use every day to live my dream life, I hope you can see that the key to success is having clarity in what you want and taking action. It's not just about what or who you know, but *what you do* with that knowledge and those relationships. The cemetery is full of unfulfilled dreams. Why? It's not the lack of dreams but the lack of *action* that holds people back. Remember, "someday" is never guaranteed; "someday" is today!

So, today is your chance to start the business you've been called to, send your invitations out into the world, and connect with potential partners. Today is the best day to start living with purpose! You have everything you need, so stop looking for shortcuts and embrace the challenges. Everything you desire is on the other side of a decision, disciplined effort, and determination.

My greatest wish for you is to become the best version of yourself and achieve your dreams! These ten superpowers have transformed my life, and if you follow them, you'll see a transformation in yours, too.

LEADING LADIES

Remember: to achieve something new, you must do something you've never done before. I wish you all the beauty in life, and I look forward to meeting you—living your best life, on the beaches of the world!

Watch Johanna's Video Now!
LeadingLadiesCourse.com

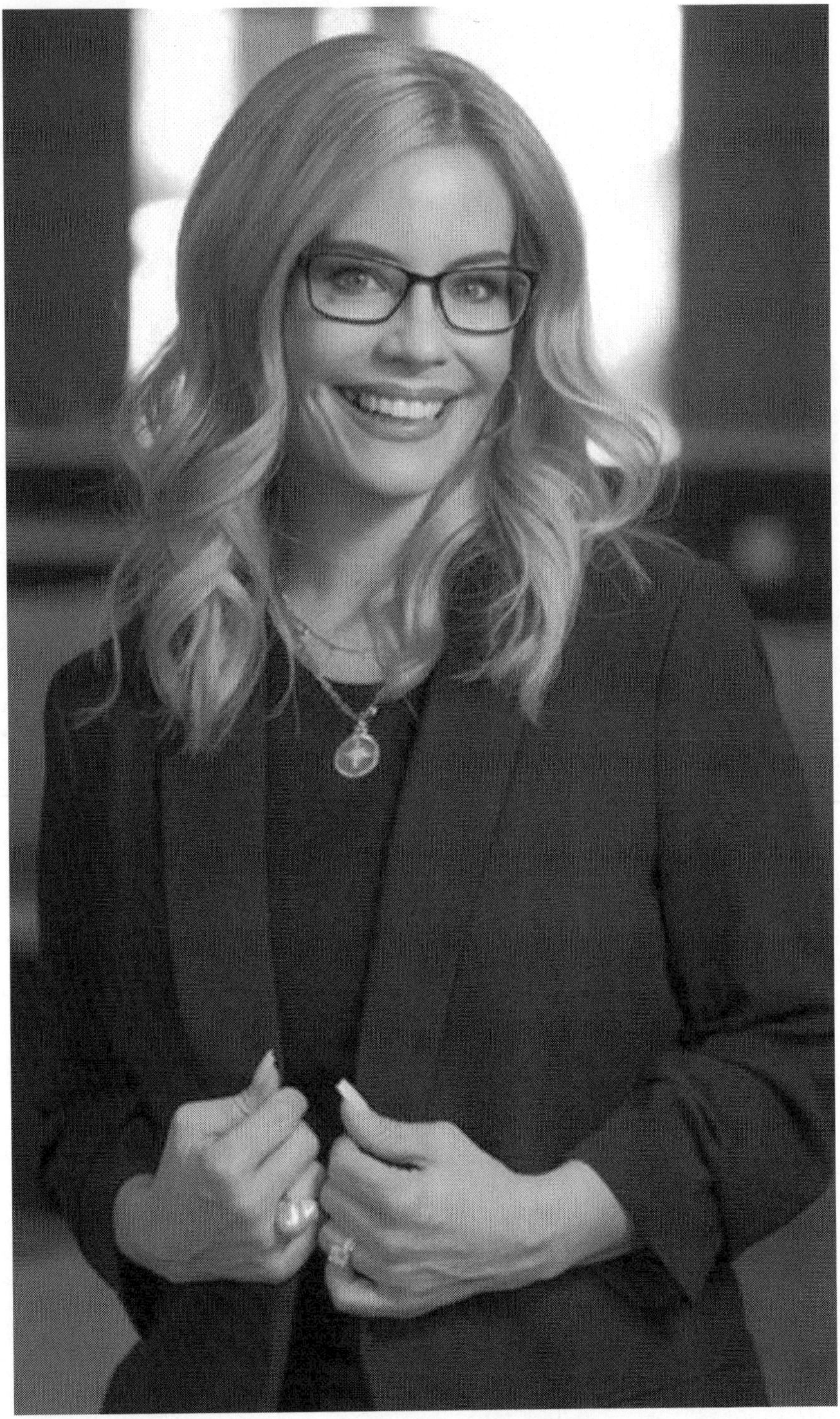

6

If It's To Be...

The Network Marketing 'Personals' That Shape Your Path To Success

Misty Lavertu

🌐 MistyLavertu.com
ⓕ Facebook.com/misty.lavertu
📷 Instagram.com/mistylavertu
♪ Tiktok.com/@mistylavertu

If It's To Be...

Misty Lavertu

Hello, everyone! I'm thrilled to have the opportunity to connect with you in this book, filled with the insight and experience of twenty-one other amazing women! In this chapter, we're going to explore a topic that's very close to my heart: the transformative power of Network Marketing and the personal development that comes with it.

As my mother taught me, *'If it's to be, it's up to me!'* So, at the end of our time together, I hope to leave you with a deeper understanding and appreciation of how far this amazing profession can take you in both your career and personal life—if you do the work! So, let's dive right into the heart of our discussion—what I call the 'Network Marketing Personals,' and the significant role they play in paving our road to success.

To some, the concept might seem a bit abstract, but I assure you, the path I'm about to outline is straightforward, practical, and, most importantly, *proven*. It's a journey I've taken myself, alongside countless others, and the path is laid out right in front of you, too!

Before we begin, a brief introduction might be in order. I'm a mother, a wife, an entrepreneur, a life coach, a business coach, and a seasoned

Network Marketing professional. Like many of you, I wear numerous hats, each important in its own right. Yet, what defines me most is my dedication to leading, mentoring, and empowering others in a way that's genuine, transparent, and authentic.

My adventure in Network Marketing spans over 15 years, during which I've cultivated a thriving team and crafted a life filled with options and peace of mind for my family. Don't get me wrong, this journey hasn't been without its hurdles, but the strategies and stories I'm eager to share with you have been my roadmap through every challenge.

Together, we'll delve into several key areas essential for personal and professional growth. We'll explore how mindset and personal development shape our essence, how taking responsibility and ownership empowers us to make decisions aligned with our values, and how a clear vision and mission guide us toward our goals. We'll discuss the importance of consistency in our daily actions and the impact of our social circle on our standards and aspirations.

So, are you ready to dive deeper and discover how these principles can shape your path to success? Let's now break down each component and journey through the transformative power they hold in crafting a life and career you love. Join me, and let's unlock the potential that lives within each of us!

Mindset & Personal Development

At the heart of our journey lies the cornerstone of personal and professional growth: mindset and personal development. This is where my enthusiasm is truly ignited! The concept of a strong mindset isn't just a skill to acquire; rather, it's an art form to perfect. It's absolutely essential in our profession, and it influences our identity, our achievements, and the joy and fulfillment we derive from life. Essentially, our mindset determines how we navigate our existence.

Consider mindset and attitude as the foundations for growth, resilience, learning, and improvement. Not only is a positive mental attitude (PMA) beneficial, but it is also transformative, shaping our success, happiness, and approach to life. Personal development, on the other hand, involves cultivating self-awareness, enhancing skills, and recognizing our strengths and weaknesses.

Think about the challenges you've experienced in your life—in other words, the phases where you were forced to grow. Can you pinpoint the parts of your story where a positive mindset or a lightbulb moment from personal development led to an ultimately beneficial outcome? Often, it takes difficult circumstances to finally move us into a space where we *must* choose heightened self-confidence, reduced stress, clearer mental focus, and more efficient time management.

Now, imagine *not waiting for a crisis* before adopting these positive mental frameworks. I encourage you to become obsessed with mindset and personal development in the good times and the challenging times. This is a surefire way to find fulfillment in both your personal life and your business endeavors.

Some years back, a woman joined my team who showed an initial outpouring of drive and determination. We were excited to have her in the group, and we were looking forward to watching her on her path to success! However, after some time, life's trials—including becoming a single mother with three young children and overwhelming debt—cast a shadow of self-doubt and limiting beliefs over her mindset. She felt destined for failure due to her circumstances.

I valued her place on the team, and I didn't want her to give up on her potential, so I scheduled a one-on-one call, where I shared stories of women I knew who had overcome similar adversities. These stories offered her a glimmer of hope, and so, she immersed herself in personal development activities—reading, listening to podcasts, and practicing affirmations. I made sure to check in with her daily and give her reassurance when she needed it, but, for the most part, her journey into personal development was self-sustaining! This marked the beginning of her transformation from despair to hope and determination.

Within a year, her dedication to personal growth catapulted her through the ranks. Not only did she become a top performer, but she also became a source of inspiration for others who were in similar situations. Her story is a powerful testament to the impact of a positive mindset and continuous personal development.

From this experience and many others, I've distilled three critical steps for overcoming limiting beliefs and fostering a growth mindset:

1. Identify your limiting beliefs. Start by acknowledging what holds you back. Write them down and get clear on these obstacles. If you find this challenging, seek support from someone you trust, but remember not to skip this step, as understanding your starting point is crucial.

2. Seek out development resources. Actively pursue personal development and mindset enhancement. Don't delay; start immediately! This kind of material is available everywhere—on social media platforms, YouTube, blogs, podcasts, and more. Schedule and plan your growth journey and immerse yourself in it.

3. Celebrate every step of progress. Recognize and celebrate every achievement, no matter how big or small. We often overlook the significance of small wins, waiting instead for monumental successes. However, these daily victories are the stepping stones to greater achievements.

By embracing these practices, you will embark on a transformative path. Mindset and personal development aren't only about reaching a destination; they are also about growing through the journey, learning from every experience, and continuously striving for betterment. Let's commit to this growth together and witness the incredible impact it can have on our lives and careers!

Responsibility & Personal Ownership

Diving into the realm of responsibility and personal ownership, we uncover another layer essential to both personal life and professional ventures. Being accountable is a choice, and it's a necessity that impacts our outcomes, positively or negatively, as well. In all my years of experience, I've found that those who wholeheartedly embrace responsibility most always find themselves on the path to remarkable success.

When we encounter individuals who adopt an "I own this" mindset, the difference in their approach and outcomes is stark compared to those who deflect and blame others for their circumstances. Embracing responsibility and personal ownership sets off a transformation, opening doors to growth, learning, and the creation of a future we all yearn for.

Responsibility involves a conscious effort to navigate life's decisions and actions with integrity. It emphasizes being accountable for our thoughts, actions, and the resulting consequences. Personal ownership, on the other hand, is a commitment to control our reactions and attitudes towards various challenges, taking *active* steps to steer our lives. This activeness is crucial; it's not about passively observing life but engaging with it, making decisions, and assuming ownership of our paths.

Transformation through responsibility and ownership is a dynamic process. It's about converting challenges into opportunities for growth and learning, which, in turn, empowers us to sculpt the future we envision! How you handle life in the face of difficulty speaks volumes about what kind of leader you can become.

Years ago, a member of my downline quickly climbed the ranks, amazing everyone on the team by embodying the essence of leadership. But once she was at the top, an unpredictable shift occurred. She had seemingly stepped away from the leadership principles of accountability and responsibility that had taken her so high in the organization, and instead, she started blaming others for her setbacks. This not only affected her performance but also divided her team. She was at a critical crossroads: would she continue to blame others, or could she be guided to see the broader picture?

Through conversations focusing on the importance of responsibility and learning from her mistakes, I introduced a framework for personal accountability that was built upon goal setting and self-evaluation. She was willing to do the work, grow, and evolve—and her shift away from finger-pointing and towards a proactive mindset enabled her to learn from setbacks, continuously improve, and ultimately, reclaim and even enhance her leadership credibility.

As you can see, success isn't merely about what we achieve but how we navigate the journey. To cultivate this mindset, here are the following action steps:

1. Understand your role. Clearly define your responsibilities and the expectations you've set for yourself. This clarity is foundational!

2. Incorporate guidance. Seek advice from trusted leaders and mentors. Learning from those who have walked the path before you is not only about outsourcing your journey but enriching it with their wisdom.

3. Reflect and learn. Embrace every outcome as a learning opportunity. Mistakes are not just inevitable but also incredibly valuable, serving as stepping stones for growth.

By embedding these principles into our lives, we not only steer toward success but also nurture a culture of accountability and growth, both for ourselves and those we lead. Responsibility and personal ownership aren't just strategies; rather, they are the bedrock of enduring success and leadership!

Personal Vision & Mission

Crafting a personal vision and mission is comparable to setting the sails on your journey through life and business. It's an exercise I hold in the highest regard, and I'm constantly refining and building upon it in my own life. The importance of dedicating time to formulate a clear vision and personal mission cannot be overstated—it's about visualizing your destination, instilling a sense of purpose, and aligning your values with long-term aspirations. This alignment inspires perseverance and serves as your North Star, guiding you through life's challenges.

Creating a vision requires deep introspection to identify your passions and envision a future that aligns with your personal goals. This process should be exciting and inspiring! Similarly, defining your personal mission involves crafting a statement that encapsulates your purpose, guiding principles, and intended actions.

The benefits of having a clear vision and mission are many—but perhaps most important are the ways they provide resilience to overcome obstacles and serve as a beacon throughout your growth journey. And keep in mind, these are living, breathing concepts you shape for yourself as you go through life. As you evolve, your insights will evolve as well, enabling you to master the art of maintaining a purpose-driven life filled with clarity and determination.

I once had a business partner who overcame personal hardships in her life and dedicated herself to uplifting others. Her vision and mission centered around empowering women both financially and personally, which became the cornerstone of her approach to Network Marketing. Her focus on empowerment over mere sales and numbers enabled her to recruit and mentor with a unique passion, encouraging a sense of community and success not only for herself but for the women she guided.

At one point, corporate leadership strongly encouraged her to work more with company messaging in her recruiting process. However, despite pressures to alter her women-centric approach, she remained steadfast in her belief that her success and that of her team were intrinsically linked to their mission of empowerment. Her unwavering commitment to her values and mission led her team to consistently achieve top numbers in the company, all while fostering a strong community of empowered women.

So, you might be wondering, how do we embark on this journey of creating a personal vision and mission?

1. Start by reflecting on your values, motivations, strengths, and passions. Look back on moments in your life that filled you with a sense of empowerment and use these insights to craft a personal mission statement.

2. Consider both your short-term and long-term goals. Ensure they align with your values and passions.

3. Incorporate these elements into your daily routine. Allow them to guide your decisions and actions. Remember, this is a dynamic process that can be refined as you grow and evolve!

By integrating your vision and mission into your daily life, you establish a framework for decision-making that is clear, direct, and deeply personal. This intentional approach to life and business paves the way for not just financial success but also a fulfilling sense of community and belonging.

Consistency & Personal Drive

The essence of achieving long-term success in any endeavor can be simplified into two critical components: consistency and personal drive. Consistency isn't merely a practice; rather, it's the backbone of transformation, turning the ordinary into the extraordinary through steadfast and intentional effort. If you pair this with personal drive—the inner fire fueled by ambition, determination, and focus—then you've got the makings of a high performer! This combination is powerful, fostering motivation, encouraging risk-taking, and sustaining persistence. Together, they form the bedrock of success and growth, enabling individuals to achieve their objectives more swiftly and effectively.

One standout example of the impact of consistency and drive involves an associate of mine, a woman brimming with potential. Initially, her journey was a rollercoaster of high energy and subsequent periods of inactivity, leading to unpredictable outcomes. This pattern affected her growth as well as showcased the critical need for a structured approach to her work.

After identifying the lack of consistent structure as the root cause of her challenges, she began to implement a daily method of operation (DMO), setting achievable goals and tracking her progress meticulously. This structured approach to her daily activities fostered a reliable work ethic and led to significant improvements in her performance. Her earnings and influence grew remarkably in a short period, a testament to the power of consistency and personal drive.

To harness this power in your personal journey, consider the following action steps:

1. Define clear goals. Start by articulating what you want to achieve and writing it down. Specific goals provide direction, reduce distractions, and enable you to aim your efforts at one target.

2. Establish a consistent routine. Your Daily Method of Operation (DMO) should be sacred. Treat it with the utmost importance, as the consistent execution of this routine is critical for your business's survival and growth.

3. Implement a tracking system. Utilize tools such as journals and online platforms, or work with a mentor for accountability. Tracking your progress is essential for identifying areas of improvement and celebrating successes.

Remember, clarity is key. A confused mind is stagnant, so it's vital to have a clear, organized approach to your goals and daily tasks. By embracing consistency and fueling your drive, you will set the stage for unparalleled growth and achievement!

ntwrkr.com

People & Your Personal Circle

The influence of the people in our personal circle is all-encompassing. This influence is far-reaching and expands to every aspect of our lives from our sense of well-being to our professional growth. Early in my journey, I learned that good company brings less stress, more harmony, and a sense of being understood, which, in turn, creates an environment ripe for growth and happiness.

Our personal and professional circles significantly shape our outlook, growth, and well-being. Being around kind, positive, and ambitious people encourages us to embody similar traits, and the opposite is certainly true! Think about the decisions you've made in your life, both the good and the bad, and then recognize who you were influenced by at those times. I think most people can agree that positive associations lead to new opportunities, ideas, and ventures, challenging us to elevate our standards and aspire to greater achievements. Negative associations will likely lead in the opposite direction.

There are dozens of commonly used phrases that underscore this concept, such as "You are the average of the five people you spend the most time with," and each one highlights the importance of carefully choosing our company. This selection process is paramount to our development and success, as our network significantly influences our net worth and overall life trajectory.

Once, I had a team member who faced ridicule and a total lack of support from the people closest to her. This mockery and emotional isolation took a severe toll on her, leading to self-doubt and a decline in her professional performance. However, when she opened up about her struggles, our team rallied around her, sharing our own experiences of overcoming similar challenges. The active choice she made to lean into this new support network rekindled her passion and confidence, prompting her to thrive in her business and find a sense of belonging and purpose. So, the lesson here is: never doubt the power of a truly supportive community!

To cultivate a positive personal circle, take the following actions:

1. Take inventory of your relationships. Assess who in your life truly deserves a place at your table. Not everyone is deserving of your time and energy, so be selective in nurturing quality relationships.

2. Build and strengthen connections. Engage with people from diverse backgrounds and cultures and focus on building trust and mutual respect. Show genuine interest and listen actively to find common ground and build from there.

3. Address misunderstandings quickly. Tackling issues as they arise prevents misunderstandings from festering and negatively affecting relationships.

Implementing these strategies can lead to deeper, more meaningful connections in your community. Remember, each relationship is unique, so it's crucial to find how (or if) it fits into your life. Surrounding yourself with the right people paves the way for more fulfillment and success and enhances your life along the way!

Okay! As we wrap up our exploration of the Network Marketing 'personals' and their pivotal role in shaping a successful journey, I hope it's clear that the integration of key strategies, which include: mindset and personal development, responsibility and personal ownership, vision and personal mission, consistency and personal drive, along with the influence of your circle, are the backbone a successful Network Marketing career. These elements, each one significant on its own, create an unstoppable force towards achieving your goals!

The mantra we started with, *If it's to be, it's up to me,* serves as a profound reminder of the power of personal agency. It not only encourages self-reliance but also emphasizes the importance of personal growth and commitment—because ultimately, this profession is inherently personal, reflecting the cumulative effect of our actions, decisions, and the company we keep.

I'm grateful for the opportunity to share these insights with you. Remember, the power to shape your outcomes lies within you! Embrace every challenge, celebrate every victory, find strength in adversity, and cultivate resilience to achieve greatness. When you close this book, the very next moment is an invitation for *you* to author the next chapter of your life: one marked by growth, purpose, and meaningful contributions! And remember, today only happens once, so make it truly amazing, ntwrkrs!

Watch Misty's Video Now!
LeadingLadiesCourse.com

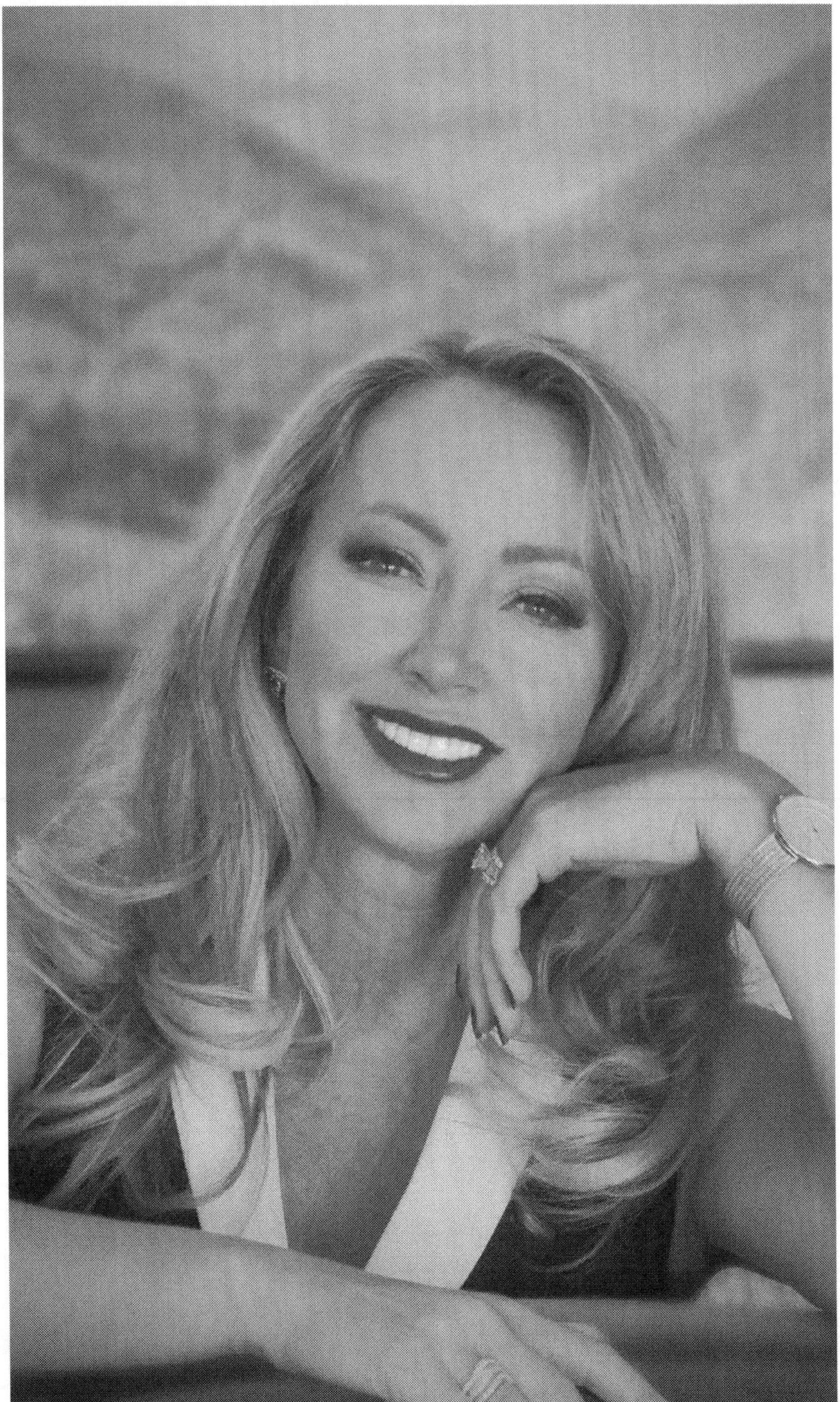

7

The Art Of Seeing

How To Cast Your Personal Vision & Create A Legacy That Inspires Generations

Deni Robinson

🌐 DeniRobinson.com
📘 Facebook.com/61553627481083
📷 Instagram.com/denirobinson
🎵 Tiktok.com/@denirobinson

The Art Of Seeing

Deni Robinson

Hello, ntwrkrs! It brings me immense joy to be here with you on these pages. I'm truly honored to have the opportunity to share my story with you, because in this world of Network Marketing, stories like mine—and soon, yours—take flight and *soar*. Together, let's embark on an exploration of vision casting and legacy creation that will inspire generations. So, grab a pen and paper, find a cozy spot, and join me on this journey!

In Network Marketing, we often hear about the *glory* but rarely understand the full story. In this chapter, I'll share a bit of my own tale, taking you all the way back to the humble, initial chapter of my life. I hail from a bustling household of seven children, where I stood as the sixth sibling. Life threw its curveballs early on, starting with my once-successful father's sudden illness, which then plunged my family into financial instability. This forced me and my siblings to mature quickly, instilling in me the value of hard work from a tender age.

By twelve, I was working to meet my basic needs, and by fourteen, I was purchasing my own clothes. Then, tragedy struck again at age fifteen when I lost my little sister in a car accident. Unfortunately, the following year, my boyfriend, the basketball team captain, became a quadriplegic as the result of a similar wreck.

These hardships filled me with sorrow and pain, prompting an instantaneous shift within me. I became laser-focused on changing my circumstances. This unwavering determination propelled me to graduate high school at sixteen and subsequently pursue college, standing independent and financially self-sufficient.

Yet, the challenges persisted. My journey has been marked by many personal losses, from my daughter's battle with cancer to surviving a near-fatal car accident myself. These trials brought me to my knees, teaching me resilience and the harsh realities of life. Through it all, one lesson resonated deeply: to play the hand I was dealt, no matter the cards.

I firmly believe that while fate gives us the cards, it's our destiny to play them wisely. It's about taking 100% responsibility for our lives, forgiving our pasts, and charging forward with a mission. When you do, the world makes way for you. Opportunities and circumstances align, and before you know it, you're on the path to greatness.

And friends, this belief has catapulted me to heights I once only dreamed of! Today, I'm writing this chapter as a seven-figure yearly earner in Network Marketing, having spoken on the biggest stages in this profession about my passion: empowering young women to shatter glass ceilings instead of fitting into glass slippers. I've built not only a thriving business, but a lasting family legacy as well: I've raised four children who are now amazing adults, and I'm a grandmother to thirteen wonderful grandchildren.

My career in direct sales began when I was a young mother, barely twenty years old, living in a forty-foot travel trailer. This journey from imagining just earning $300 a month to now making millions more has been incredible. So, you might be wondering, how did I do it? I did it in the same way you can: *by making a steadfast decision and acting on it.* And now that I have a business that spans thirty-three countries and a beautiful family by my side, I'm here to share the principles that guided me to where I am today.

Are you ready to take this transformative journey with me? We'll dive into five key principles that not only shaped my path but can also propel yours. From envisioning your success to living in the present while aiming for the future, each principle is a stepping stone to your success. Let's explore how you can reach your destination, one visionary step at a time!

See It First

Let's start with a fundamental truth: to achieve your goals, your mind must arrive at the destination *long before* your body does. Remember this: nothing significant is ever accomplished without first planting the seed of that accomplishment in your mind. I've come to understand, with every fiber of my being, that visualization is key. Imagine the complete environment of your success. The sounds, the smells, the people around you, and even what you're wearing. This vivid vision is your first step towards a life of achievement.

I've learned that the universe molds itself to the thoughts that we empower with our deepest convictions. When you align your heart and mind with unyielding passion and action, the universe conspires to turn your visions into reality! And I have personal proof that this works.

A few years ago, while starting out with my current company, I experienced a moment of unexpected clarity. On a strenuous run, struggling up a steep hill near my home, I envisioned myself crossing the stage as a new Diamond rank at the company. I felt the embrace of the founder, whom I deeply admire, and the warmth of other leaders whose lives and transformations I'd observed from afar. This vision was so vivid, so tangible, and so emotional that it brought me to tears. Yet, at that moment, I was just Deni, positioned at one of the lowest ranks in the company. But that powerful vision was the motivating force I needed. Within that same year, the scene I had envisioned became my reality.

However, to be able to reach that far without falling down, I had to balance the vision with the understanding of where I actually stood at that moment. So, I encourage you to embark on this journey of discovery. Identify what keeps you awake at night, the dreams that roll around in your head, or the aspirations that surface during your daydreams. Understand whether you are running from a nightmare or towards a dream. This insight will be the catalyst for the rest of your journey! Here are your action steps:

1. Identify your vision. What is that compelling dream for you? What are those aspirations that constantly occupy your thoughts?

2. Embrace the feelings. Make your vision so precise, real, and vivid that you begin to feel the associated emotions even before your dream materializes.

3. Balance vision and reality. While keeping your eyes fixed on your vision, remain grounded in your current reality, understanding where you stand today.

As we delve deeper into these principles, remember that your journey to success begins with a vision so clear that you can almost reach out and touch it. You really can mold your thoughts to shape your future!

Do This, Get That

In Network Marketing, the axiom "do this, get that" represents a powerful truth: each specific action yields a corresponding reward. This principle underscores the direct link between our efforts and the outcomes we achieve, whether they're tangible rewards or personal growth.

At the age of nineteen, my foray into Network Marketing started with a Tupperware party, marking the beginning of a transformative career. The concept they were offering was simple yet compelling: host parties, make money, and earn rewards. Intrigued, I dived in headfirst. The result? Within just three months, not only did I earn more money than I ever had, but I also earned my first company car. I was convinced, and I adopted "do this, get that" as my mantra for achieving all my aspirations in life.

However, the journey wasn't always straightforward. My career in this profession has been a series of beginnings and start-overs. Relocating to new cities meant leaving behind established networks and starting fresh. Each time, I applied the "three-foot rule," which meant that I would engage with anyone within a three-foot radius. This consistent effort in networking was a practical application of the "do this, get that" principle—every time I talked to people in my three-foot radius, I got new customers, which translated into the growth and success of my business in each new location.

Later in my career, I noticed the budding of a strong personal desire: renovating the kitchen in our first house. My husband agreed to the renovation but left the financial aspect to me. I knew that if I wanted that kitchen badly enough, I was going to have to find the money! Applying the "do this, get that" principle, I calculated what was needed to fund this project. I calculated how many more parties I would need to have, and how many people I needed to recruit. And with the goal in mind, the effort I put in led to the realization of my dream kitchen.

Still, that was just a one-off project, and I had bigger plans than just a kitchen! A more significant goal I had for my family was to be able to retire my husband from his successful thirty-year career as a CPA with a master's degree. Through consistent and focused effort in scaling my business, I created enough financial stability for both of us, allowing him to retire and join me in the journey of Network Marketing. It was a testament to the power of "do this, get that," as my efforts in the business provided us with the freedom and lifestyle we desired: traveling the world together, visiting places I'd only imagined, and supporting the teams and newfound friends our business has brought us.

Here are the action steps you can take to implement a "do this, get that" mindset in your business:

1. Visualize your desired outcome. That's right, we're talking about visualization again! This exercise is key in so many of these principles. Begin by envisioning the reward you aim to achieve through your efforts in Network Marketing.

2. Set specific, achievable goals. Outline the actions needed to reach your desired reward. Make these goals specific and achievable.

3. Implement consistent actions. Consistently apply the steps necessary to achieve your goals. Remember, every action should bring you closer to your desired outcome.

4. Track and adjust your approach. Regularly review your progress and be prepared to adjust your strategies as needed to stay on course towards your goals. Remember: plan, do, review, and implement action.

I believe that the "do this, get that" principle is a roadmap to success in Network Marketing. It represents the direct connection between effort and reward. By understanding and applying this principle through focused actions, you can turn your aspirations into achievements, whether it's paying bills, earning a new car, renovating a home, or achieving financial freedom! Embrace this principle, and let it guide you to the success you envision.

Look Forward, Not Backward

The principle of "forward, not back" in Network Marketing and life is a powerful reminder that our past does not define our future. It's an acknowledgment that while we cannot change what has occurred, we wield complete control over our next steps! The journey forward entails expanding our horizons, establishing new goals, and crafting a life centered around our true priorities.

Reflecting on my upbringing, financial scarcity loomed large in my childhood home after my father fell ill. I remember him drawing the outline of my feet on paper and taking it to a bargain store to buy me shoes. Once a year, I'd get a closed-toed pair for winter and a pair of sandals for the summer. We had a saying at home: "Use it up, wear it out, make it do, or do without." And even though I now have more resources than I'd ever imagined and can buy anything I desire, I still have a sign in my house that displays that very phrase.

Later, when I was in junior high, my father took me to Kmart to buy new school clothes. Until then, I had never been to a mall or a department store, so this was very exciting for me! I had so much fun trying on all of the cute clothes! I went and found my parents to tell them about all the outfits I was going to buy, but my father told me that I only had twenty dollars to spend. That's right—twenty dollars, for an entirely new school wardrobe! At that moment, I realized I was going to have to become financially independent. The experience, while certainly humbling, was incredibly valuable because it fueled my desire to create a future where I could afford the things I wanted.

It also helped that even though we didn't have a lot, my father instilled in me that I could be, do, and have anything I wanted if I was willing to work for it. This was so empowering to me as a young person, and it became my driving force. Despite coming from a small town with limited exposure to big thinkers or affluent lifestyles, I refused to let

LEADING LADIES

my past dictate my future! This belief propelled me through the toughest days and the biggest challenges, reminding me that my imagination and dreams were the keys to building the future I desired.

Here are steps to ensure you're looking forward, not backward:

1. Make peace with your past. Acknowledge your history without letting it hold you back. Every experience, good or bad, has contributed to who you are today. Never curse the journey.

2. Create a vision board. Visualize your future goals. Put them on a vision board and use it as a daily reminder of what you're working towards. Look at them daily.

3. Stay focused on your goals. Like a racehorse with blinders, keep your focus straight ahead. Don't get distracted by obstacles or detours; stay committed to your path. Focus on the step in front of you rather than the whole staircase!

4. Seek inspiration from others. Look for evidence in your network and beyond that others have overcome their pasts. Draw inspiration from their stories of triumph over adversity.

5. Write your own story. Actively shape your future. Don't let your past circumstances limit your potential. Remember, interesting lives are often forged through challenges and friction.

In life, as well as in Network Marketing, recognizing that your past does not define your future is critical! You have the power to turn doubts into determination and dreams into reality. By focusing forward, making peace with your past, and taking inspired action, you can create a future that far exceeds the limitations of your past experiences. Your journey forward is an opportunity to redefine your life on your own terms.

Do What You Can

"Do what you can" is all about the power of taking action within your current capabilities while keeping your ultimate vision at the forefront of everything you do. It's about recognizing that your current scope of vision, no matter how limited, is the starting point for a journey that can lead to greater horizons. This principle teaches us that progress, not perfection, is the key to success.

In my early days in Network Marketing, it was challenging as I tried to balance motherhood and career. It was heart-wrenching to leave four young children at home, sometimes with tears in their eyes, latched onto my leg begging me not to leave. I remember the nights I stopped at gas stations to change into my work attire or express milk for my baby, questioning if the sacrifices were worth it. Now, looking back, I'm immensely grateful to my younger self for her tenacity and vision, because it laid the foundation for the life I have today.

I know so many mothers who have dealt with similar challenges. Debbie, a member of my team, faced her own set of obstacles as a single mother on the brink of losing her home. Clearly, she had very little time to spare, but she knew that she could come to her own rescue if she *did what she could* with diligence and consistency! With only twenty minutes a day to focus on her business, she prepared for that small window of time and worked diligently, making calls and setting up meetings.

You can probably guess what happened: her dedication and efficient use of limited time turned her life around after just a few months, saving her home and eventually leading her to a six-figure income—and then to becoming a multimillionaire. Her story is a powerful example of doing what you can with what you have! So, if you're wondering how to "do what you can" in your own life, here are some action steps:

1. Start where you are. Begin your journey with whatever resources and time you have available. Your starting point does not define your potential.

2. Prepare and plan. Be like Debbie and get prepared! Set yourself up for success by planning your actions and knowing your goals. Organize your tasks and time efficiently.

3. Set non-negotiables. Determine your non-negotiable activities and stick to them. Decide how many hours you'll work, and how many people you'll reach out to, then follow up consistently.

4. Persist despite rejections. Remember, rejections are not failures; they are steps towards success. Keep moving forward regardless of the number of 'no's' you encounter.

5. Be the CEO of your life. Run your life and your business with the mindset of a CEO. Understand that bad days are part of the journey, but they do not define your path. Allow yourself to reset and start

ntwrkr.com

afresh when needed. Remember, no matter what happens, you're the boss!

The principle of "do what you can" is about embracing your current situation and using it as a springboard for future success. It's about understanding that your vision *can and will* expand as you progress. By preparing, planning, and persisting, you transform challenges into stepping stones for success. Remember, the discomfort you face today will be the currency for the dreams you're building for tomorrow!

Stay In The Here And Now

The "here and now" principle emphasizes operating in the present while keeping an eye on the future. It's about recognizing that vision and imagination, while powerful, need to be grounded in daily actions. It might be easier to daydream and think of what could be, but mastering the mundane and small tasks that collectively move the needle in your business is what ultimately paves the path to success.

Early on, one of the skills I learned was the ability to zoom out to see the big picture and then zoom right back in on the minutiae of daily tasks. Remember that four-mile run I wrote about earlier, where I had the vision of walking across the stage? Well, after lingering in that amazing moment, I snapped back to my reality. It was clear that there was a significant distance in between where I was in my life that day—and where I wanted to be.

I started by mastering and scaling a lower rank before moving up the ladder. This approach was not about chasing shiny objects but building a consistent and stable business. So, if you find yourself unable to get out of the clouds and into the mundane daily tasks that will move your business forward, here are some action steps to get you into a place of progress:

1. Focus on the present. Identify the tasks that need to be done *today*. Operate in the present, taking steps that align with your future vision.

2. Master the basics. Become brilliant at the basics. Know exactly what you need to do daily and teach these skills to your team.

3. Schedule and commit. Every successful person you see in this field started the same way: with a starter kit and the willingness to reach out to people. They didn't open the box and find customers inside! Just like they did, you need to commit to the process. Schedule your tasks, and don't leave details to chance. Remember to be prepared to work regardless of the circumstances.

4. Overcome fear of rejection. Accept that rejection is part of the process. Look for people who resonate with your vision and are eager for change, and don't worry about the rest. I never let anyone's 5-second 'no' steal my joy or my vision for myself.

5. Plan for consistent growth. Understand your next achievable rank and what it requires in terms of team size and volume. Commit to this plan with consistency—marry high conviction with high activity.

Embracing the here and now is crucial for success in Network Marketing. It involves balancing your long-term vision with the actions you take today. By mastering mundane tasks, focusing on the present, and scheduling your efforts, you lay the foundation for future success. Remember, every big achievement is a sum of small, consistent actions. Keep your eye on the future but let your actions in the present lead the way.

As we near the end of the chapter, I want to emphasize that this journey through Network Marketing is as much about personal transformation as it is about professional success.

Are you ready to transform any doubts you may have harbored at the beginning into the determination to change your life today? Remember, the power to decide your future lies within you, not in your past, not in your circumstances, nor in the voices of naysayers. Your vision should be so profound that obstacles become mere stepping stones on your path to success. As Henry Ford stated, obstacles are what appear when we lose sight of our goals. Keep your focus sharp and unwavering.

Embrace the realization that the true outcome of this journey is not just income; it's about what you overcome and who you become in the process. The stories and experiences shared in this book are testaments to the fact that success is achievable. They are a reminder that through overcoming, you become a stronger, more capable version of yourself.

Recognize that there's a time for sowing and a time for reaping, and they do not occur simultaneously. Patience and continuous effort are key. Your journey in Network Marketing is about planting seeds, nurturing them, and then enjoying the harvest.

This profession presents an opportunity for all people. It offers a home for everyone, regardless of their background or current skill set. It's about changing lives with products, earning through rewarding compensation plans, and growing personally and professionally. You now know about this incredible opportunity, so take it, share it, and make a difference boldly.

All of us have had the experience of looking back to a time when our younger self did something that we are now very thankful for. We look back at those moments and understand that if we hadn't walked out the door, if we hadn't made that one phone call, if we hadn't made a promise to ourselves and kept it—our lives would be very different. So ask yourself: what can you leverage, or decide to cut from your life, that your future self will be thankful for one day?

As you step forward, remember that your success is limited only by your belief in yourself. I believe in you and in the effort you're willing to put forth. Go out and create a legacy that will rock the world. When you achieve your goals, know that I, along with many others, will be cheering for you! Until our paths cross again, I wish you all the success you deserve and believe you can achieve. You can do this!

Remember: Some people succeed because they are destined to...but most people succeed because they are *DETERMINED* to! See you soon, ntwrkrs!

Watch Deni's Video Now!
LeadingLadiesCourse.com

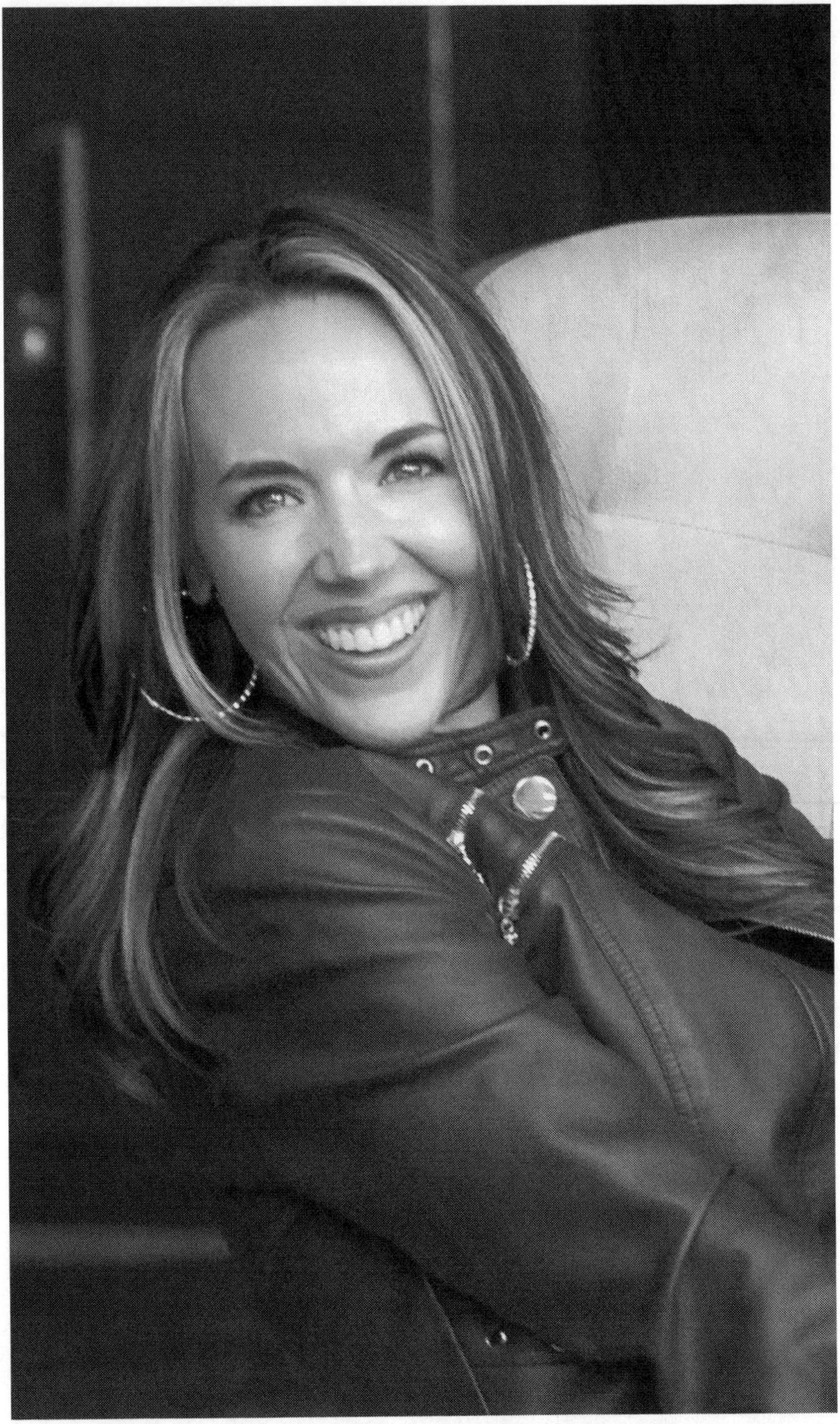

8

Alignments Before Assignments

How The People You Align Yourself With
Dictate Your Life & Business Success

Heidi Black

🌐 HeidiBlack.com
🅕 Facebook.com/heidiblackpro
📷 Instagram.com/meetheidiblack

Alignments Before Assignments

Heidi Black

I remember the day that changed everything. It was a warm July afternoon, and I found myself stepping into our daylight basement, where my husband, Brad, was taking a break between sales appointments. My heart pounded as I prepared to share my most recent decision with him, and honestly, with myself.

"Brad, I've decided I don't want to be married to you anymore. I can't even think of one thing I like about you. We were just kids when we walked down the aisle, and if I had the chance to do it all over again, well, I wouldn't. Our paths have gone in different directions. I'm seeing other men. I don't want any of this any longer—I don't even want to be a mom anymore. It's time for me to start my new chapter and live my best life."

Looking back today, I recognize how utterly lost that version of me was. So, when the writing team for *Leading Ladies* asked me which critical piece of information I would share with readers if I could only choose one, I knew immediately that it would be this: *Our alignments determine our assignments.* And that's what my chapter is all about—because your circle, the people you align with, shape not just what you believe is possible but ultimately who you become! My

ntwrkr.com

journey, filled with missteps and victories, taught me the invaluable lesson that who we let into our lives matters. I am beyond grateful to be joining the other amazing authors in this book, sharing a twenty-five-year path that's been anything but straightforward.

But let's not dive in just yet, ntwrkrs! I'd like to backtrack a bit so I can share some highlights from my personal history. I grew up in the Northwest, the oldest of seven, in a home that was filled with love—but not drive. In my family, generations of people were taught that the 'right' path was to go to school, get a job to pay the bills, and then one day retire with enough money to (hopefully) live on.

From a young age, none of that resonated with me. I felt different. There was a spark in me that wanted more. I paid more attention to the world around me and my dreams of a future than to my homework, and I barely graduated high school. I wasn't dumb, by any means, I was just bored! And after high school, it didn't get much better. I didn't see the point in going to college, and soon my feelings of boredom turned to rebellion. I went through the motions as an elementary school teacher's aide while I tried to figure out what I was going to do with my life.

One afternoon, the sweet school librarian approached me in the break room. She said, "Heidi, there's something special about you. I think you should meet my daughter." Later that week, I was introduced to Cindy, my first mentor. I learned that Cindy was a top leader in her company, which was a candle-based Network Marketing company. I learned that she set her own hours and made great money on her terms, which was exactly the kind of career I was looking for! Meeting Cindy sparked a flame in me, so to speak, and I dove headfirst into learning about

LEADING LADIES

leadership and business.

Fast forward a few years, and I met Brad: a goal-oriented man who shared my passion for growth. We started a life together, brimming with passion and ambitions. And despite the zigzag journey to the success that we have now, at 43 years old, and married for 23 years, I can finally look back and appreciate everywhere we needed to go to get here. But those decades were rife with challenges. I had to learn the hard way that listening to the wrong voices would take me to the wrong places in life, and that only the right voices would lead me to where I belonged.

And now, living in one of America's most prosperous cities with my family, I lead a successful company in a male-dominated industry with my husband and am a top leader in a global Network Marketing company. My path to success hasn't been easy, so I'm dedicated to helping others by spreading the message about the power of right alignments—especially when it comes to business and Network Marketing!

Tom Challan once told me that Network Marketing is all about dealing with the 'junk in your trunk' and transforming your baggage into your stepping stones for growth. I couldn't agree more, and I believe that the right alignments are key to making this transformation happen. It's said that in 5 years, your future will be determined more by the 'who' than by the 'how'. So, as you read the following pages, I want you to think about your current inner circle.

Consider this: are the people you spend the most time with living the kind of life you want? Do they possess the relationships, health, mindset, and financial stability you seek? What do *their* lives say about *your* future?

In this chapter, I'm going to delve into four key areas: Core Values & Principles, Goals & Aspirations, Morals & Standards, and Faith & Spirituality. These are not just words; rather, they are the pillars that uphold the structure of our lives. As we journey through these concepts, I encourage you to listen intently, pause, reflect, and perhaps even re-read if something strikes a chord within you. This isn't just a lesson; it's a transformation waiting to happen!

Ask yourself: are you living a life that excites you every morning, or are you just drifting along, settling for less than your potential? It's time for introspection, for digging deep. So, grab your favorite drink, a fresh notebook, and a pen, and let's go on this adventure together!

Core Values & Principles

Our journey begins with core values and principles. Picture these like the compass that guides every decision we make. From who we marry to our business alignments, these values are the bedrock of all significant life decisions. And because I wasn't clear on my values or principles in young adulthood, I had to learn the hard way. My unhindered early career ambitions led me away from deep down what I knew to be important in life. I chased temporary gains and immediate gratification until everything around me fell apart, and it took hitting rock bottom to realize the critical nature of having clear, established values in life. So, I hope I can save you from this heartache.

As a young, goal-oriented Christian woman, I often pondered what a successful Godly woman should look like. I didn't have any real-life role models as an example, so I focused on outward appearances, mistaking surface-level attributes for true values. But the more I pursued what I should look like externally, the less I concentrated on who I was becoming on the inside.

Early in our marriage, Brad attended college while I worked a daytime desk job and spent my evenings and weekends with my new side hustle. We were committed to pursuing our goals to build a business and hoped to one day make it our full-time careers. But soon my ambition would take a dark turn when, at the age of twenty-five, I was introduced to a man who owned a Network Marketing travel company. This presented itself as an opportunity to use all the skills I'd developed in an industry which rewarded my drive.

In this new company, I was quickly recognized as a rising leader and became the face and voice of the company. This was the attention and admiration that I had been looking for! I was rewarded and celebrated, and before I knew it, I began traveling with the owners all over the country. However, this kind of close interaction led to my becoming entangled in a toxic relationship with one of them. He bought me gifts, took me out to nice dinners, and made sure to let me know how fond of me he was. And one unfortunate evening after an event in Las Vegas, he put something in my drink. I woke up unaware of what had happened, full of mixed emotions. I felt shame, embarrassment, and anger—but mostly, I felt trapped. I couldn't tell anyone that I, a young married woman, was engaging in a risky relationship.

I wish I could say that this was the end of that story, but it wasn't. Believing that this was just an inherent part of being a successful woman at the company, I once again became comfortable with it. I was leading a double life. When I was working and traveling, I was the bold, exciting, important woman I'd always dreamed I'd be, but I felt obligated to interact in ways I was uncomfortable with. And when I was at home, I was the good Christian wife I'd signed up to be, but I struggled with the dishonesty and disloyalty I was hiding from my husband.

Living this double life was exhausting, unsustainable, and devastating. I was trapped in a cycle of shame, manipulation, and self-compromise. This period of time became a defining battle—a struggle between the person I was at home and the person I became on the road. I didn't know my values or my worth, and I had mistakenly aligned myself with the wrong people, places, and situations to get my temporary fix of validation. My identity became tied up in the false belief that success in Network Marketing meant I needed to win the favor of my male leaders by whatever methods necessary. I told myself that I was in control, but really, I was being controlled. I had become a counterfeit version of myself that I didn't even recognize in the mirror.

I want to pause here and address the goal-driven women reading this book: If you're in a similar situation, whether it's like the one I described, or one of addiction or abuse, I want to impart to you that recognizing these toxic patterns is crucial. I'm here to tell you that no matter how long you've been unknowingly participating in this destructive cycle, it's never too late to change. Speak up, reach out to someone you trust, and make a commitment to align yourself with healthy, growth-minded individuals. This toxic pattern doesn't have to be your story—your future self will thank you!

Today, right now, it's critical to define your core values. The first step to realignment is recognizing when something doesn't match up with your vision of your best self, so you have to get crystal clear on these! It will be the new GPS for your life. For example, my core values are a Kingdom Mindset (God First), relationships, creativity, fun, and personal growth.

After I became clear on these, they ultimately became my guide for every decision I made, whether it revolved around a relationship, a company to partner with, or a new opportunity. Rediscovering my core values was a turning point in my life, but defining these values wasn't an overnight process—it took years to clarify what mattered most to me.

I encourage you to take the time to define your own core values. They will become your decision-making guide, helping you choose friends, business opportunities, and life paths that align with who you are and who you aspire to be. And to take this a step further, if you have a significant other, take the time to define your family core values as a team. Have a meeting every month with the people in your family to review these values and redirect choices and behaviors where necessary together.

Goals & Aspirations

With a clear understanding of our core values and principles, we can now focus on our goals and aspirations. I grew up in a home where big goals and dreams were not encouraged, which I know is a common theme for many. If anything, most of us are taught from a young age to be realistic, and that money doesn't grow on trees. But to achieve greatness, we must first allow ourselves to dream big. And remember, the people you surround yourself with can either support or hinder your growth. It's proven that what you believe is possible is nurtured and reinforced by the people you spend the most time with! If they aren't aligned with your goals and dreams, you're setting yourself up for failure and frustration.

Ten years ago, my family and I made a bold move from Oregon to Texas. This wasn't just a change of location; it was a complete reset of our lives. We were in a state of surrender, in large part because of the reckless choices I had made. I prayed that God open doors that would be right for us while slamming shut those that were not. New state, new community, new beginnings. Sometimes, to achieve drastic change, you must be willing to take massive steps. This move marked a turning point for us, a line in the sand that paved the way for a future aligned with our true values and aspirations. We became incredibly intentional with our alignments and our faith, and we prioritized the health of our marriage, the health of our bodies, our businesses, our vision, and our legacy. It was a stark contrast to where we had been a decade before.

However, when I emerged from the chaos I had created, I found myself hesitant to dream or set goals. My past choices had eroded my trust in myself, and I attempted to squash any urges to dream big.

I'll take this moment to remind everyone reading that the concept of forgiveness—for others and for yourself—is vital. It may sound unrelated to goals and aspirations, but if you haven't forgiven yourself for negative choices you've made in your pursuit of goals in the past, it will keep you from setting new goals. Despite any mistakes, missteps, or downright catastrophes you've experienced in your life, you must forgive yourself and let go of shame to allow yourself to dream again. This truly is the first step first toward healing and success!

I'll share a personal story from about a year ago to illustrate just how powerful specific goals continue to be in my life. One day, as I was cleaning out a storage bin, I found a recipe box with note cards of goals I had written nearly fifteen years beforehand. My life was in absolute turmoil at that time, but somehow, I'd managed to gain clarity about what I wanted. One of my goals was to live in a beautiful home with a tree-lined driveway. And today, I'm living in that exact dream. We live on a wooded acre at the end of a private cul-de-sac. This shows the immense power of our minds and the importance of being specific with our aspirations.

As I wrap up this part of the chapter, I want to offer some advice on how to handle relationships during this stage of alignment. As you gain clarity and start working towards your goals, be prepared for resistance, especially from those you thought were supportive. Growth can be uncomfortable, not just for you but for those around you—and some of the people who were closest to you might pull away because this version of you is new and different. Despite this shift, stay strong! When these situations arise, think of what it will mean to you to become the person you know you're created to be. Remember, your journey to greatness might require you to reevaluate your relationships. These are the changes that are required for your God-sized goals and dreams. And don't worry, the people who truly support you will remain by your side!

Morals & Standards

Though similar, morals and standards are distinct from core values and principles. They dictate not only what we decide to do but how we show up in the world. In my twenties and thirties, my moral compass was skewed, leading me astray. I recall a trip to Miami for a conference that epitomized this misalignment. It was for a Network Marketing company that was known in the industry for throwing the best parties. That weekend, I indulged in every desire, losing myself in the chaos: dance clubs, bottle service, and staying up all night, and sharing a hotel room with co-workers. One morning, my co-worker found me lying on the bathroom floor, and another morning, I had fallen asleep in the hallway of our hotel. Both times, I didn't know how I'd gotten back to the hotel or who I'd been with the night before. I'd blacked out and blocked out all the memories. And while my co-workers were concerned, I shrugged it off as no big deal since it was common behavior for me, and I considered it fun.

Coming off of that weekend high, I returned home and announced to my husband that I was ready to live a fast and furious party life, and that I didn't want the responsibility of being a mom and wife anymore. It sounds crazy, but this story is living proof of just how far we can go off track when we aren't living by a moral code. Little by little, compromising and spending time with the wrong people, my heart had become so hardened. It didn't happen overnight; it was a gradual process of aligning myself with the wrong people in the wrong places at the wrong times until I was unrecognizable to myself and those I loved most.

Our alignments have a profound impact on our morals and standards, and my journey is a testament to this. In all the stories I've told you, the common denominators are the people that I chose to align with and do life with. Ultimately, their lives modeled for me a way of thinking and being in the world. And this influenced my decisions and led me to adopt habits and behaviors that were not true to who I really was.

Establishing strong morals and standards is about knowing who you are, what matters to you, and refusing to compromise your integrity for short-term gains or pleasure. Think of them as guard rails on the curvy, mountainous highway of life: without them, you risk veering off the path to your detriment and destruction. Your alignments really are that powerful.

Faith & Spirituality

Without a foundation of faith, knowing that you were created on purpose, with purpose, life can feel pretty meaningless. Shortly after my trip to Miami, after I'd announced my intent to depart from family life, my husband could have just let me leave. He had, after all, endured seven years of being put through hell, and he had every right to tell me to leave. But he chose to stay. He fought for me, for our marriage, and our family. He fought for our future and everything we could become together.

And though my husband is a strong man, I realized that this choice was not made in his strength alone. His foundation of faith in Jesus overrode his human emotion in that moment. Brad led me and our family with such strength in that decision. And it was then when a friend and confidant he knew through bible study reached out to us with a contact—a new alignment, you could say—named Vicki Norris.

Despite my initial reluctance and a heart heavy with skepticism, I agreed to drive into the country and meet with Vicki at her homestead, Dream Acres. We sat at a table in her office, and she reached out her hands and asked to pray with me. As someone who had only been going through the motions in church for many years, I found the genuine, prayerful environment overwhelming and uncomfortable! All the numbing effects from years of self-inflicted spiritual apathy started to melt away, and I couldn't help but sob as she continued to pray. My heart softened and I began feeling remorse for what I'd done. And I also felt hope for the first moment in a long time.

Vicki's prayer was more than mere words; it was a conduit for power and hope. She introduced me to the Sozo Ministry, a healing and deliverance ministry that I've referred many people to since experiencing it myself. Vicki also introduced me to the concept of Biblical Entrepreneurship, igniting a journey towards understanding our role in bringing God's kingdom to Earth. This newfound comprehension reshaped my perception of faith—it was no longer about passively waiting for the afterlife but actively participating in God's plan here and now! And that mindset forced me to examine all aspects of my life: work, relationships, and everything in between.

Emboldened by these revelations, Brad and I embarked on a bold path, giving up our former lives to embrace a new beginning. We moved in with my in-laws for six months and prayed for direction. It finally came, through an invitation from our longtime friends Tom and Kim Challan. They invited us to visit them in Texas for two weeks, and after that short period of time, we knew it was where we wanted to call home. Though the choice appeared abrupt to everyone around us, we had faith that this was the catalyst for tremendous growth and realignment with our true values and purpose.

In Texas, our integration into the Elevate Life Church and mentorship under Pastor Keith Kraft further solidified our understanding of living a life aligned with our core values and faith. It was here that we learned the immense power of right alignments—how they shape our life's assignments, open doors at the right time, and amplify our impact in both life and business. And this has made the ultimate difference in the way we live our lives.

Each and every one of us has a unique path in life, and that means that every person's alignments will be different based on our priorities, morals, core values, and faith. However, I believe there are a few key universal action steps that will help you become more rightly aligned at this very moment.

1. Take time to get clear on your priorities. This will help you establish core values based on what matters most to you. And those core values will help you make every decision you're faced with, whether that's a relationship, a job offer, a move, etc.

2. Take inventory of your current alignments. Look closely into the people and companies you're aligned with. Are those alignments taking you closer to or further from the person you want to become?

3. Begin to bring your relationships, life situations, and work into closer alignment with the core values you've established. This is not an overnight process, and it can take years to achieve. But you can trust me when I say that it's worth it!

If, during the time you've spent with me in this chapter, you've decided that you want to focus on improving your alignments in life to better your assignments in life, I commend you—It's not a small decision. It has the power to change your life in ways that I could only begin to describe in the stories I've shared.

I hope this chapter has deepened your understanding of the significance of your alignments. Let my story be a catalyst for intentional living, for as you rise up, you'll either see your inner circle elevate with you or gracefully fade, unable to match the heights you're destined for. Remember—as you forge ahead, do not settle! You are on the cusp of your next great adventure, and I am wholeheartedly cheering for you. I'll see you out there, ntwrkrs!

Watch Heidi's Video Now!
LeadingLadiesCourse.com

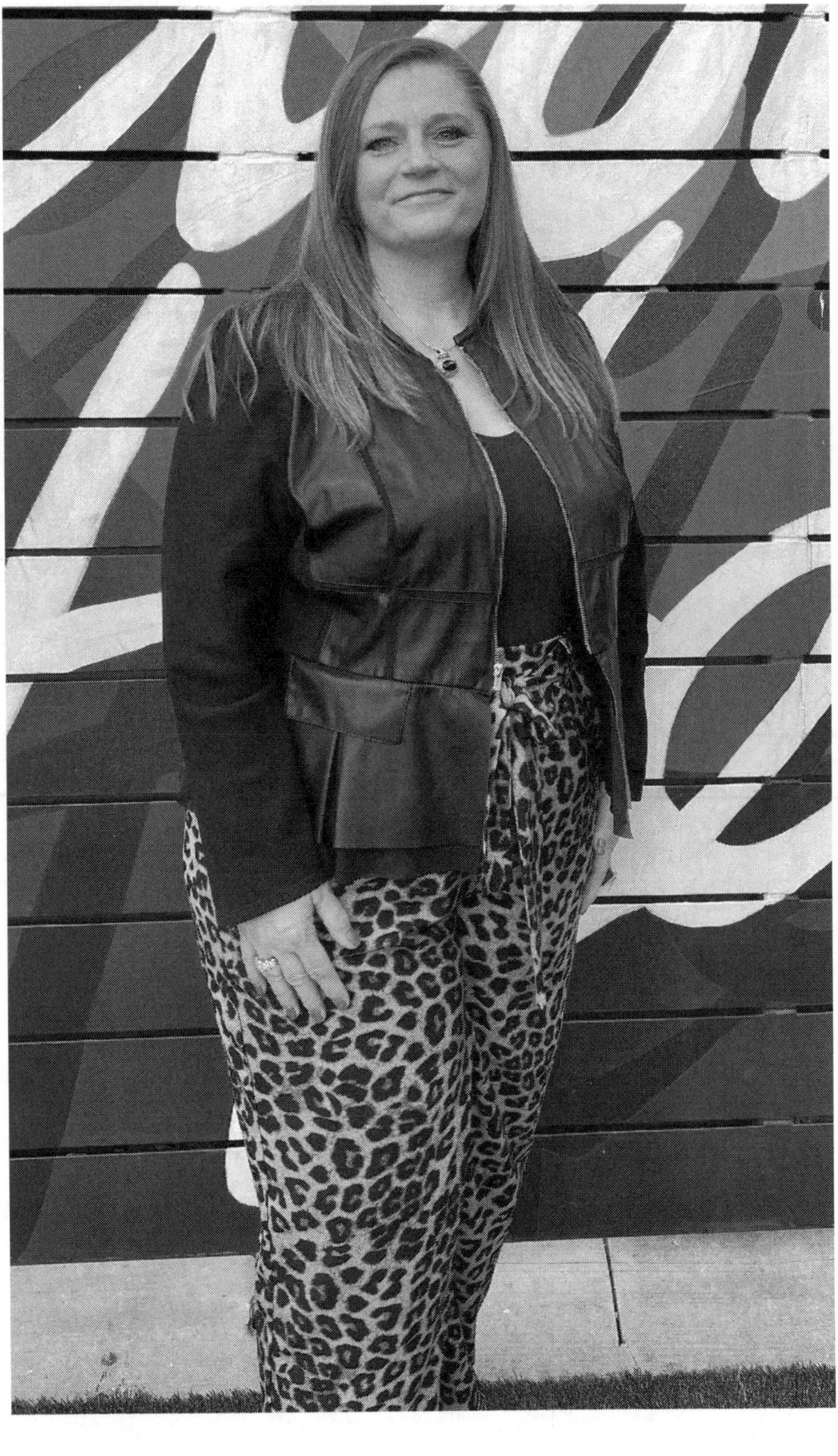

9

Life's Leverage

Unleashing Life's Hidden Leverage Points For Maximized Living

Diane Hochman

🌐 DianeHochman.com
f Facebook.com/DianeHochmanTraining
📷 Instagram.com/dianehochman
♪ Tiktok.com/@dianehochman

Life's Leverage

Diane Hochman

Hey, ntwrkrs! I'm excited to share some great stuff with you through this incredible book, full of expert insights and valuable advice. Over the past two decades, I've dedicated myself to the home business sector, specifically focusing on the dynamic world of Network Marketing. It's been an incredible journey, enabling me to help countless individuals, much like yourself, unlock their potential and achieve remarkable success.

In this chapter, I'm going to introduce a foundational concept that has been a cornerstone of my success: the power of leverage. Surprisingly, this principle remains unfamiliar to many! It's not something that's typically taught in schools, and it's unlikely that our parents have passed this knowledge down to us. Yet, understanding and applying leverage in your business can be transformative, propelling you toward the success you've always aspired to achieve. It has the potential to truly set you free.

But what exactly is leverage? Well, let's take a look at an example from our childhoods. Are you familiar with a seesaw or teeter-totter, or whatever it was called in your neck of the woods? I'm referring to the playground contraption that lets small children lift other kids, or even adults, off the ground. And all that up-and-down fun is made possible by the triangle in the middle: the fulcrum.

It defies what seems possible, right? A kid shouldn't be able to lift the adult on the other side of the see-saw off the ground. But they *can*, because of that fulcrum and the magic of leverage. I'm going to show you how to use leverage in your business, so you can win your time back and earn large quantities of money. This formula will allow you to work just a few hours per day, affording you the freedom to prioritize family time, travel, or pursue any of your other passions.

As we explore this concept together, I'll guide you through four critical areas essential to mastering leverage in your business. These areas include building meaningful relationships, maximizing exposure, creating a library of content, and generating residual income. Each of these components is a vital piece of the puzzle, and when integrated effectively, they can redefine your business and, ultimately, grant you the freedom to live the life you've always envisioned.

So, let's get started!

Relationships

One of the foundational pillars I've emphasized to my teams and students throughout my career in Network Marketing is the undeniable power of relationships. While it's true that not every person you meet will be a direct prospect for your business, it's important to remember that every person you meet *knows someone who is!* Every interaction is an opportunity to expand your reach, as each person you engage with likely has connections who would benefit from what you offer.

When I initially entered the world of Network Marketing, business was done completely offline. I was a busy mom of two children who were just transitioning from elementary school to middle school, so my life was a whirlwind of activity. I was the quintessential "mom mobile," ferrying my kids to various activities, assisting with homework, and fulfilling all the other responsibilities that come with parenthood.

Amid this hectic season of life, Network Marketing started to move from the offline space to the online space. I adapted quickly, creating a digital marketing program specifically for our profession. However, I needed to connect with other professionals who could help me broaden my audience and draw more people to my program! I decided to travel to a prominent marketing event, knowing that it would be a gathering place for some of the most influential people in the industry. Once I was there, all the Network Marketers huddled up together, and before I knew it, I was breaking bread with all of them.

The relationships I forged at that event were nothing short of transformative! Despite being relatively unknown at the time, my new relationships led to invitations to be a guest trainer on one of the most prominent online networking sites and to speak at an event attended by over four thousand people. The moral of the story is, it doesn't matter what you're looking for—speaking on stage is my forte, but no matter how you're looking to be recognized or utilized, building relationships is where you start. And it's not just about the immediate connections you make; it's about the doors those connections can open.

So, yes, you want to meet as many people as you can, but you also want to build relationships with people who already have warm markets that are full of potential connections. Real relationships are built on reciprocity and trust. This trust is not something that can be rushed or forced—it takes time and genuine interactions, along with a sincere desire to contribute to the success of the other person.

To foster these relationships, here are some actionable steps you can take:

1. Commit to meeting people. Set a goal to meet as many people as possible! This could be through social media platforms like Facebook, TikTok, or Instagram, or in-person events and gatherings. If you're able to dedicate full-time efforts to your business, aim to meet at least ten new people each day. If you're balancing other responsibilities, set a target of five daily interactions. Now, notice I didn't say pitch these people; rather, simply get to know them!

2. Seek out successful individuals. Surround yourself with people who have achieved the success you aspire to. Attend industry events, join relevant groups, and engage in communities where you can connect with accomplished professionals. These people can provide invaluable insights and may open doors to new opportunities. And distance doesn't matter! You can jump on a plane and get to an event, or stay local by finding your chamber of commerce, church group, or real estate meeting.

3. Focus on serving others. Approach each new connection with a mindset of offering support and adding value. By prioritizing the needs of others and offering your support, you will create a foundation of goodwill that often leads to mutual benefit. This approach can lead to unexpected opportunities and partnerships that have the potential to propel your business forward.

As you can see, the power of relationships in Network Marketing cannot be overstated! By prioritizing meaningful connections, seeking out successful mentors, and adopting a service-oriented mindset, you can unlock a world of possibilities for your business. Remember, the journey to success is not a solo endeavor; it's a collaborative effort built on the strength of relationships.

Exposure

Exposure might sound like a complex idea, but it's something you're probably already familiar with. Consider how you network in your everyday life. When your child needs something, you instinctively start asking around for recommendations. You seek advice on the best teachers, the most reliable orthodontists, and more. Networking and building relationships are skills that you already possess, and they form the basis of exposure.

In the context of Network Marketing, exposure occurs when someone with a following introduces you to their network and speaks highly of you. It's as simple as someone you trust telling others about you. We all do this when we recommend a great pizza place or a skilled massage therapist to our friends. The objective is to increase visibility so that more people become aware of you and what you have to offer.

So, when we recruit someone, we want to work through their warm market, encouraging them to introduce us to the people they know. This expands our reach to individuals who might not have come across us otherwise but are willing to listen because of their relationship with our mutual contact.

For instance, If I sign Mary into the program and she hosts a house party, all the attendees will be open to hearing from me, even though they don't know me personally. This is because of my relationship with Mary and the implied trust that's already there. When we talk about exposure, what we're discussing is the *leveraging of existing relationships* to widen our circle of influence.

In the previous section, I wrote about getting on a plane—to Los Angeles, in fact—and meeting influential people in the Network Marketing space. We connected personally, and our mutual trust led them to introduce me to their online audiences. No longer limited by in-person events or geographical locations, this exposure transformed me into a household name in the industry, seemingly overnight!

Just imagine what your business would look like if everyone in your town knew you had the best product, that you were able to work from home and spend more time with your kids, and that the extra money you were making afforded you to take your family to Disney World. Word-of-mouth endorsements would spread, attracting people who desire what you offer.

Exposure acts like a magnet, drawing the right individuals to you without the need for exhaustive one-on-one searches. While building a relationship may be the first step to leverage, as it's a connection with someone you trust and can seek help from, exposure can amplify this by introducing you to a broader audience, transferring trust through the person who introduced you.

So, how can you increase your exposure?

1. Look for opportunities to get in front of your contacts' contacts. Whether it's a small gathering of five people, a Zoom party for twenty, or a speaking engagement in front of a hundred people, every bit of exposure counts! Find out where your contacts' contacts are getting together and find a way to offer value.

2. Get involved in local or online groups. What are your interests? Where do you have a sphere of influence? Anywhere you have a presence, like the PTO, the Chamber of Commerce, or even Mardi Gras Krewes in places like Louisiana where I live can provide a fun way to build your warm market, which is paramount for gaining exposure.

Exposure is about leveraging your relationships to broaden your reach and attract the right people to your business. It's a powerful tool that, when combined with trust, can significantly accelerate your success in Network Marketing.

Content

Content creation has become deeply integrated into our daily lives, thanks to platforms like social media. Essentially, content can take the form of audio recordings, videos, or written pieces like blogs, all of which you share with your audience via emails, social media posts, or other platforms. For Network Marketers, becoming a prolific content creator is a step toward gaining significant leverage.

The beauty of content creation lies in its flexibility. You can generate content every day, depending on your availability and commitment, producing anywhere from one to ten pieces of content. Each one, whether it's a short-form video like a TikTok or Reel, a graphic accompanied by insightful words, or a well-crafted blog post, serves as a building block in your online presence. By consistently posting across various social media platforms, you not only engage your audience but build a substantial library of content that can be repurposed repeatedly.

Life is unpredictable, filled with unexpected challenges that might hinder your ability to operate at your usual pace. In my own life, I faced unforeseen circumstances such as divorce and COVID-19, temporarily affecting my ability to run my business the way I was used to.

During those challenging times, having a reservoir of content became my lifeline to my business. When the coronavirus sent me into the ICU, I was upfront with my audience about what was going on. The outpouring of prayers, flowers, cards, and well-wishes still warms my heart! But to the rest of the world, my business was functioning as it had for years. I recycled the hundreds of posts I had in my content library, and even though I wasn't out at events or actively recruiting, my business was still able to grow.

On the other hand, during my divorce, I wanted that season of my life to remain very private. I wasn't my normally perky or motivated self. I didn't want to see or talk to anyone. I just wanted to sit on my couch and watch *Gilmore Girls!* And that was okay *because I had a content library.*

Once again, I used that content library to maintain my presence online, and I'm telling you—not even my team knew I was gone. Every piece of content I had created added to the treasure trove of 'reruns' that I could share with my audience, ensuring that my voice remained heard even if I wasn't actively creating new content.

These experiences taught me a very important lesson: content creation is not solely about immediate engagement. It's also about preparing for the future, creating a safety net that allows your business to thrive even during challenging periods. It's a strategic move that provides leverage and resilience, ensuring the continuity of your Network Marketing business!

To help you build your content library, here are some actionable steps:

1. Embrace daily creation. Dedicate yourself to producing and sharing new content every day for the next ninety days. Experiment with various formats such as posts, stories, short-form videos, or graphics. Consistency is key!

2. Utilize creative tools. Make the most of platforms like Canva for designing graphics and explore the world of Reels or TikToks for engaging videos. These tools can significantly streamline your content creation process, allowing you to create more content in less time!

3. Organize your content vault. Develop a system for storing and organizing your content. Whether you use cloud storage or a specific folder on your computer, having an organized collection will make specific content types easy to find, and simplify the process of repurposing content in the future.

4. Recycle and refresh. Don't hesitate to republish old content. As your audience expands, new followers will appreciate discovering your earlier work, while long-time followers will enjoy revisiting your past valuable insights.

By implementing these steps, you'll not only enhance your engagement and visibility but also fortify your business against life's inevitable fluctuations.

Residual Income

Residual income is a term that resonates deeply within the Network Marketing community, as it symbolizes the gateway to financial independence. For those primarily focused on direct sales, the concept of building a team and generating residual income might seem like uncharted territory. It certainly was for me! I remember my early days in this profession, when I was solely dedicated to selling products, unaware of the opportunities that team building and residual income could provide.

As I delved deeper into the concept, I learned that residual income, in its essence, is simply earnings that continue to flow after the initial effort has been made. It's the recurring revenue you receive when customers make regular purchases or enroll in auto-ship programs. The power of this income stream is often underestimated. Some people may dismiss smaller amounts of residual income, such as $200, $300, or $500, as insignificant. However, when you consider the substantial investment needed in traditional financial instruments like stocks or mutual funds to generate similar passive returns, the value of even modest residual income becomes impossible to ignore.

The benefit of residual income extends beyond mere financial gains; it offers a safety net during life's unpredictable moments. During the seasons of divorce and illness in my life, where my ability to actively work in my business was severely hindered, my residual income served as a financial lifeline, ensuring a steady stream of income when I wasn't able to devote much attention to business.

One of the most remarkable aspects of residual income is its reliability. Whether you're going on a family vacation, celebrating an anniversary weekend, or attending to the health needs of a loved one, the assurance that your residual income will continue to support you is life-changing. It's a reward for the hard work and dedication you've invested in building your business, providing peace of mind that your financial well-being is secure, even in your absence!

To fully harness the power of residual income, take the following powerful action step:

1. **Focus on nurturing your relationships and ensure customer satisfaction.** One of the most common mistakes I see Network Marketers make is overlooking the importance of follow-up after a sale is made. Cultivating long-term relationships with customers and team members is key for sustaining and growing your residual income! Regular follow-up ensures that your clients remain engaged and

satisfied, which, in turn, supports the longevity of your residual income stream.

Understanding the value of residual income, prioritizing customer relationships, and consistently nurturing your business are key steps to unlocking your full income potential and achieving the financial independence you desire!

As we conclude this chapter, I want to reiterate that leverage can transform the way you work, enabling you to achieve more than you ever thought possible. While the idea of working from home or anywhere else with such flexibility might seem too good to be true, I assure you, it's a reality! Of course, there will be times when you're doing a launch or a special event when your focus intensifies, and you might find yourself working longer hours. However, generally speaking, the freedom to manage your time and the assurance that your income continues to flow is a direct result of leveraging the four key principles I've outlined.

Begin with relationships. The foundation of any successful Network Marketing business is the connections you make. It's about meeting people, engaging with them genuinely, building relationships with people and their warm markets, and serving their needs. Remember, the more you give, the more you receive. Start by offering value, and the rest will follow.

Next, leverage comes into play through exposure. It's not just about the person you directly interact with; it's about who that person can introduce you to. Build a relationship so strong that they're eager to share your message with their network. When the right people hear what you have to offer, they'll naturally be drawn to it without the need for hard selling.

Content creation is the next critical aspect of leverage. Those who know me often joke about my morning routine, which involves posting and creating content, regardless of where I am. Whether I'm on a cruise or in a hospital, if I can move my fingers, I'm creating content! And with the tools available today, much of this can be automated, allowing your presence to be felt even when you're not actively working.

Lastly, focus on residual income to attain the lifestyle you desire. By consistently working on building streams of residual income, you secure your financial freedom and ensure that your hard work continues to pay off long into the future.

To you ntwrkrs out there, remember, you truly are incredibly awesome. I may not have a profound closing statement, but what I do know is that it's been an absolute pleasure to share these insights with you! I wish you tremendous success in your journey. Congratulations on deciding to empower yourself with this knowledge! Stay connected with the ntwrkr community (special shoutout to my co-authors and everyone who contributed to this book!), get out into the world, and leverage your way to the top! See you out there!

Watch Diane's Video Now!
LeadingLadiesCourse.com

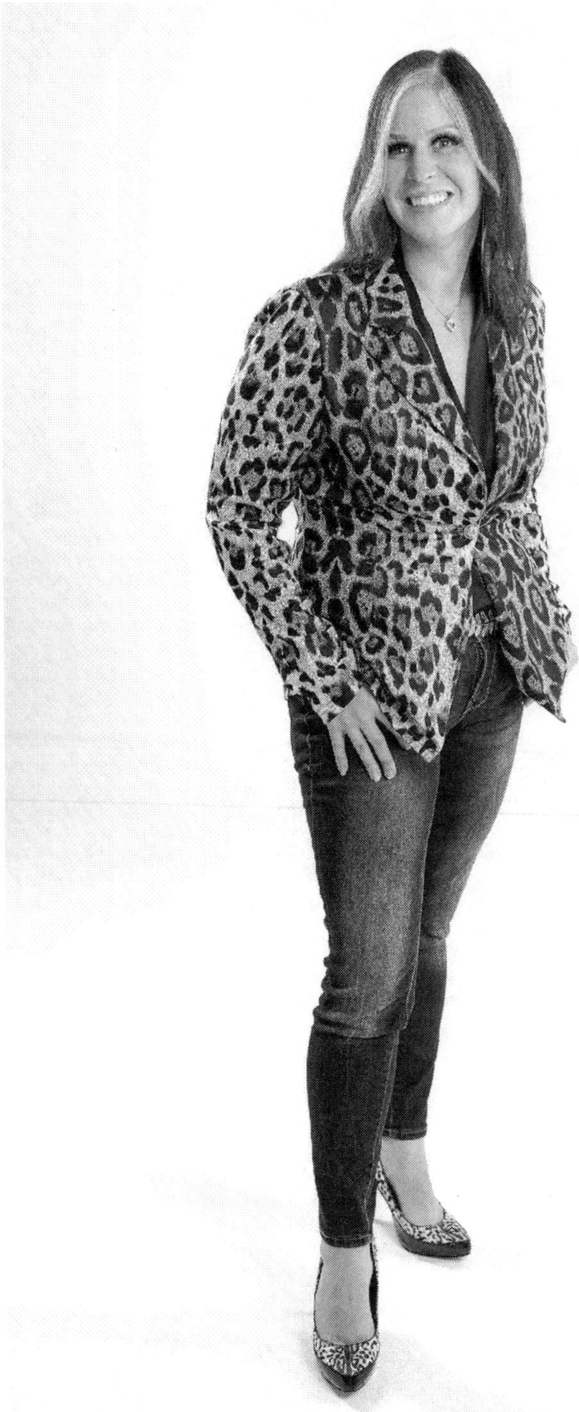

10

Be A Gold Digger

5 Ways To Excavate Greatness From The Women In Your Tribe

Alisha Lindsey

🌐 AlishaLindsey.com
[f] Facebook.com/alisha.lindsey.5

Be A Gold Digger

Alisha Lindsey

Hey, everyone! I'm so pumped to be writing this chapter in *Leading Ladies* about a concept that's super close to my heart. Before we dive in, I want to express my gratitude to each of you for reading these words and taking the initiative to enrich yourselves by going deeper into the captivating world of Network Marketing. And second, I want to give you a quirky piece of advice that might raise an eyebrow—and that's to *"Be a Gold Digger."*

Now, hear me out, because it's not what you think! I'm not going to tell any of you to chase after wealthy men to get rich, as the term "Gold Digging" commonly implies. Instead, we're going to dive head-first into five transformative strategies that will unearth and nurture the potential in the amazing and talented people around you. That's right! By using these methods, *you're going to get pure gold out of your team!* Intrigued? Let's get into it!

First and foremost, I want to share with you a little bit about my background so you can understand where I'm coming from. I'm a proud Black Diamond earner with my company where I've had the privilege of sitting on the council for the past six-plus years! My journey in Network Marketing has led me to several platforms and stages, both within the USA and internationally, providing me with opportunities to share and learn from thousands. Milestones in my career have included multiple appearances in *Prosper* and *Behind Her Brand* magazines, training with industry legends like Darin & Jennifer Dowd, Jeremy & Mindy Deeble, Geoff & Kathryn Belleville, and Ray Higdon, just to name a few. My husband Josh and I were also selected to be official Ambassadors for Dr. John C. Maxwell, the world's foremost author on leadership, as we advised him on his first and only book on Network Marketing, *The Power of Five!*

Beyond these professional achievements, I'm a devoted mother to two incredible kids, and I've been a wife for almost twenty-two years. Here's a fun fact: I married my husband just three weeks after meeting him! Our journey has been extraordinary, with both of us building our legacy together. While he's the academic achiever, with a Doctorate in Business Administration and a recent certification in plant medicine from Cornell University, I've always been the more visible face of our endeavors, particularly in the world of social media. We live in Montgomery, Texas, where we're surrounded by a rich history and an environment that instills the values of freedom, family, and faith that we hold so dearly. These values have not just shaped my personal life but have also guided my leadership style.

Growing up, I was never fond of traditional classroom education, so Network Marketing was a perfect fit for me based on the fact that learning was based on real-life experiences. If there's one thing I'd emphasize to anyone new to the profession, it's this: You're either "green and growing" or "ripe and rotting." In other words, if you're not learning, you're going backward. You can't pour from an empty cup, after all, and so, if you're going to pull gold from your team on a continual basis, then you'll need to place yourself into situations where you can be poured into, and it's up to you whether that's digital or in-person! The bottom line is, surround yourself with mentors and plenty of opportunities for training!

The great part is, if you're lifting yourself up in that way, the inevitable will happen—those around you will level up, too. I love the phrase, "A rising tide lifts all ships," and that philosophy has always driven me to do more. By enhancing our individual capacities, we are sure to elevate everyone around us. My mission has consistently been to provide education, not just within my own team but to everyone eager to learn in this profession. I believe that empowering leaders is the most paramount step you can take to ensure a long-lasting and successful team. So, as we embark on this journey of "Gold Digging" together, I'm going to guide you on the path to understanding the ways you can extract the absolute best from the ladies you lead!

Map Her 'Why'

To begin, we need to understand the motivation behind your team member's involvement in Network Marketing in the first place. The 'why' connects all the dots! It's the foundation of a person's drive and ambition, and it's about more than just financial goals—*it's about what those finances can accomplish.* I've had so many new team members tell me that they just want to earn more money, but when I dig a bit deeper, I find out what that money will do in their lives or the lives of others.

Often, a powerful 'why' can bring tears to your eyes. In my case, my 'why' was to change my family's financial habits, retire my husband, and give my daughter opportunities we couldn't provide her with before, like dance lessons or private school. Sure, on the surface, the focus seemed to be about money—and it certainly involved money, but the *actual* 'why' was that I wanted to bring my family closer together, enrich their lives, and develop their gifts.

And it's not just important for you and your career—it's critical for those you're guiding. Knowing someone's precise 'why,' the reason for someone's drive and determination, can be the difference between their success and stagnation. 'Whys' are emotional and felt from the heart. Remember, if they're not crying, you haven't found their 'why' yet!

Here are my favorite ways to map her 'why'!

1. Create a private and comfortable environment. People will only open up to you if they feel emotionally and physically safe to do so. This is best done in person, but as a close second, a quiet video call will work just as well.

2. Be present and engaging. When you're diving deep into someone's dreams and aspirations, make sure you're actively listening and showing her that you understand how seriously you are taking the conversation. No one wants to feel ignored when they're being vulnerable!

3. Gently push her to go big. Most people are hesitant to think in grand terms, so they'll give you the breadcrumbs of their dreams at first. When this happens, try to shift the conversation from basic necessities to larger goals. Encourage her to dream beyond her immediate needs, and to aim for legacy!

4. Get permission to remind her of her 'why' when things get hard. Her 'why' can be a powerful motivator when she's thinking of backing away or giving up. Make sure you get the go-ahead to bring it back up to her!

Identify Her Shiny Strengths

As you're listening to her tell you about herself and her 'why,' listen for her to subtly reveal her hidden strengths. It's rare that you'll find someone who will tell you what they're great at right out of the gate, so it's your job as a leader to tug on the threads of greatness when they show up in conversation.

For instance, if you're talking to your team member about her 'why,' she might tell you that she's been through a ton of hardship in her life—maybe she's had to care for a sick family member or step into the role of single mom suddenly. The important thing to remember is that what she's *not* telling you out loud is that she is an incredible nurturer, leader, and healer.

Make sure you point these strengths out to her! Remind her that she has innate problem-solving skills that she's used to find forward motion in her personal life, and that anyone on your team would be fortunate to collaborate with her. By recognizing and emphasizing these qualities, you're highlighting her invaluable attributes.

Here are my favorite ways to identify her shiny strengths:

1. As she talks about her 'why,' listen to the history of what she's been through. Even if she doesn't realize it, she's telling you all about her strengths as she recounts what she has survived and what she does best.

2. Capture those strengths so you can reference them later. Write down her strengths so that during challenging times, you can remind her that she's powerful!

Believe The Gold Is There

In addition to their strengths, everyone has weaknesses, or what I consider to be areas of growth. The problem is when we decide that, because we've made those mistakes, we must not be worthy. That's when we become our own worst enemy.

The truth is, we've all made mistakes in our bumpy pasts. However, despite those setbacks or weaknesses, our intrinsic value remains. So, if someone on your team is trying to tell you why they don't think they can achieve a big goal, or why they can't use their strengths to help others, it's critical to use positive language to shift negative self-talk around fears and past failures.

I once spoke with a colleague who'd endured verbal abuse from family members, leading to diminished self-worth. By highlighting her resilience and passions, I aimed to shift her perspective, and I reminded her that her survival in that situation was a testament to her strength!

Here are my favorite ways to help someone believe the gold is there:

1. Ask her about what's holding her back—the fears, doubts, and past failures. Active listening is the cornerstone of this step, paired with affirmation that you see strength even when she doesn't.

2. Redirect her negative self-perceptions by offering a fresh perspective. Remind her that every setback is just another lesson—another step closer to success. It's about perseverance, believing in the potential that's clearly visible to others, and helping her see it, too.

3. Replace her self-doubt with genuine self-belief. By reflecting on what she's shared, emphasize her strengths, challenge her misconceptions, and replace her self-imposed limitations with limitless possibilities. This process can revolutionize her mindset and, consequently, her life!

Refine One Nugget At A Time

The journey to self-betterment is rarely straightforward. It often requires a laser focus on a single facet of our character, refinement of it, and then magnifying its potential! Take, for example, the task of refining a hidden strength that is overshadowed by a limiting belief. When a person recognizes this buried potential, it's just like realizing there's gold beneath her feet! However, *recognizing the strength* and *harnessing its value* are not one and the same.

ntwrkr.com

Let's say you've found a team member's strength that you want to develop. Don't wait to get started! Letting an opportunity or newfound realization sit idly by, collecting dust, is much like a pioneer discovering gold but refusing to dig. It's of the utmost importance to give her a tangible task—a real and immediate action. Something as simple as this can often create a ripple effect of confidence!

In the many times I've 'refined gold' over the course of my career, a large number of women have confessed their deep-seated fear of going live on social media. If you're comfortable on camera in front of a lot of people, it might seem like a trivial fear to you, but for some, it's a very real phobia and can be debilitating. When this was the case with a fellow lady on my team, I challenged her to just do one simple, one-minute live video. The topic? Anything under the sun, from the chirping birds outside to her favorite book. And once she embarked on this challenge, I asked her to tag me, ensuring I would bear witness to her brave action. And what happened afterward was magic: this woman who was afraid before now had a win under her belt, and she gained the confidence to conquer more challenges. It's so encouraging to realize that the very things we dread the most often transform into our strongest assets!

Here are my favorite ways to 'refine her gold,' one nugget at a time:

1. Identify her most prominent fear or weakness. What is she shying away from most? Sometimes she won't be able to tell you, and you'll have to observe it for yourself.

2. Focus only on the development of that area. We can't fix all the things at once, can we? No! So, focus only on this one area and know that the rest of the nuggets will get refined in due time.

3. Take actionable steps toward a small win. It doesn't have to be a huge accomplishment; it just needs to be enough to give her the confidence that she can improve and succeed.

4. Review, reassess, and seek a new challenge. When you're finished with the first one, move on to the next! Just remember, this step is a never-ending cycle, and it's one that promises growth, confidence, and a life governed less by fear.

Commit To The Dig

Commitment is essential to any successful venture. As leaders in Network Marketing, we see this first-hand when we find team members who aren't getting the results they want because they struggle with dedication to their business. When this happens, taking proactive steps to keep them accountable can be absolutely transformative. It not only encourages their commitment, but it also demonstrates how invested you are in their growth! The metaphor of 'committing to the dig' is about continuing to uncover the potential that's often hidden under layers of doubt and fear.

In the early stages of my career, there was a period where face-to-face meetings were my primary mode of interaction. And while this strategy actually led me to a high rank within my company, I realized that with success came challenges. There were nights of long drives and unsuccessful meetings, leading to weeks where I felt like I was spinning my wheels. And in the midst of this professional whirlwind, I felt like I was missing out on valuable time at home with my family.

One night, after one of the worst weeks I'd had out there on the road (I hadn't closed *anything!*), I walked through the front door, exhausted, and I realized that my daughter, a toddler at the time, had decided to cut her own hair while my husband was in another room on a business call. I had been waiting to give my daughter her first haircut, and now all her baby curls were on the floor. I was pushed to the brink, and I went into my closet and bawled my eyes out. I was questioning every choice I'd made, and I considered quitting right then and there.

But it's moments just like these when the value of a mentor shines brightest. My husband immediately called my mentor and got me on the phone with her. She listened to my struggle, reminded me that there were going to be hard times, made me acknowledge the wins I had already made, and then shared some of the challenges of her own journey. Her stories of missed family events, and the eventual freedom and opportunities her success afforded her, painted a vivid picture for me: I could either quit and miss out on the life I'd imagined for my family, or I could keep going through the challenging times to see that life come to reality.

So, I buckled down. I asked different family members to watch the kids, I hired babysitters, and I even asked fellow church members to fill in at home!

This is the essence of commitment: pushing through despite the odds, lifted up by the belief in yourself and the support of those around you. As leaders, it's our responsibility to guide our teams through these inevitable challenges.

Here are my favorite ways to help her commit to the dig:

1. Remind her of her 'why'. Remember this from the first step? Here's where you're going to bring it back up (as long as she already gave you permission to do so!). Ask her if something has changed. And if she says she wants to quit, ask her if she has a new plan to achieve that 'why.' It's rare that she does.

2. Share your personal stories of challenging times. If she can understand that you've overcome obstacles to your success as well, she'll believe she can do it, too.

3. Fix her vision. Success is rarely linear; in fact, most of the successful people you encounter will tell you that their path has been all over the place! Help her see past the obstacles to the life she's imagined for herself.

Don't Abandon The Mine

In the ever-changing world of Network Marketing, it's easy to feel discouraged when members of your team or potential customers seem to vanish into what I like to call 'ghost mines.' These are the people you're trying to partner with who, for one reason or another, become inactive or unresponsive. But here's the golden rule: never abandon the mine!

When team members become ghosts, resist the urge to interpret their silence as disinterest. Instead, keep the communication channels open. Drop them simple, heartfelt messages, such as, "Hey! How are you? I want you to know I'm here for you." By doing so, you're letting them know that their well-being as a person matters to you more than a number in a business.

Years ago, a friend of mine was pursuing a significant business opportunity. The potential partner expressed initial interest but then went silent for months. When she came to me and asked for advice, I suggested a different approach. Instead of inquiring about the business, I recommended sending a message that simply read, "Are you okay?" To her surprise, she received a response within minutes. The potential partner had been out of the country, and this simple gesture reopened the line of communication, leading to a fruitful business partnership. While outcomes like this aren't guaranteed, they illustrate the power of genuine concern.

And this speaks to a larger principle: people value authenticity! When you show genuine interest, you're communicating that you see someone as more than just a business transaction. This personal touch is what sets successful Network Marketers apart. Remember, people don't truly understand how much you care until you show them.

My favorite ways to make sure I don't abandon the mine are:

1. Ask genuine questions, one at a time, and be patient. Questions like, "Are you okay?" and "Have you given up on this project?" are powerful in their simplicity and open-endedness.

2. If she responds negatively, offer support instead of judgment. Remind her of her 'why.' Encourage her to type out her 'why' and share it with you. Later, when she needs motivation, remind her of her 'why' by sending it back to her. A simple gesture, like sharing a captured memory of her ambition, can reignite her passion.

3. Continue to engage with her even if she seems distant. The phrase, "fortune is in the follow-up" holds true, but it's about more than just persistence. It's about care, consistency, and authenticity—so, go ahead and like, share, and comment on her posts.

4. Always remember the power of public visibility. You never know who's watching you online, so be active on social media! I've been surprised multiple times by 'ghosts' on my page who, after a period of silent observation, finally reached out because they were inspired by my public posts. You might be the beacon someone needs, so keep shining, and keep going!

Watch Out For Bandits

As we move into our final lesson, I'd like to share a vital insight, which is to always be cautious of those who might obstruct your journey toward success. Just as miners guard their treasures against bandits, you must shield your ambitions against doubters and detractors!

Consider your aspirations to be much like a gold mine. There will always be people who will try to discredit your findings, insisting that what you've unearthed is mere fool's gold. Such doubters might be motivated by their own insecurities, maybe even by their failure to dig deep enough in their ventures to ever find anything. Or perhaps they are driven by envy, so they refuse to rejoice in your success.

These so-called 'bandits' come in various forms, and I'll go through them one by one:

Well-Intended Mis-informers: These are people who genuinely care for you, but they lack the expertise or experience to do so. Their intentions are rooted in the fear of seeing you get hurt, even if their worries are baseless. These people are usually family members and close friends.

Singular Path Advocates: This is the group that believes their way is the only right way. While their advice might be valuable in some contexts, it's important to remember that multiple paths lead to success! And their way is *not* the only way to get there.

Crab Potters: This term comes from a unique phenomenon observed when crabs are piled into a bucket. When one crab tries to escape a bucket, others pull it down instead of working together so they can all have freedom. Similarly, some people would rather see you confined to their limitations rather than see you soar!

So, who can you take advice from? An essential piece of wisdom I've adhered to in my journey is this: only take advice from those whose lives you'd willingly trade places with, at least in the specific domain in which they're offering advice. If someone excels in parenting but struggles financially, take their parenting advice but leave their financial guidance.

Remember, when you adopt someone's advice, you implicitly accept the outcomes and consequences of their choices. This doesn't only apply to finances but extends to all areas of life, from cooking to parenting to professional endeavors!

For instance, I have family members who have earned considerably, yet their work-life balance is skewed. Despite their financial success, I wouldn't trade places with them because I value a balance that allows me to dictate my schedule.

So, that's it! We've gone through all the ways to begin getting the best gold out of everyone you lead! Let's review:

Map Her 'Why': Before anything else, find out why she's pursuing her goals. This 'why' should be profound, emotional, and authentic.

Identify Her Shiny Strengths: Every woman possesses unique strengths, the 'shiny' aspects of their character. Recognize and harness them.

Believe The Gold Is There: Be confident in the value of what you're pursuing. Everyone has a reserve of gold within; it's all about unearthing it.

Refine One Nugget At A Time: Focus on one strength at a time, refining and honing it to perfection. Then, move on to the next!

Commit To The Dig: Stay dedicated to your quest, nurturing your strengths and seeking continuous growth.

Don't Abandon The Mine: Reach out and ask simple questions to those who have become distant, and make sure to stay connected via social media regardless of whether they re-engage right away.

Watch Out For Bandits: Naysayers will always be around, attempting to belittle your dreams or impose their insecurities upon you. Whether their intentions are to protect, or their attitude is born out of jealousy, or if it's a mix of both, the decision to heed their advice lies with you. Remember to get mentors who you'd trade lives with!

Always remember—your worth transcends the limitations others might try to impose on you. I wholeheartedly believe in your potential! Stay blessed, stay driven, and thank you for joining me in this chapter!

Watch Alisha's Video Now!
LeadingLadiesCourse.com

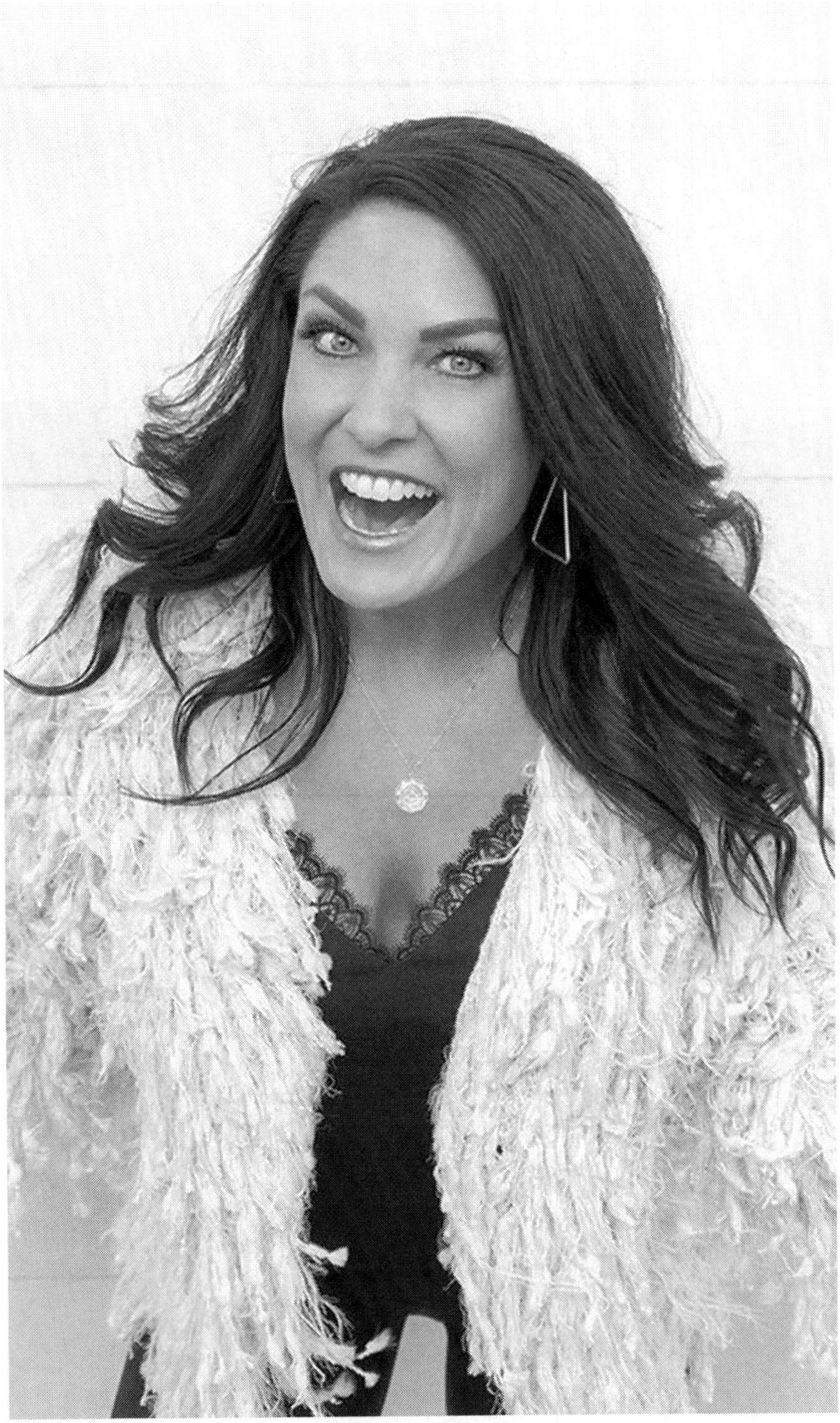

11

You Are What You Think

The Path From Thought, To Feelings, To Action, To Results

Michelle Barnes

🌐 MichelleBarnes.com
f Facebook.com/MichelleBarnesSuccessCoach
📷 Instagram.com/michellebarnessuccesscoach
♪ Tiktok.com/@tiktokladyboss

You Are What You Think

Michelle Barnes

Hello, ntwrkrs! Ever since I learned I would be writing a chapter in this book, I've been jacked out of my mind with excitement to share this life-altering concept with you. The insights I'm about to unveil aren't just theories; they're the very principles that have radically transformed my life and continue to do so every day. I am convinced, without a shadow of a doubt, that embracing and acting upon these insights will have a profound impact on your life! Throughout these pages, I'll lead you down a transformative path: from your thoughts and feelings to your actions, ultimately shaping your results.

Now, you might wonder, who am I to guide you? Why should my words carry any weight? Well, for twenty-eight years, I've been fully immersed in this profession, living and breathing the very essence of Network Marketing. Like many of you, I was raised on the conventional wisdom of success: get good grades, go to college, and climb the corporate ladder. I diligently followed this path and became the first in my family to attend university.

I graduated with a degree in Sociology and Criminology from the University of Colorado before venturing into law school. However, amidst the legal jargon and case studies, I had an epiphany—this was not my calling. Have you ever experienced that internal alarm, warning you that you're off track? That happened to me, and the alarm was *loud.* My inner GPS shouted, *Stop! You're heading in the wrong direction!*

Unexpectedly, my journey led me to Network Marketing—a field I had never envisioned for myself. I started with a modest goal to make an extra $500 to $1000 a month, but soon, I fell in love with the profession. It was about more than just selling products; it was about improving people's health, their financial situations, and most importantly, a change of mindset.

My first year in the business was eye-opening. Despite grappling with $80,000 in student loan debt, residing in a one-bedroom apartment, and juggling two other jobs—one as a waitress and another as a personal trainer, I managed to earn $102,000. By the age of thirty, I had made my first million dollars. This isn't to boast but to illustrate a point—if I could do it, so can you! Remember, being broke is a temporary state, not a permanent one.

Fast forward twenty-eight years, and here I am, a proud single Mom and sole provider of two amazing boys, still as passionate about this business as ever. I've seen it all: the good, the bad, and the ugly! And it's this wealth of experience that I bring to you today.

So, are you ready to embark on this transformative journey? What we will explore together is not just about individual success; it's about impacting your team, your organization, your family and friends, and even your community. In these unpredictable times, we, as entrepreneurs, are called to be the beacon of hope, the light in the darkness to others. This chapter will empower you to be just that.

I'm here to teach you the art of reframing your circumstances—to become what I like to call a 'Spin Master'. It's about transforming your thoughts, feelings, actions, and ultimately, your results. We're going to dive deep into these concepts, so get ready, take notes, and let's jump in with full commitment. Are you all in? Because I certainly am. Let's start this transformative journey together!

Thoughts

Let's delve into the concept that "thoughts are things." What we think, we become. Our thoughts are essentially our internal dialogue, shaping our reality and the world around us. I learned a profound lesson from reading Dr. Shad Helmstetter's book, *What Do You Say When You Talk To Yourself?* which emphasizes the power of self-talk, and that is: we experience around 75,000 thoughts daily, and astonishingly, 91% of these are repetitive and often not positive! If our thoughts forge our reality, and most are recurring and negative, it's evident that a transformation is needed.

The crux lies in understanding that every thought emits a frequency, like an echo, creating a vibration that we project into the universe. What we think, we attract. This concept highlights the necessity of being the gatekeeper of our minds, diligently monitoring our thoughts to ensure they are empowering rather than disempowering.

Imagine having a day where everything goes wrong: the alarm clock doesn't go off, you stub your toe, you get in the shower and knock the shampoo all over the bathroom floor, you cut yourself shaving your legs, and the day spirals downwards. You shake your fist in the air and yell, "Are you kidding me!?" Well, this series of negative events often stems from our initial thoughts. If you start your day thinking, "I'm having the worst day," the law of attraction ensures it manifests as such.

On the other hand, imagine a day when you're excited about something, like a vacation. You set your alarm for an insanely early hour, like 3:00 a.m. The alarm goes off and you wake up energized and excited to catch that flight to Cabo San Lucas! You jump out of bed, get ready with a spring in your step and a smile on your face, and your entire day mirrors that positivity. The writing is on the wall, friends: whatever you focus on grows. whatever you focus on expands. It's like a magnet! If you focus on all the crap in your life, you will literally become a crap magnet!

So how do you get into this positive trajectory for your life? You must become what I call the 'Spin Master'—transforming every negative thought and situation into a positive one. It's about shifting our focus from negative outcomes to positive possibilities. Our invisible thoughts create our visible reality! Therefore, changing our thoughts will change our feelings, vibrations, frequencies, and ultimately, the results we achieve in life.

But I'm not simply going to tell you to think positive thoughts and move on, I'm going to give you explicit action steps to help you become the Spin Master!

1. Embrace positive outcomes. Begin by shifting your focus. Instead of fearing what could go wrong, start expecting what can go right. The switch from a negative to a positive mindset is the first step in transforming your life, and it takes practice to feel completely comfortable doing it. Start this moment, and before long, it will feel like second nature.

2. Cultivate a positive self-perception. Remember, you will never outperform your self-image. How you perceive yourself directly influences the results you achieve. Therefore, work on increasing your confidence and reducing your fears to align your self-image with your aspirations.

3. Align your inner dialogue with your goals. Adjust your self-talk to reflect your desires and aspirations—your thoughts should mirror the results you want to achieve! This alignment is crucial in manifesting the life and success you aim for.

By mastering your thoughts and being a vigilant gatekeeper of your mind, you will set the stage for massive changes in your feelings, actions, and ultimately, the results you achieve.

Feelings

Now that your thoughts and self-talk are spinning toward the positive, let's explore the realm of feelings. It's important to understand that our emotions are not just reactions but powerful creators in their own right. In every training session I do with clients or my team, I emphasize a core belief: energy is everything, and everything is energy. This is especially true when it comes to our feelings, which are essentially vibrations we emit to the universe.

In quantum physics, this concept is well-understood: our feelings emit vibrations—some high, and some low. When we express feelings like depression, guilt, or fear, they resonate at a low frequency. In contrast, emotions like joy, love, and gratitude vibrate at a much higher frequency. I want you to take a second and think about how just reading those words made you feel. Even just saying or reading the negative words creates a yucky feeling, right? And in turn, the positive ones feel good! How you feel at any moment is broadcasting a distinct energy, attracting people, events, and situations with similar energies. Remember, there's no neutral ground in vibrations! You're either emitting positive or negative vibes, and these directly influence what you attract in life.

In 2006-2007, inspired by luminaries like Bob Proctor and the principles in *The Secret,* I set a monumental goal to buy my dream home. Although I was fortunate to live in a beautiful townhome at the time, I wanted to start a family and have all the space and features I wanted. I believed so strongly in the power of visualization and positive feelings that I wrote down every detail of my dream home on blue index cards, in blue ink, because writing things down in blue seeds them into the subconscious better than typing can (yes, you can Google that!).

I wrote down every detail in each room: things like, a master shower with two shower heads, a back deck, a downstairs terrace patio, and the like—each room had a full description. And putting these statements in the present tense, using phrases like, "I am so happy and grateful now that..." signaled to my subconscious to feel the feeling of already having it.

Still, it proved challenging to keep that dream alive in such turbulent economic times. Despite the 2008 recession, I paid attention solely to my vision, shutting out negativity. I didn't let the economic downturn, the news, or the pessimists derail my focus. This unwavering positive feeling, aligned with my thoughts, helped me manifest that very home. My experience is a testament to the fact that aligning our thoughts and feelings with our desired results, rather than current circumstances, can indeed create our own economy, regardless of the chaos of the outside world. Here are some action steps to help you make sure you stay focused on your vision:

1. Visualize your future. Start by vividly imagining your desired future. Visualization isn't just daydreaming; it's a powerful tool to align your feelings with your goals! The clearer your vision, the stronger your emotional response will be.

2. Write down your goals with emotion. Use the blue index card/blue ink method. Write your goals in the present tense, as if they've already happened! This act of writing not only clarifies your goals but also embeds them with emotion. Then, put these cards *everywhere*. On your mirror, in your car, in your wallet, you get the idea! Constantly seeing your goals written down will solidify their presence in your daily life.

3. Create a vision board. Assemble a vision board that resonates with what you want to feel and achieve. Seeing these images daily will reinforce your positive emotions and keep you aligned with your goals.

ntwrkr.com

Remember, your feelings are powerful indicators and creators of your reality. By consciously aligning your emotions with what you desire, you set the stage for manifesting your dreams into reality!

Actions

Actions serve as the bridge between our thoughts, feelings, and the tangible results we seek. While thoughts and feelings remain invisible, actions are the visible steps that propel us towards our goals. To achieve what we desire, action is non-negotiable!

Taking real action requires self-discipline—it's about doing what needs to be done, even when we don't feel like it. Building self-esteem and a positive self-image comes from fulfilling the promises we make to ourselves. As Ralph Waldo Emerson wisely said, "Do the thing and you shall have the power." This principle holds especially true in the realm of action: consistently doing the necessary tasks, even those we might not enjoy, builds the foundation for success.

When I began my journey in Network Marketing, I was $80,000 in debt, juggling multiple jobs as a waitress, bartender, personal trainer, and legal intern, and I was far from the path of financial independence. However, attending a life-changing three-day event shifted my mindset. I saw leaders who were living the life I aspired to, and I resolved to emulate their actions.

I committed to picking up the phone and not going to bed until I had booked ten people a day to come to my office for a presentation (yes, this was before social media and cell phones!). Often, this would take hours of "smiling and dialing," and a whole lot of rejection at first. But taking this simple yet consistent action, even when I didn't feel like it, was instrumental in earning $102,000 in my first year. By embracing the mundane, confronting the initial discomfort (or what I like to call *embracing the suck*), and focusing on improving my skills daily, I transformed my life! It can happen for you, too, and you can start this transformation by taking the following steps:

1. Embrace discipline and resilience. Self-discipline is the key to turning aspirations into achievements. Embrace the challenging parts of your journey, and understand that they are essential for growth.

2. Set clear daily targets. Define actionable and specific goals for each day. Your DMO (Daily Method of Operation) is everything! Make sure you are intentionally blocking out chunks of time to do the IPA's (Income-Producing Activities) that are necessary to move your business and life forward on a daily basis. This clarity will give you a roadmap and a sense of purpose each day.

3. Align actions with thoughts and feelings. Ensure that your actions are in harmony with your positive thoughts and feelings. This alignment is key to attracting the results you desire!

Action is the tangible manifestation of our inner world. Without it, any potential success will stay trapped in your own head! By committing to disciplined action, setting clear goals, and aligning these actions with our thoughts and feelings, we pave the way for remarkable transformation and success.

ntwrkr.com

Results

Alright, friends! We've laid the groundwork, and now it's time to dive into the realm of results. Results are the culmination of our thoughts, feelings, and actions. They are the tangible evidence of our internal processes manifesting in the external world. Throughout my twenty-eight years of experience building a business and coaching others to achieve their goals, one story resonates deeply: that of Kelly, a seasoned Network Marketer.

Kelly's story exemplifies the power of aligning thoughts, feelings, and actions with desired outcomes. While she was achieving decent results initially, they fell short of her true aspirations. Many come to me claiming to be doing everything required for success, yet they are missing the mark. The distinction often lies not in the actions themselves but in the energy and belief behind those actions.

Initially, Kelly mechanically performed her daily tasks without the conviction or positive energy needed to attract success. This is a lesson that it's not enough to go through the motions; rather, the vibrancy of our energy is what truly resonates in the universe! In Kelly's mind, it was enough to check off the boxes of her DMO checklist. But I urged her to be honest about her thoughts and feelings regarding the company she partnered with, the products she was selling, and most importantly, *herself*.

She realized that despite going through the motions, those actions weren't fueled by positive beliefs. It took some re-tooling, but she eventually was able to infuse her actions with positive thoughts and feelings—and her desired results poured into her life. She committed to achieving elite status within the business, and her determination to have positive thoughts influence her feelings, and have those positive feelings direct her actions, was nothing short of life changing. Unlike before, her energy and posture reflected a deep-seated belief in her goals, making her success inevitable.

This story illustrates a vital point: Network Marketing, at its core, is a platform for personal growth with a compensation plan attached. The most significant barrier to success isn't a lack of knowledge or skills, but a failure to apply what we've learned consistently. Personal development is crucial, but without action, it's like hoarding treasure without ever spending it! So, if you want to get incredible results like Kelly, here are your action steps:

1. Change your self-talk. The dialogue you have with yourself shapes your reality. Cultivating a positive inner voice is essential for fostering empowering thoughts and feelings, leading to better results.

2. Embrace repetition. Mastery stems from repetition, and repetition is the mother of all learning. Regularly practicing positive thoughts, feelings, and actions will transform them into habits, which will reshape your reality quietly in the background.

3. Act 'as if'. Begin embodying the success you seek now. Adjust your posture, speech, and actions to reflect where you want to BE. This alignment between your current self and future self accelerates your journey toward your goals.

Results are not the end product of just any action—they're a reflection of the entire journey. It's a cycle that starts with your thoughts, influenced by your feelings, translated into actions, and manifested in your results. By understanding this cycle and actively participating in each stage, you position yourself not just for success in Network Marketing but in any endeavor you pursue!

Be A Spin Master

Now that we've explored this journey of personal and professional growth, I want to emphasize the concept I wrote about at the beginning of this chapter: the action paradigm of becoming the *Spin Master*. Without exception, positive input leads to positive output. And vice versa, negativity in any of the domains—thoughts, feelings, or actions—breeds negative outcomes. Being the Spin Master isn't just a concept; it's a way of life that stems from the realization that our perception shapes our reality.

In my own experience, this realization traces back to one of my earliest childhood memories: a lesson in positivity from my mother, who raised me as a single parent after divorcing my father when I was only nine months old. We had very few material possessions, just a mattress on the floor and a stereo that we'd listen to music on. However, despite our humble living conditions, my mother instilled in me the invaluable lesson that our circumstances don't define our happiness or our potential.

I was four years old when I realized the way we lived was different from other people. I had just played at a neighbor's house down the street. Kimmy lived in a big house and had tons of toys, Nike shoes, and all the latest trendy clothes. When I returned home and questioned my mom about our lack of furniture, she didn't put her head down in shame or try to explain that we didn't have much money. Instead, she looked me straight in the eye and asked, "If we had all that furniture, where would we dance?"

My mother's confident and empowered response highlights the essence of being a Spin Master. It was her way of transforming a seemingly negative situation into a positive, focusing on the joy and freedom we had rather than what we lacked. That day, she taught me that happiness is an internal state, independent of external circumstances. It's a reminder that we all have the capacity to be Spin Masters in our own lives, to turn every negative thought and situation into a positive one.

And before you question whether the action paradigm of being a Spin Master is just about forcing a positive outlook, I'll impart the next step of the process: it's about genuinely shifting our perspective to see the potential for growth and joy in every situation. This isn't toxic positivity; instead, it's the understanding that life is a series of choices and that we have the power to choose positivity, to choose growth, and to choose success.

As this chapter comes to a close, it's imperative to grasp the profound truth that thoughts are indeed things. The sequence from thoughts to feelings, actions, and ultimately results, isn't just a theory; it's the scientific formula by which we sculpt our reality, moment by moment, day by day. Your thoughts are the architects of your experiences, continuously shaping the world around you.

So, take a look around—can you see it now? The essence of your being, the core of your reality, is a direct reflection of the thoughts you've had leading up to this moment. It's a powerful reminder that the capability to be, do, and have anything in life starts within the realm of your own mind! And if I can do it, you can, too—I wholeheartedly believe in your potential and your capacity to transform your dreams into reality. Get out into the world, become the Spin Master, and let your thoughts, feelings, and actions create the life you've always dreamed of!

Watch Michelle's Video Now!
LeadingLadiesCourse.com

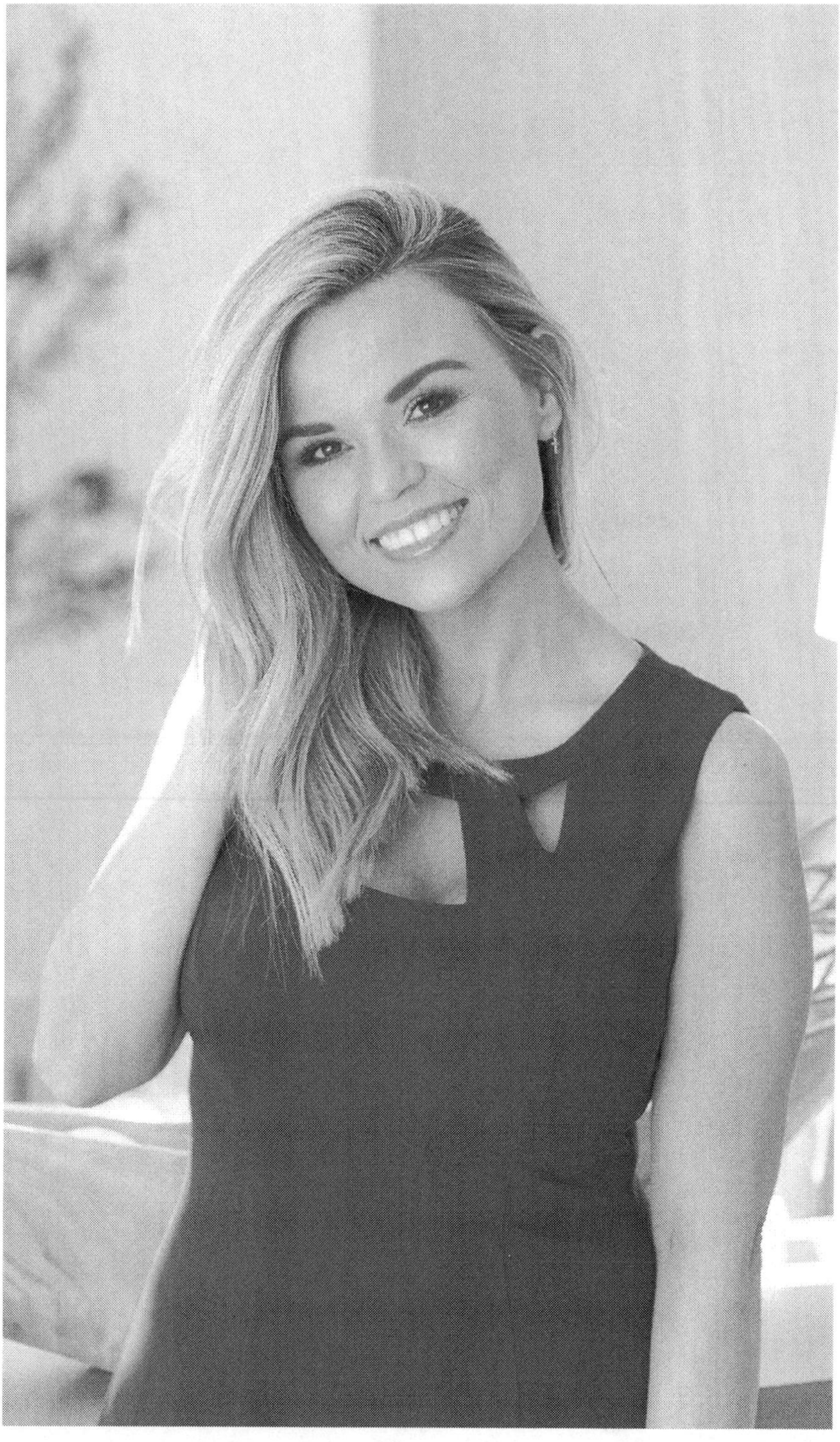

12

Building Unbreakable Bonds

The Roadmap That Transforms Your Team Into A Sisterhood

Brittany Beck

Facebook.com/100081108432129
Instagram.com/brittanynbeck
Tiktok.com/@brittanybeck022

Building Unbreakable Bonds

Brittany Beck

Welcome, fellow ntwrkrs! I'm thrilled to be here, sharing some of my personal experiences in leadership with you. In this chapter, my focus is on a topic vital to our industry—building unbreakable bonds to transform your team into a thriving sisterhood. This journey is more than just professional development; it's a roadmap to personal and collective transformation.

A brief introduction for those new to my story: I'm a dedicated wife, a mother of two incredible children, and a daughter of the Most High King. My career in Network Marketing has been a series of challenges, triumphs, and relentless pursuit of growth. I've had the privilege of building teams of over 40,000 distributors, generating lifetime sales surpassing $125 million, and achieving a multiple seven-figure income. But the true highlight of my journey has been empowering other women to realize their potential, attain financial freedom, and become the best versions of themselves.

Okay, enough about me! Let's delve into the heart of building unbreakable bonds, and why it's so crucial to your Network Marketing business. In my years of experience, the strength of a team lies not just in numbers or sales but in the depth of its connections. The sisterhood we create is our backbone—it's about supporting and being supported and understanding that this is a shared journey of growth and success. Whether you're just starting out or are a seasoned leader, building a sisterhood within your team can be transformative. Imagine a team that's not merely a group of individuals working towards common goals but a close-knit community that supports and uplifts each other through thick and thin. That's what we're aiming for!

We'll explore several key elements to building a thriving sisterhood: Proximity, Accountability, Authenticity, Vulnerability, Camaraderie, Activity, and Grace. Each of these elements plays a unique role in forging a team that's not just successful but also harmonious and resilient. So, let's dive in!

Proximity

Fostering proximity is the first step you want to take as a leader when you're building a sisterhood. Proximity means being around each other (either in-person or virtually), getting to know one another, and being an approachable and relatable leader. It's about breaking down the barriers of hierarchy to encourage open, meaningful interactions. No pedestals or velvet ropes here! You want to be in the trenches, so to speak, with your team so they can see you championing them and their businesses.

On my current team, there's a woman I've worked with for nearly seven years. We've been in three different companies together, and I consider her a sister! But it wasn't always like that. In our first company, we weren't directly connected, but she was on my team.

Even though we weren't directly connected, I always made myself available for conversations and was readily available to help in any way. I increased my level of proximity to her, and over time, our relationship blossomed from professional to personal—all because I stepped out and worked to nourish that relationship with accessibility and open communication. Now, she's an invaluable part of my sisterhood! If I had stayed quiet and kept to myself, I might never have gotten to know what an amazing woman she is. If you're looking to increase the proximity between you and your team, here are some action steps that will help you along the way:

1. Start "Taprooting." If you're unfamiliar with this term, it really just means digging down into your team, getting to the bottom of who they are and how they work, and finding the people deep in your organization who have incredible potential but just need that extra connection and support from you. Once you understand who you're working with and how they like to work, jump into the mix and start building from a foundational level!

2. Be active in team chats. This is an opportunity for your team to feel your presence throughout the day, even if it's just quick messages to ask how they are or to encourage them as they go out into the world to grow the business. When you're constantly engaged, your team will want to be, too!

3. Schedule Zoom meetings. In a world where we can't always get together in person, Zoom meetings are the next best thing. Just being able to see someone's face when you're talking to them creates a level of connection that's more intimate than communicating over text.

Accountability

Accountability within a team involves setting and pursuing goals together, but it's about more than just the initial goal-setting. Accountability is about being a cheerleader, a motivator, and sometimes, a gentle taskmaster for each other! After all—it's great to have wild, crazy ambitions in your business, but if you're not actually *doing* the wild, crazy things to make those goals happen, it won't get you where you want to go. Also, collaborating and helping your team members stay accountable adds an extra layer of excitement to our achievements. Within a sisterhood, every win becomes a collective celebration!

I have a team member who embodies this perfectly. She may not top the charts in sales, but her commitment to the team's success makes her an invaluable asset. Anytime there's a challenge, or incentive in the company, she is the one who takes it by the reins and runs with it. We rely on her to keep the energy positive and enthusiastic. We know we can depend on her to show up on every Zoom, no matter what. Her consistency and dependability have made her an integral part of our sisterhood!

Remember, when you're thinking about accountability, it's not always the high-ranking leaders or the number-one recruiters who are going to shine here. It might be the woman who just wants to make a little extra money each month but who has the time and personality to inspire the rest of the team to keep going. Here are some ways to encourage accountability on your team:

1. Do a power hour. Dedicate a specific time for your team to meet and work together to complete goal-driven tasks. Doing this collectively encourages accountability in ways that individual commitments may not achieve.

2. Create team challenges. These are a great way to energize your team, even when there's no company-wide promotion going on! Doing team blitzes, 90-day challenges, 5-day recruiting challenges, and similar activities can maintain momentum and accountability!

3. Encourage accountability partners. Pair team members to work together on their daily method of operations (DMO). This not only helps with individual accountability but also builds trust and connections among team members!

Authenticity

Authenticity is about embracing and expressing your true self, and showing up just as you are. In this business, it's tempting to feel pressure when you're rising up the ranks to look and act like the leaders you see on stage. But you need to silence those expectations and instead be true to your values, interests, and personality in order to attract your tribe.

And before you start thinking that your tribe should be a group of people just like you, you should remember that those closest to you won't agree with everything you say or share all the same opinions with you. The people in your tribe will simply love you for you, and you'll love them for them. The mutual respect and admiration come from being around authentic human beings.

I didn't always know this, of course. In the beginning of my career, I was starstruck by the amazing women I saw on stage. I thought I needed to be just like them, but as I tried my hardest to emulate these women, I realized that I wasn't capable of duplicating their success unless I brought my authentic self to the scene. From then on, I started attracting people that fit into my tribe better and began building my sisterhood.

The women in my 'girl gang' know—I might rock Valentinos on the red carpet in the evening, but by midnight, I'm hanging in the hotel lobby wearing my pajamas with my team. They'll find me headed to a Bible study one moment and jamming out to rap music on the way home. They understand that I work hard and pour my all into my business (but not before 10 a.m., since I don't get along with alarm clocks)! But that's just me, and people can love it, or people can hate it. There's no showing up as anyone other than myself. So, if you're looking for ways to step into your authentic self and build pillars around your personal brand, you've come to the right place!

1. Get quiet and figure out who you are. Sit down and write it out. What's important to you? What do you like? What do you *not* like? Get crystal clear on this and ask friends to chime in if you need to.

2. Share it out to the world. When you've got a good idea of who you really are, start spreading it consistently! You'll more than likely attract people who appreciate your unique qualities and the fact that you're willing to put yourself out there.

3. Don't be afraid to go against the grain. When you're willing to stand out in your company, or even in this industry, for being who you are, you grant others the permission to do the same and you may attract people you never would have otherwise. There are great surprises in store for those brave enough to be authentic!

Vulnerability

When you hear the word "vulnerability," some of you might assume that it requires sharing your deepest, darkest secrets with complete strangers to achieve it. However, vulnerability is not solely about showing your weaknesses; it's also about opening your heart to those you lead. It's about embracing that emotional courage to reveal your true self, and that's what can truly transform relationships from surface-level friendliness to genuine connections.

I understand that it can be scary! We all carry wounds that have left scars. You might worry about being perceived as weak, but, in reality, the opposite is true. When you share your struggles and triumphs with those around you, you become relatable and accessible. It's this honesty that deepens the bonds of sisterhood and inspires a connection that goes beyond the superficial.

I remember a retreat we had in Washington, where a diverse group of women from different backgrounds all came together. Many of these women were meeting each other for the first time, and you could definitely feel the uncertainty and nervousness in the air. But the magic happened as we sat together and shared our stories! Some were beautiful, and some were tragic. There were tears all around as we all found out what each other had been through. But each story helped us bond a little more and ultimately took us from a group of co-workers to a true sisterhood. If you want to cultivate an environment of vulnerability for your team, here are my favorite ways:

1. Create a safe space for sharing. Whether it's a local gathering or a huge retreat, create an environment where everyone feels comfortable opening up. This could be as simple as sitting in a circle on the floor where each person shares their "WHY" and their journey.

2. Encourage storytelling. Ask your team members about their motivations for joining the industry, their life experiences, and the obstacles they've overcome. This allows each person to be vulnerable and also helps others to see the strength in their stories.

3. Take your stories beyond meetings. Encourage your team to share parts of their stories on social media platforms like Facebook, Instagram, or TikTok. This is a way to extend the spirit of vulnerability and sisterhood to a larger audience, offering hope and inspiration to others facing similar challenges!

Camaraderie

Camaraderie involves nurturing deep trust and mutual respect within your team. It goes beyond creating a fun and loving environment; rather, it's about establishing a sense of safety, support, and genuine care for each other's well-being!

In my own journey, I've come to understand that camaraderie isn't based on ranks, titles, or achievements. It's about consistently showing up with the best interests of your team at heart. It's about staying in consistent conversation, leading by example, and building the kind of trust where each person knows, "I've got your back, and you've got mine."

About a year ago, I faced the challenging decision to change companies. As you may know, such a move is never easy or pleasant! However, I shared my decision with my personal leaders at the old company, not with the intention of persuading them to follow but out of honesty and respect for their careers and what it would mean if I left. Amazingly, each one of them chose to join me in this new venture, and many of them told me that it was an easy decision to make because it was rooted in the trust and bonds we had built as a team. I like to think this was because I was committed to being a servant leader, one who put the team's needs ahead of my own. I encourage you to take action in the following ways if you want to foster camaraderie within your team:

1. Get in the trenches. Lead from the front and show up consistently *with* your team. Let them know that you're standing alongside them in this constantly changing profession! Trust is built in the trenches through honesty and transparency. Most people value direct conversations over sugarcoating and beating around the bush! Leading with integrity and being willing to have hard conversations builds mutual respect and camaraderie.

2. Show off Your team. Highlight your leaders' ideas and achievements in team zooms, have fun with team-branded swag, rank-up gifts, social hours, and work to collaborate in any way possible to make your team members feel included, seen, and heard.

3. Put everyone in the same room (or Zoom room!). Bringing your team together through activities like team Zooms, dinners out, and retreats solidifies the camaraderie that you've already cultivated remotely. Gathering everyone for a dose of fun and connection goes a long way! And speaking of activities, my next topic will cover just that!

Activities

Activity, fun, and energy are all essential elements of a thriving sisterhood. These are the things people remember and talk about long after the actual events are over, creating a lasting positive sentiment of joy and excitement around being part of the team.

In today's digital age, we've become accustomed to building connections through social media. But there's an irreplaceable magic that can only be found when gathering in person! It's in these moments—whether it's laughing together, crossing off goals from our dream boards, or simply dancing and singing the night away—that we find out who we really are beyond the computer screens. For people who are introverts like me, these in-person experiences are transformative, helping us step out of our shells and forge deeper connections.

I recently returned from a trip to Charleston, a place I had never been before and one I wanted to cross off my dream board. It was a girls' trip, and one of our goals was to shake off the typical winter blues. The energy was incredible! We created reels together, shared belly laughs, and made many core memories. These experiences left us all invigorated, not just about our business but about life itself. It was through moments like these that we transitioned from being just teammates to becoming close-knit friends. So, if you want to infuse this sense of fun and energy into your team, here are some actionable steps:

1. Kick virtual activities up a notch. Regular old team Zooms can be turned into a party with themes or dress-up elements! For instance, I hosted a 'Santa Beck' Christmas event, complete with costumes and company trivia. I had everyone wear their favorite Christmas attire, and I played Santa and gave away lots of prizes! Even though it was a virtual event, it really helped bring the atmosphere of fun and connection.

2. Create shared experiences. Organize team retreats, excursions, and incentive trips. These events are not just concerned with having fun but also about building relationships and understanding each other on a deeper level. If you have a local team, plan a regular team dinner or coffee meet-up so you can have fun and build your in-person connections!

3. Utilize company events for activities. When a large portion of your team is already together for a company conference, leadership summit, etc., take this time to plan fun activities with your team! Arrive a day early if you can and plan some exciting content and reels, team pictures, and maybe an interesting local activity that can help make that event more memorable.

Grace

Grace and empathy are not just "nice-to-have" virtues for a leader—they are essential elements in creating deep-rooted bonds within your team. You can be crushing it in every other aspect of leadership, but without grace and empathy, you risk isolating your team members, which can potentially lead them away from your circle and team.

Grace in leadership means understanding and accepting that everyone has their highs and lows. There will be times when team members are buzzing with energy and fully engaged, and other times when life takes over, whether it's a new relationship, a pregnancy, or personal challenges. When their focus shifts away from their business, it's absolutely critical to show grace. Support your team members, celebrate their joyous moments, and stand with them during their toughest times. This will promote a culture of understanding and acceptance, regardless of their current engagement level with the business.

Empathy is about genuinely putting yourself in someone else's shoes, digging deep into their perspective, and responding with compassion. It's recognizing that what might seem trivial to you could be everything to them! Every interaction should be approached with an intention to understand and support, rather than judge or dismiss.

There was a time in my Network Marketing career where lack of empathy from a leader had a serious impact on my path. One particular month, I lost a huge bonus due to a technical issue in our back office. When I asked my upline to run it up the chain and try to help me, her response was, "Oh, sorry, I guess you should work harder next time."

I was crushed. Here was this person who I trusted to really show up for me, to root for me, and to help me when things got tough, but she didn't. That was it for me; it was over. Once this trust was broken, I couldn't move even another inch forward with her. This experience taught me the importance of empathetic leadership, which is not just about business outcomes, but about nurturing trust and respect. In order to integrate grace and empathy into your leadership style, here are some practical steps:

1. Be present in good times and bad. Whether a team member is celebrating a milestone or facing a challenge, show up for them. Your consistent presence reinforces your commitment to their well-being.

2. Offer support proactively. If a team member is going through a tough time, find ways to help. This could be as simple as a one-on-one encouraging call, sending a thoughtful gift, or just a message to let them know they're loved. Also, stand in the gap for their team. There's nothing worse than needing to take a step back and experiencing fear about what will happen to your business during your absence. This is your opportunity to step up and be there for her team so she can focus on getting through the challenge.

3. Encourage open communication. Create a space where team members feel comfortable sharing their struggles without fear of judgment. This openness nurtures a supportive environment and strengthens team bonds, leading to a sisterhood that is unbreakable, no matter what life throws at them!

Okay, friends, we're nearly finished! Remember that these elements—Proximity, Accountability, Authenticity, Vulnerability, Camaraderie, Activity, and Grace—are what create a truly remarkable team. In fact, these elements create a sisterhood. Team building is more than achieving business success; it's about making a lasting impact in people's lives.

This era, more than ever, calls for genuine connection and deep relationships. By applying these principles, you're not only paving the way for long-term business success but also enriching lives, including your own!

Thank you for being here on these pages with me. You have the power to create a positive ripple effect in the world of Network Marketing and beyond! So, let's go out there and build sisterhoods that not only stand the test of time but also bring joy, fulfillment, and unparalleled success. See you out there!

Watch Brittany's Video Now!

LeadingLadiesCourse.com

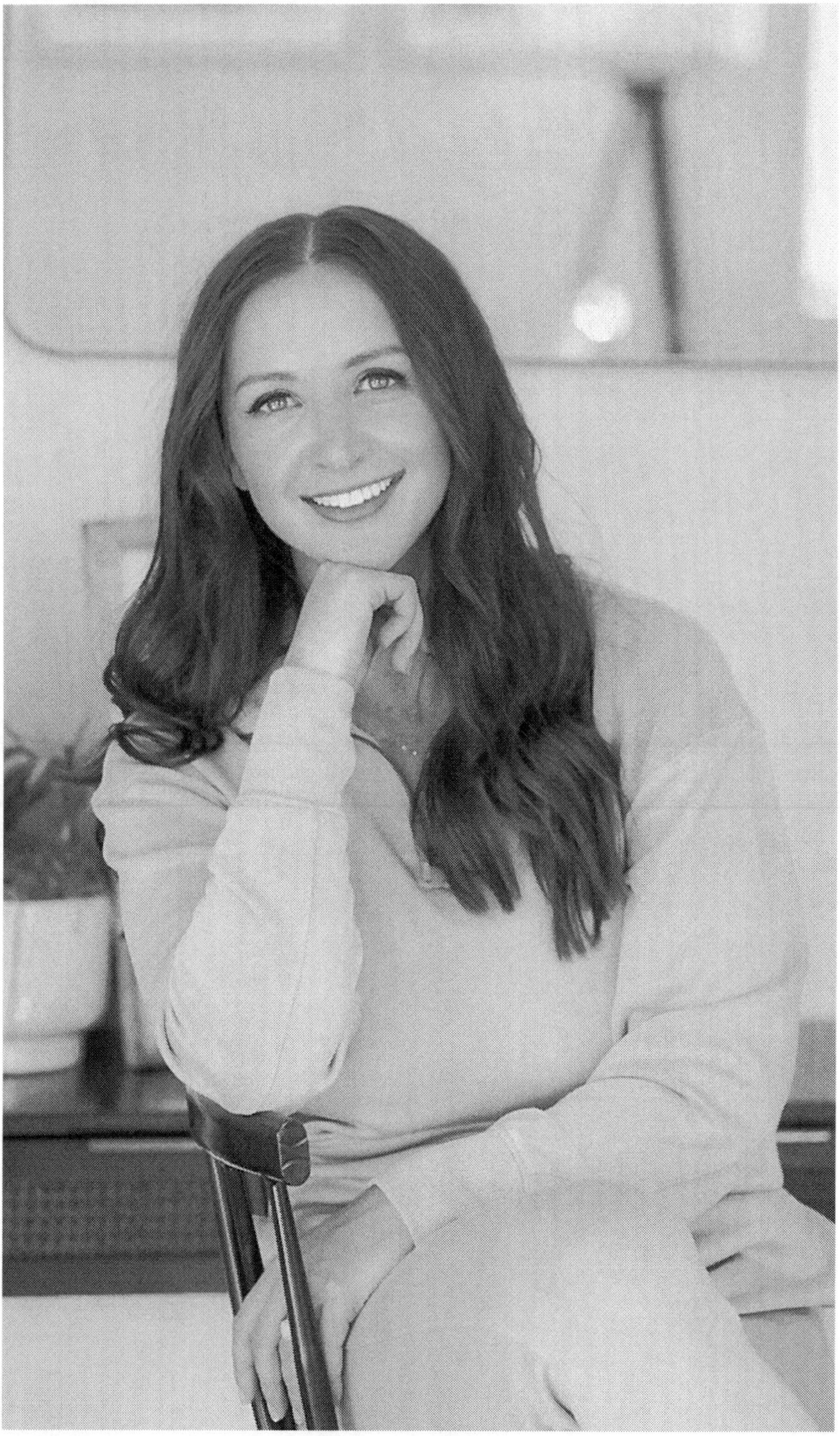

13

The Time Is Now

7 Reasons To Start Chasing Your
Dreams This Second

Alyssa Favreau

Facebook.com/alyssafavreau33
Instagram.com/alyssa_favreau

The Time Is Now

Alyssa Favreau

Hello, fellow ntwrkrs! Ever since I received the news that I'd be contributing a chapter to this incredible book, I knew exactly what I wanted to share with you. Now that I'm here, I'm thrilled to present you with a concept that I believe is critical for success in business and in life: the best time to chase your dreams is *right now.*

My Network Marketing career has spanned eight years, but I've always been surrounded by the dynamic, powerful nature of this profession. This is, of course, thanks to my mom, Deni Robinson, who has had thirty-five years of experience in this field. Make sure to check out her chapter in this book, too! I guess you could say I was brought up on Network Marketing, so I've spent a lifetime observing successful people in the field and figuring out their day-to-day habits and long-term strategies.

A standout realization about the way these successful people treat their businesses is this: they understand that there's no time like the present to pursue their dreams. This moment, right now, is ripe for living, dreaming, shining, and reaching for those aspirations that stir your soul. And if you don't take it, it's gone.

Think about the cost of unfulfilled dreams—it's not just the loss of those dreams but also the potential inspirations they could have sparked in others! Your destiny is in your hands, and you have the power to craft the life you desire. This all hinges on how seriously you take your dreams and the decision to pursue them without waiting for what you perceive to be the perfect time.

In this chapter, I'll walk you through seven compelling reasons to immediately start chasing your dreams. We'll explore why embracing failure is a pathway to success, the chaotic nature of life's unpredictability, the necessity of dedicated effort to realize dreams, the power of compounding your skills, the unalterable truth of aging, the lessons in every life experience, and the relentless pace of technology. These insights are not just observations but catalysts for action and change.

So, let's link arms and explore each of these reasons to immediately start pursuing your dreams, outlining actionable steps to empower your journey. Buckle up—we're in for an exhilarating ride!

Failing Your Way To Success

Let's dive into our first powerful insight: failing your way to success. It may sound paradoxical at first, yet, here's the truth: in our society, we're often taught to fear failure, to see it as a stop sign. From our days in grade school, where an 'F' was something to avoid at all costs, we've been conditioned to equate failure with defeat. But I'd like us to shift our perspective, especially in the entrepreneurial and Network Marketing world you've bravely ventured into.

In this dynamic space, failure isn't a setback; it's a stepping stone. In fact, it's a part of life that molds us into better versions of ourselves. Successful people embrace it, understanding that every failure is valuable feedback. It's about winning or learning—both are incredibly valuable—and often, you learn more from failures than successes.

I gleaned this firsthand lesson from observing my parents—my amazing and successful mom whom I mentioned earlier, and my dad was a successful entrepreneur in accounting. But both faced their share of failures while I was growing up.

My mom had to restart her direct sales business five times in new locations, each time feeling like she was back at square one. She didn't let that stop her, though. Instead, she used the lessons from experiences to propel herself forward. When she finally joined Network Marketing, she appeared as an overnight success. And what many didn't see were the lessons learned from starting over multiple times, which ultimately contributed to her rapid success.

My dad's journey in growing his CPA firm wasn't smooth sailing, either. He was constantly navigating the challenges of hiring the right employees and adapting to technological shifts, moving from paper-based systems to digital. However, he knew that each hurdle, each moment of discomfort and perceived failure, was an opportunity to grow and adapt, and this attitude led to the eventual tripling of his firm's revenue.

It may sound counterintuitive, but I promise, that embracing failure and discomfort is where the magic happens and where growth is sparked. It's about taking risks, learning from them, and stepping out of your comfort zone to reach new heights! So, how can you start changing your mindset around failure? Here are three actionable steps:

1. Self-assess exactly why you're stuck. This is important because often after a failure, you settle into what I like to call a 'post failure pause.' Of course, it's normal to pause for reflection after a setback. However, I'd like you to ask yourself, are you still pausing for constructive reflection, or is it fear of failing again holding you back?

2. Identify and act on 'that one thing'. What is that one thing you've been hesitant to do because of fear of failure? Write down the immediate next step needed to progress towards that goal. Remember, it's about taking one step at a time, rather than seeing the entire journey from the start.

3. Take the next step immediately. Now I'd like you to put down this book and act on that next step, whether it's reaching out to more people, improving a skill, or following up on leads. The key is action, no matter how small the step may seem. Then pat yourself on the back and jump back into this chapter!

Let's embrace our failures as the lessons and stepping stones to success that they actually are. It's time to redefine failure—not as an end but as a pivotal part of your journey to success. Now, take that brave step forward!

The End Is Near

Next, let's discuss a somewhat sobering yet profoundly significant realization: *the end is near.* This isn't meant to be morbid, but rather, think of it like a wake-up call to the unpredictability and preciousness of life. It's about understanding that life can change in an instant, flipping our world upside down. In moments where we face this reality for ourselves or a loved one, as challenging as they are, offer us a chance to slow down, reassess our priorities, and make sure we're not just getting swept away in the daily grind.

I was recently struck by the sudden loss of a legend in the network marketing space, Jessie Lee Ward. Her passing, although we weren't close friends, shook me to my core. It made me realize the true legacy of a person lies in the impact they leave behind—and Jessie's impact was so vast that it touched lives far beyond her immediate circle. She had a profound ability to inspire and transform people's lives—including mine.

Back in 2016, I was at a Network Marketing event listening to Jessie speak from the stage. To be completely honest, her words didn't resonate with me. At all! Yet over the years that followed, I watched her grow immensely, and her message and methods began to have a strong influence on me. I was fortunate to be part of her accelerator program, and I experienced a tremendous amount of growth and change under her instruction.

The transformation from the woman I saw on stage in 2016 to the mentor who profoundly impacted my growth was nothing short of incredible. Jessie Lee, who was only a year older than me, embodied the essence of living each day to the fullest, making the most of the time we have.

Her passing was a stark reminder that tomorrow isn't guaranteed. It forces us to ask ourselves, why aren't we more grateful for each day? Why don't we seize every moment as if it's our last? Jessie Lee's legacy lives on in many ways, including many of her followers announcing they will #bossleeup when life's challenges seem insurmountable. It's an inspiration to make an impact, to live fully, and to embrace each day with gratitude and purpose. In honor of this realization, I encourage you to embrace these simple yet powerful steps:

1. Meditate on the fact that tomorrow is not guaranteed. Consider how this phrase impacts your decision-making. Does your current lifestyle align with your true purpose and reason for living?

2. Identify your top five priorities. Make a list of the five most important things in your life right now. This exercise is about gaining clarity on what truly matters to you.

3. Focus and strategize on just one of those priorities. Choose one priority from your list. Each day, take deliberate steps to make this a more significant part of your life. It's about moving the needle, no matter how small the steps may seem!

Let's take this opportunity to #bossleeup in our own lives, drawing inspiration from those who have shown us the way. Remember, while we can't predict the end, we can live each day with intention, and we can make sure that our actions and choices reflect what matters the most to us.

Dreams Don't Happen Just 'Anyway'

It's time to tackle our third key insight: *dreams don't just happen just 'anyway'*. Instead, they become a reality through dedicated effort, through a balance of learning and doing. In Network Marketing, it's easy to fall into the trap of thinking about our dreams, affirming them, and even attending trainings, while not taking the necessary actions to make them a reality.

I'd like to share a concept from Fraser Brooks, a remarkable trainer in our field. He talks about the importance of having both a left foot and a right foot in our business journey. The left foot represents our beliefs, education, and affirmations. The right foot symbolizes action. Trying to step with only one foot leads to going in circles, not forward! It's about finding the right balance between knowledge and action.

When I joined this profession, I initially thought success in Network Marketing would naturally come to me, being the daughter of a successful Network Marketer. I believed that my mother's success and wisdom would somehow magically transfer to me! However, I overlooked the years of effort, skill development, and massive action she had put into her career. Success isn't something that can be simply passed down; rather, it requires personal commitment and action. So, let's get practical with some action steps:

1. Assess whether you've only been using one 'foot'.

- Have you been accumulating knowledge without applying it? Do you have notebooks filled with ideas that have become mere 'shelf help'? Recognize whether you have knowledge and beliefs that you need to act on.

- Do you need to strengthen your belief in yourself, or do you need to enhance your knowledge or skills? If you've been taking action without the right education, you might need to focus on education.

2. Identify areas of entitlement. Where have you felt that success should have been handed to you? This could relate to your upline, your sponsor, or previous experiences. Identify these areas and understand that success in Network Marketing is earned, not given.

Remember, dreams don't just happen 'anyway!' They require a balanced dance of belief and action. So, identify which foot you need to move forward with, and take that step, whether it's gaining more knowledge or taking bold action towards your dreams. Step forward in your journey, not just dreaming, but actively shaping our dreams into reality!

Compound Your Skills

Another vital part of the journey to success is understanding how to compound your skills. In Network Marketing, as in any field, skills are assets. They appreciate and compound over time, and they open doors to new opportunities and greater mastery.

Consider this analogy from Alex Hormozi, an influencer who dominates the realm of entrepreneurship and growth. He urges his audience to understand the progression of skills like this: understanding math leads to learning accounting, which opens the door to tax work, then to understanding insurance, and eventually to becoming a Chief Financial Officer. Each skill builds upon the previous one, expanding your capabilities. Similarly, Network Marketing is an excellent gateway to entrepreneurship, particularly due to its emphasis on human psychology and sales skills. I've always believed there is no better on-ramp to entrepreneurship than Network Marketing!

When I started in this profession, I was unsure if it would be my ultimate career path. Like many, I wasn't dreaming of becoming a Network Marketer from a young age. However, I recognized the immense value of the skills I would gain in this field, skills that would be useful in all future endeavors.

Initially, my passion wasn't for the profession itself, but for the company and products I represented. It took time and experience to see the effectiveness of Network Marketing as a vehicle for success. This realization dawned upon me after I graduated with a bachelor's degree and landed a job in corporate marketing, where I found a lack of fulfillment. Luckily, a mentor suggested that I compare the two fields and then reassess my career path.

I compared the lives of my corporate superiors with those of successful Network Marketers like my mother. The differences stared me right in the face: Network Marketing offered the potential for significant income, impactful work, and most importantly, time to enjoy life, while corporate marketing could only offer me financial gain. This realization solidified my commitment to the profession, knowing that the skills I developed would be invaluable, regardless of the immediate outcome. So, if you're wondering how to compound your own skills, here are a few actionable steps:

1. Assess your commitment. Are you fully engaged in your Network Marketing business, or are you holding back because you're unsure of your final destination? It's time to increase your level of commitment, regardless of whether you see yourself doing this long-term.

2. Adopt a skill acquisition mindset. Recognize that hard work and skill development in Network Marketing will pay dividends in all areas of your life, no matter where land in your career. Success, in any field, is intentional, not accidental!

3. Revisit your initial 'yes'. Reflect on why you said yes to Network Marketing in the first place. Reconnect with those reasons and recommit to your journey, focusing on enhancing and compounding your skills.

Remember, the skills you develop in Network Marketing are not just for this moment or this career path; they're assets that will continue to grow and serve you in countless ways. Embrace the process of skill compounding and watch as it transforms not just your business but your entire approach to life and success.

You're Not Getting Any Younger

Now, let's address a truth we often overlook: *we're not getting any younger.* Despite all the anti-aging products and health supplements we fill our medicine cabinets with, time marches on, and life actually becomes *more* complex with age, not less. This reality brings us to a crossroads: either we get pushed around by life's demands, reacting to each new challenge, or we choose to strengthen ourselves, take control, and proactively pursue our dreams!

As a mother of three young children, including a six-month-old, I know firsthand about the chaotic beauty of life. In the early days of motherhood, I thought about setting aside my dreams, hoping for a calmer future to pursue them. However, conversations with parents of teenagers and empty-nesters revealed a stark truth: life doesn't get easier; rather, the challenges just change shape.

This realization, while initially overwhelming, taught me a crucial lesson: there's never a perfect time to start something new or to prioritize my dreams! Waiting for that 'ideal' moment is an illusion. I learned this after my first child was born. I planned to re-engage with pursuing my dreams when he was six months old, thinking I'd be more rested and he'd be out of the newborn phase. Yet, as he grew, new challenges crept in and took the places of old ones, showing me that life doesn't pause or simplify for our convenience. So, now that you understand the reality of this, what can you do to navigate it? Here are some practical steps:

1. List out everything on your plate. Write down all your responsibilities, from household chores to professional tasks. Remember, there's no responsibility too small! It's essential to visually acknowledge everything you juggle daily.

2. Determine what's essential and delegate the rest. Decide what tasks are crucial for you to handle personally and which ones you can delegate. This could mean hiring help or asking for support from your network.

3. Redefine your schedule to include your dreams. Once you've delegated non-essential tasks, reassess your schedule. Identify pockets of time that can now be dedicated to pursuing your dreams and goals.

Accepting that I couldn't do it all alone was transformative. I chose to hire help for tasks like laundry and house cleaning, freeing up time for my Network Marketing business and personal aspirations. This decision became my motivation to succeed in this profession, ensuring I could afford the support I needed.

Your approach may vary—it could be seeking more help from your support network or hiring assistance. Whatever it looks like for you, the key is to recognize that achieving your dreams often requires offloading some of life's burdens.

Just remember, the complexity of life doesn't diminish with time! Embrace this fact, reorganize your life accordingly, and you'll find that pursuing your dreams becomes a more attainable and fulfilling journey.

There Is A Lesson In Every Experience

Next, let's explore the idea that every experience in life, especially those that are challenging, holds a lesson. Life's difficulties are opportunities for growth, skill development, empathy, and resilience. They can build our confidence and reinforce our trust that things will improve. And yes, I know that it's easy to say the words but not so easy to put this mindset into practice, but it's the best way I know how to overcome what has seemed insurmountable in my life.

I'm a big fan of Tony Robbins, and his perspective on this has been a game-changer for me. He says, "It's vital to view life's events as happening *for us*, not *to us*." This mindset shift can be transformative, especially during tough times. Along those same lines, the principle that 'what we focus on expands' is not just a motivational quote; it's a reality. Simple experiments in your day-to-day life can help you build a case for this concept.

Take, for example, the moment you buy a new car, like my family did with our Chrysler Pacifica. Suddenly, you start noticing that same model everywhere. Were they there before? Sure, they were! However, now you're noticing them without even trying. The same is true for the opportunities and results we choose to think about. This phenomenon is a testament to how our focus shapes our perception and experience.

Many people don't know this about me, but when I was twelve, I was diagnosed with Hodgkin's lymphoma. I would battle this disease over the next six months, and it took a serious mental, emotional, and physical toll on me during what should have been my most fun, free, and formative years. In my later teens, I often looked at my life situation and questioned why this was my reality. I fell into the mindset that I wouldn't get the things I wanted or deserved in life because of what had happened to me.

However, over time I realized that the experience of fighting cancer—of having to be brave and courageous even when things were at their worst—was instrumental in shaping the strong young woman I had become. Once I learned that seeing the experience as happening *for me* instead of *to me*, I was unstoppable.

Some people, even after reading this chapter, will continue to let difficult experiences define them and limit their potential. Others, however, will learn to use their negative experiences as fuel to transform and empower their lives, seeing every challenge as a chance to grow stronger, more resilient, and more patient. I want you to be the type of person who becomes empowered by these types of events. To put this into practice, here are some steps you can take.

1. Identify a traumatic experience. Think of a challenging or negative experience from your past. Write down the negative feelings associated with it on the left side of a piece of paper.

2. List your strengths. On the right side of the paper, list your strengths and positive traits. Then, try to draw connections between the traumatic experience and these strengths. Often, our greatest strengths are born out of adversity!

3. Zoom out for perspective. When facing a current challenge, imagine a 'future you' explaining this experience and what you learned from it to an audience ten years from now. This helps you gain a broader perspective and see the potential lessons.

4. Assess recurring patterns. Consider if your current challenge represents a recurring pattern in your life. If it does, it might be the lesson you need to learn to prevent its recurrence.

5. Have gratitude for life's experiences. Lastly, strive to view your life experiences, especially the challenging ones, with gratitude. If it's difficult to feel grateful for them now, that's okay. It's a journey, and with time and reflection, gratitude can emerge.

Remember, all of life's experiences, the good and the bad, are happening *for us,* not *to us.* They shape us, teach us, and prepare us for the future. Embracing this perspective can transform how we view and handle life's challenges!

Tech Never Sleeps

Finally, let's discuss an unavoidable reality of today's world: *technology never sleeps.* This profound truth doesn't just apply to the world at large, it especially applies to the Network Marketing profession! Success in this field is built on relationships and communication—and as the vehicles for those two things change due to technological advances, it's just not an option for Network Markers to fall behind.

If you're wondering if it's as serious as I make it sound, let me share some staggering statistics with you:

⇨ The AI industry is growing by 16% annually
⇨ 40% of the global population has access to the internet
⇨ 90% of the world's online data was generated in the last two years (read that again!),
⇨ 5 billion people own a mobile device,
⇨ 2.65 billion people use social media
⇨ Every day, the world becomes more reliant on smartphones

I'm not just relying on numbers here; in fact, I have evidence from my business that this is true. A few years ago, a woman who had been very successful in Network Marketing a decade earlier joined my team. She had financial, social, and career success for many years, but then she decided to stop and raise her family full-time. When she came to me, she was excited about getting back into the profession she had loved and excelled in.

However, the Network Marketing landscape had drastically changed since her days of house parties and in-home meetings. She was overwhelmed by the emergence of Facebook groups, Zoom meetings, and social selling. Despite her past success, she struggled with the steep learning curve of modern technology. And despite the coaching from me and others, she almost quit the profession on a few occasions when it felt like she would never grasp the breadth and depth of the online world she needed to participate in. Ultimately, she had the motivation to stay the course, but it took her almost a year to get into a comfortable place with the 'new' Network Marketing field.

This serves as a reminder that if we don't keep up with technology, we risk feeling alienated in our own industry. While the core principles of Network Marketing remain constant, the methods of execution evolve. Falling behind in technology can leave us overwhelmed and ineffective. To ensure you're not left behind, try these actionable steps:

1. Identify the online habits of successful leaders. Select five network marketing leaders you currently admire. Observe their online presence and take notes on what they're doing that you aren't.

2. Learn and implement. Choose one skill or strategy they use and learn just enough to get started. Commit to taking one action every day to improve your business in this area, even if it's not perfect!

3. Repeat and grow. Once you've integrated one skill, go back and choose another. Implement it in the same way, embracing imperfect action over inaction.

Remember, in the fast-paced world of technology, taking consistent, albeit imperfect, action is key. This approach will yield more benefits than waiting to act perfectly. Embrace technology, adapt to its changes, and use it to enhance your business. And remember—this is ongoing, for the rest of your life and career!

So, let's wrap this chapter up! We've journeyed together through seven themes that will enhance your success in Network Marketing and in life. Let's briefly recap these pivotal points:

1. Fail Your Way to Success: Embrace failure as a valuable learning experience. Remember, every setback is a setup for a comeback.

2. The End is Near: Reflect on your current priorities. If tomorrow isn't guaranteed, are you focusing on what truly matters?

3. Dreams Don't Happen 'Anyway': Dreams require action and skill development. Nurture your dreams with decisive steps and continual learning.

4. Compound Your Skills: Your skills are invaluable assets. Invest in them, and they will appreciate over time, opening new doors of opportunity.

ntwrkr.com

5. You're Not Getting Any Younger: Life doesn't necessarily get easier, but you can get stronger. Prioritize your time effectively and surround yourself with the right support.

6. A Lesson in Every Experience: Every challenge you face is an opportunity to learn and grow. Stay open to these lessons and let them guide you.

7. Tech Never Sleeps: In our technology-driven age, adaptability to technological advancements is key. Use technology as a tool to bolster your network marketing efforts.

I sincerely thank you for taking the time to explore these ideas with me. And I want you to acknowledge the effort you've put into gaining these insights and commit to applying them! Don't let these lessons be more 'self-help' that never gets acted upon; transform them into 'self-action.'

Remember, the path to success is a journey, not just a destination. It's about evolving, growing, and embracing every step of the way! I have full faith in your potential and your journey ahead. Thank you for allowing me to be a part of it!

Watch Alyssa's Video Now!
LeadingLadiesCourse.com

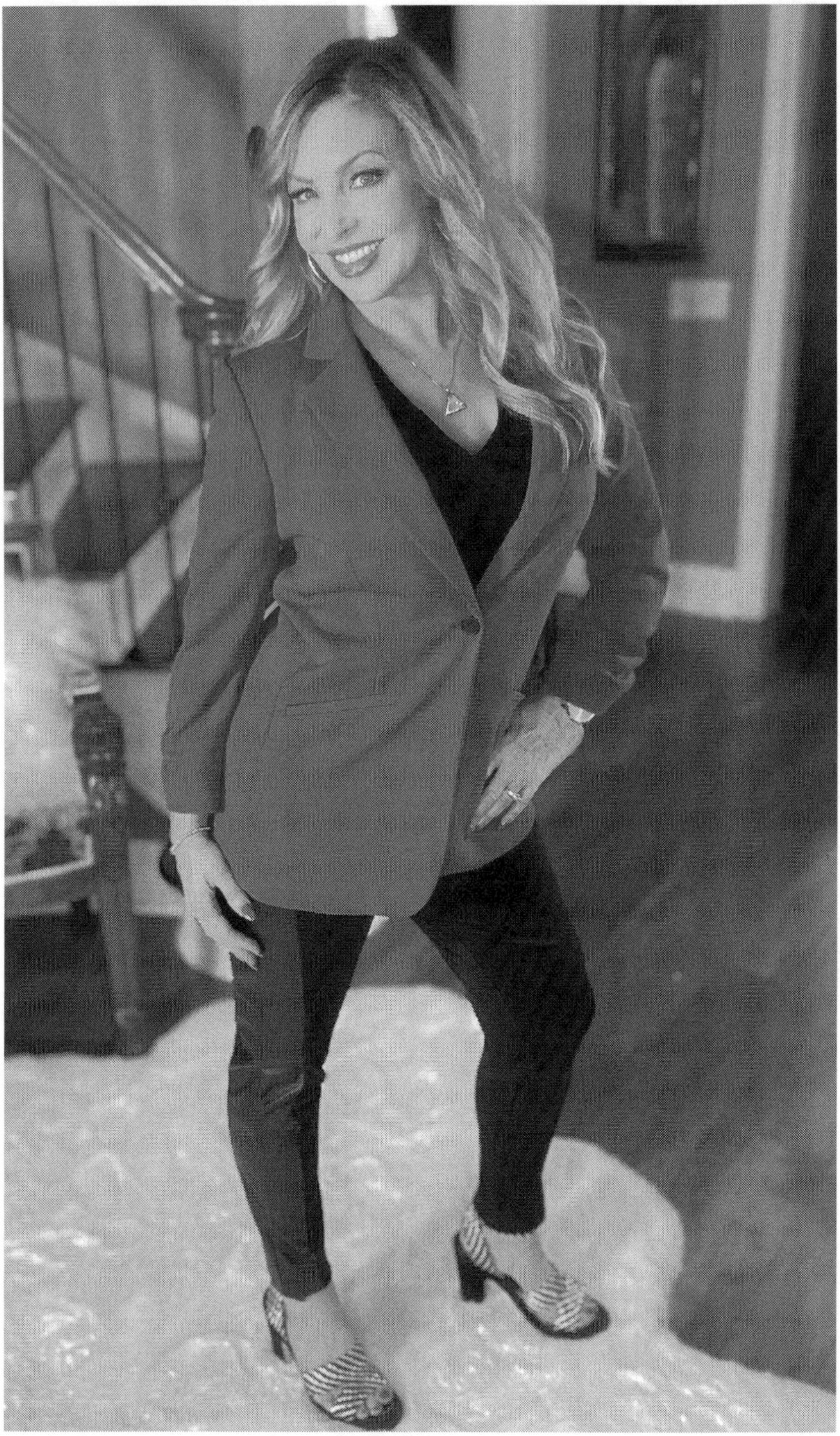

14

From Surviving To Thriving

Turning Your Traumatic Past Into An Empowered Future For Yourself & Others

Danielle Singh

Facebook.com/thedaniellesingh
Instagram.com/thedaniellesingh
Tiktok.com/@thedaniellesingh

From Surviving To Thriving

Danielle Singh

Hello, fellow ntwrkrs! I'm genuinely thrilled to share my story with you in this remarkable book, alongside so many distinguished women in the Network Marketing profession whom I deeply admire and respect. I'm looking forward to sharing my journey with you, and I hope that it will positively impact your life and help you become an even better leader in both your professional and personal life.

I've been involved in Network Marketing for nearly a decade now, and before that, I held high-level marketing positions in the natural health and fitness arena and have been a holistic health advocate, published writer, coach, athlete, and fitness competitor. Inspired by my late father, Charles, a certified executive chef, I combined my passions and started my own personal chef, nutrition, and meal-planning business many years ago.

I have resided in the beautiful Tampa Bay area of Florida for over twenty-six years, and I'm happily married to my soulmate and best friend, Dave, for nearly twenty years. Together, we've built and co-owned a boutique dental practice, share a passion for rescue dogs, and are now embarking on a new journey together in Network Marketing—helping others achieve their dreams.

I'm passionate about living a holistic lifestyle, healthy gourmet cooking, gardening, dancing, concerts, biking, nature, and everything the Florida lifestyle offers. But what truly brings me joy is helping others to overcome their past traumas, embrace their authentic selves, and find their unique strengths by sharing their stories in an empowering way.

You may wonder why you should listen to me about turning your traumatic past into an empowered future. Like many women, I've had to heal from a traumatic past, including childhood sexual abuse, to create the amazing life I have today.

Sharing my story on these pages has been a challenge, but I knew it was necessary to positively influence others and help create change in their lives. My belief is that everyone deserves to live life without feelings of unworthiness or shame. My dream is to help women of all ages embrace their traumas early on so they don't endure the decades of torment that I experienced.

If you've faced trauma or hardships, know that you're not alone, and it's never too late to overcome the challenges in life and turn your pain into power and purpose. This subject is important because women need to know they can rewrite their narratives, embrace their authentic selves, and use their stories to inspire others.

Think of it this way: we are not defined by our past but instead refined by it. In this chapter, I'll teach you to meet the woman you are today, find the lesson in your trauma, discover how to love yourself completely, unleash your inner warrior, and empower others through your journey.

LEADING LADIES

So, who's ready to dive in? Let's do this together!

Meet The Woman You Are Today

Have you ever felt like you're just getting by? I know I have. It's easy to get caught up in the daily grind of work and family responsibilities, forgetting to take a deep inward look. We often find ourselves merely surviving, not realizing we're on autopilot.

We go through the motions but not the *emotions,* especially when in survival mode, without addressing our past traumas. We need to ask ourselves: what makes us who we are? What are our character strengths and beliefs that help us navigate life's challenges? We often don't take the time to understand why we fall into bad habits and patterns.

Instead, we keep repeating them. However, I'm here to tell you that it doesn't have to be that way. We can take control of our lives, thoughts, and actions, and become more intentional about our choices and decisions. And the best part is, understanding ourselves better can lead to a more balanced and fulfilling life.

For me, this journey of self-discovery has been key to my success in my Network Marketing business. By understanding my strengths, I can help others do the same. The woman I am today is a result of all the trials and triumphs I've experienced. Every moment, good or bad, has shaped me.

This realization allows us to reframe experiences to heal and set ourselves on the right path toward freedom, self-love, and success, which includes our Network Marketing businesses. As we embrace our authentic selves and share our stories, we attract like-minded women into our businesses who share our core values and vision, ultimately becoming better leaders and role models.

Now, I'd like to share a story of overcoming unworthiness and starting anew. After a difficult childhood and adulthood, including a divorce, I found myself at thirty, leaving everything behind for the second time. I rented a small U-Haul with very few belongings and towed my car from Pennsylvania to the Gulf beaches of Florida without a plan or even a place to stay, but in my gut, I knew it was time to focus on my health, happiness, and wellness.

I soon found a small apartment near the beach and started working at a restaurant. I began running on the beach, training rigorously to feel better about myself. I became obsessed with fitness and loved my new beach life. Finally, I felt like I was finding myself. This led to a new career in health and fitness as an athlete, fitness competitor, and spokesmodel for a women's worldwide fitness competition, as well as an incredible journey of self-discovery and personal growth.

As I trained for the competition, I never imagined being more than just a competitor. Then, I became the VP of marketing for this very competition—traveling across the country, attending numerous health expos, and promoting the event. I was even scheduled to be interviewed for Fox Sports News! And while this was certainly an exciting opportunity, I couldn't shake the feeling that, even after all I'd accomplished, I didn't deserve to be on television talking about the competition.

LEADING LADIES

I had achieved so much in the previous year, including organizing a charity event for St. Jude's Children's Research Hospital, procuring over 80 sponsors, organizing a trade show, creating marketing materials, and raising a significant amount of money. I was also featured on the front page of the *Tampa Tribune* Sports section and placed in the top twenty out of one hundred ninety-two women athletes at the competition! But still, no matter what I did or how much I accomplished, that nagging voice of imposter syndrome wouldn't go away.

The day of the interview finally came, and I felt like a nervous and insecure wreck! However, that televised interview, which I initially felt was a disaster, ended up being one of the best things that ever happened to me. It gave me the confidence to believe in myself and led to amazing opportunities. When I mustered the courage to watch the playback, I was surprised at how composed I appeared to be. That visual confirmation, along with listening to myself talk effortlessly about all I'd accomplished, finally cemented my belief in myself.

I then became a nutrition and healthy eating influencer, featured in commercials and interviews, and wrote for health and fitness publications. I started my own personal chef and meal planning business, and I also represented a women's fitness wear line. Looking back, I was able to recognize and celebrate my accomplishments, but it took inventory and self-reflection to realize my worthiness and reform my old beliefs. My mindset, self-love, and self-talk now began to reflect the woman I am today.

So, to meet the woman you are today, I encourage you to try the following action steps:

1. Sit somewhere quiet and write down a list of your achievements. It doesn't matter if you think your accomplishments weren't a big deal (even though I promise you, they were!). Write them down anyway!

2. Identify the strengths and qualities that allowed you to accomplish each one. When you're done reflecting on your strengths, reach out to a friend or family member and ask them what *they* think your greatest strengths and achievements are. Do you notice any consistency?

3. Take ownership of the amazing things you've done. Accept the fact that yes—you really achieved those things, and they helped shape the woman you are today!

Recognizing and embracing the woman you are today is essential for personal and professional growth. Reflecting on your achievements helps you move forward with confidence! Celebrate your journey and use it as a foundation to excel in life and business.

Find The Lesson In Your Trauma

Growing up, I was living what may have seemed like the American dream with a loving family in a beautiful neighborhood. We had a great life, but my parents struggled with alcoholism, which led to constant arguments and my father's infidelity. Eventually, this took a toll on their marriage and our family.

I vividly remember coming home one day to find a "for sale" sign in our yard and being told by my parents that they were getting divorced.

Back then, divorce was frowned upon, and as a result, we were ostracized from our community. Our lives quickly crumbled, and my mom, brother, nana, and I ended up living in a small duplex, separated into two apartments.

I was moved to a new school where I was bullied on a daily basis. My mother struggled to work full-time and provide for us. Things worsened when my mother remarried, and during this time, I became a victim of childhood sexual abuse. I blocked this trauma out to protect myself, but I can now clearly remember the day the darkness crept in.

The abuse started with what seemed like normal affection but turned into something no child should ever have to face. I was only eight or nine years old, and I felt shamed, dirty, violated, alone, and scared. The abuse happened in secret, and I felt isolated and too afraid to tell anyone. I began blaming my mother and I wanted to run far away from home. My mother always seemed angry about something, and I was terrified to tell her about the abuse. I prayed for help and a better life, which I now know I received.

At age eleven, I finally told my mother about the abuse, but she called me a liar and screamed at me. The house went silent, and this continued until we went to therapy. However, therapy brought more distress as my mother and the therapist disregarded my claims and insisted I was making up stories. I was labeled a bad girl, a liar, and promiscuous, which left me feeling sad, lonely, and unwanted.

I then started running away from home and got involved with the wrong crowd, turning to drugs and addiction to escape my pain. Despite my young age, I promised myself that I would break free from this toxic environment. I began working various jobs from the age of 11 and eventually became emancipated at fifteen.

I completed high school despite the odds, and even became a restaurant trainer by age seventeen. Surviving an abusive childhood gave me incredible strength and resilience. I'm sharing my story here with you to show how we can find lessons in our hardships and persevere.

Here are three steps to help you find the lesson in your trauma:

1. Find a safe space. Choose a calm and safe place to reflect on your experiences. It can be helpful to have trusted friends or family members with you for support. When I shared my past, God brought the right people into my life who truly cared about my well-being, like my husband, my friends, and even new online friendships with people I had never met in person.

2. Acknowledge your past. Confront your traumatic experiences and recognize that they don't define who you are. Instead, focus on how you managed to survive those tough times.

3. Create a positive narrative. Shape a positive story about how you helped yourself through those difficult moments. You are incredible, and it's important to remember that you are the author of your own life story and the director of your life's movie. The way you frame your story is crucial and can make a significant difference. You have the power to rewrite it and portray yourself as the hero!

By following these steps, you can transform your perspective on your past and empower yourself to move forward with grace, strength, and resilience.

Love Yourself Completely

Many of us believe that we fully love ourselves, but in reality, we only embrace the positive aspects of our lives. True self-love, however, involves accepting and cherishing every part of ourselves, even during challenging times.

It's easy to feel good about ourselves when we're achieving our goals and everything is going smoothly. But what about when we face setbacks, make mistakes, or struggle with our mental health? It's actually in these moments that self-love becomes crucial. Embracing all facets of ourselves, including our flaws and imperfections, is essential to living our lives fully. This means forgiving ourselves for our mistakes and being gentle with ourselves during tough times.

Practicing self-love starts with treating ourselves with kindness and compassion, just as we would a friend. We need to prioritize our own needs and care for ourselves physically, mentally, emotionally, and spiritually. Additionally, it's important to push back against negative self-talk and focus on our strengths and achievements.

Self-love is a journey that takes time and effort. It's about learning to love ourselves unconditionally and recognizing our worth. As we embark on this important journey, we open ourselves up to new possibilities and opportunities.

My personal road to self-love has been challenging. I endured childhood abuse, unhealthy relationships, and I struggled with self-worth. I found myself in a cycle of abuse and self-sabotage. At nineteen, I reached a breaking point and decided to change my life. I moved away from my hometown and started anew.

In my new life, I finally began to face the pain and trauma of my past. I started sharing my experiences and embracing them as part of my journey. This process allowed me to develop incredible survival skills and I finally believed that I deserved better.

By following four action steps, you can also embark on a journey of self-discovery and self-love:

1. Find a safe space. Reflect on all aspects of yourself, including those you typically avoid or view negatively.

2. Embrace your experiences. Accept that your unique experiences are part of your journey. Find value and strength in them.

3. Give thanks. Appreciate the lessons learned from your experiences and recognize how they've shaped you into the strong woman you are today.

4. Reconnect with your inner child. Offer love and support to the younger version of yourself. Promise to protect her worth and value.

Your unique experiences and stories can serve as a survival guide for others. Embracing your past and learning to love yourself completely can inspire others to do the same.

Unleash Your Inner Warrior

Do you ever find yourself overwhelmed by negative self-talk or doubt? If so, it's time to tap into your inner strength and arm yourself with resilience. This metaphorical armor protects you from the harmful effects of negative thinking and helps you move forward in life.

For me, the armor of God is what works best. In other words, I surround myself with positive affirmations, engage in prayer and meditation, and make sure to stand firm in my beliefs. Your armor, however, might look different. It could involve setting boundaries with toxic individuals or practicing daily self-care.

The key is to find what empowers you and keeps you strong. You were born to be a leader. Don't let negative self-talk or doubt hold you back, and remember to embrace your inner strength and protect yourself. You've got this.

However, I understand that maintaining self-love can be challenging when negative thoughts and criticism creep back in. It's essential to recognize and protect yourself from these harmful thoughts and old habits that can hinder your progress and prevent you from reaching your full potential as a leader. I refer to this as putting on your armor of God, which includes strategies and practices to ward off negativity.

I was once at a conference as an attendee when the CEO unexpectedly called me on stage to share my story. This caught me off guard, and I was instantly filled with fear and doubt. As I approached the stage, trembling and with a quivering voice, I turned inward, took a deep breath, and prayed for the right words. My goal was to resonate with at least one person and make a positive impact in their life.

On that stage, I shared my story of my father's recent passing, the depression I faced afterward, and how I eventually found my way back to feeling good again. The response was overwhelming, and I received applause, hugs, and tears. One person even thanked me for helping them. In that moment, I knew it was all worth it, and I felt God working through me. Despite feeling unsure of myself, listening to the recording afterward allowed me to appreciate the authenticity and flow of my words.

In the past, when speaking on stages, I often felt disingenuous because my focus was mainly on promoting a product or an event rather than openly sharing my personal experiences. However, this time, I spoke authentically from my heart, sharing a deeply personal story about my father's passing and my journey through grief. This vulnerability had a profound impact on those who approached me afterward.

Unfortunately, self-doubt and negative thoughts crept back in shortly after that, attempting to shake my belief in my own story and worthiness to be on that stage. It became crucial for me to put on my armor and fiercely combat these negative voices to protect my newfound way of life. My armor consists of various practices such as prayer, breathwork exercises, meditation, positive affirmations, motivating self-talks, visualization, journaling, and honest self-reflection.

Here are four actionable steps to unleash your inner warrior and strengthen your own armor:

1. **Surround yourself with positivity.** Build a supportive network of people who inspire, encourage, and motivate you. Distance yourself from negative influences and seek motivation from mentors, coaches, or experts in personal growth.

2. **Set boundaries and nurture yourself.** Learn to say no and set limits to maintain your well-being. Recognize your trigger points and arm yourself with knowledge of your strengths to overcome negative self-talk.

3. **Establish a positive daily routine.** Create healthy habits for your mental, physical, and spiritual well-being. Consistent practice leads to growth and resilience, strengthening your inner warrior.

4. **Embrace forgiveness.** Forgiving yourself and others frees you from past hurt and trauma. Forgiveness is a gift to yourself, allowing you to move forward in life and heal.

By following these steps, you can protect yourself from negativity and embrace a life of positivity and growth. Remember, your story and voice are meant to be heard and can inspire others on their journey to self-love and acceptance.

Empower Others Through Your Journey

Empowering others through your journey means reaching out to those who might not be as far along in their own path. By sharing your experiences, knowledge, and authentic stories, you can support and guide others to reach their full potential. This not only contributes to their growth but also enhances your own Network Marketing business.

A key aspect of personal leadership is perseverance. It's important to stay committed and not let internal doubts or external negativity deter you from achieving your goals. By staying true to your path, you become an inspiration to others. Your ability to overcome obstacles and remain resilient sets a positive example, encouraging others to believe in their own potential.

For me, empowering others means using my experiences, including overcoming childhood sexual abuse, to inspire and uplift those around me. I no longer let these experiences define or hold me back. Instead, I use them as a source of strength and as stepping stones to thrive in both my personal life and my Network Marketing business.

Sharing your unique and authentic journey can have a powerful impact on others in your Network Marketing community. By persevering, you become a source of inspiration, encouraging others to do the same.

You might be surprised to hear that there was a time last year when I almost quit Network Marketing. I faced challenges with companies and colleagues that didn't align with my core values, and my father's declining health and passing made me pause and reflect on my life. During this period, I slipped into depression. However, a friend introduced me to a new product that reignited my passion for life and Network Marketing. This experience led me to align with a company and community that resonated with my values and mission. It also opened up an opportunity to contribute to this book, allowing me to reach and help others in a new way by sharing my unique and authentic story.

Despite the painful yet transformative experiences that brought me here, I am grateful for this journey. It's amazing how opportunities arise when you align with your true self and purpose and never give up. By using your personal journey as a tool to uplift others, you not only contribute to their growth but also find fulfillment in making a difference in their lives.

Here are three action steps to empower others through your journey:

1. Understand that your story is important for others to hear and relate to. Even if you think there's no one out there who could connect with your story, I promise—hearing your story will be the 'lightbulb moment' for at least one person in the world!

2. Find people and opportunities that align with your core values. When you find a company and team that speaks to the things you hold most dear in life, plant yourself there. They will be the soil, sun, and water that will allow you to grow, blossom, and impact others.

3. Use those platforms to be authentic and honest. When you feel safe in an organization, you can be vulnerable, empowering others with the truth of your story.

4. Share your journey with others as a tool to connect and inspire. Don't be afraid to be authentically you and share your story with the world. Your story matters, and it's time to share it.

As this chapter comes to a close, let's review what we've learned. We've been inspired to embrace the women we are today, find the lesson from our trauma, love ourselves completely, unleash our inner warrior, and empower others through our journey.

I never imagined that I would be sharing my experiences in a book, or that my stories would have an impact, but I know that if I can help even one person see their life in a positive light despite the challenges, then it has all been worthwhile! Everyone has a story to share, and it's important to learn from our experiences, view them positively, and be willing to share them with others. Applying what you've learned here in your life can be a transformative experience, both personally and in your Network Marketing business, as it has been for me.

Remember: the traumatic events of our past don't *define* us, they *refine* us!

I want to express my heartfelt gratitude for your time and for this safe space that has allowed me to share my vulnerable past and the future I have built for myself. I learned that it's possible to move from merely surviving to thriving by following these steps.

If any aspect of my story resonates with you, please know that you are not alone, and you can indeed turn your life into your own success story. I'm cheering for you, supporting you, and sending you love. Take care, and may God continue to bless you on your journey.

Watch Danielle's Video Now!
LeadingLadiesCourse.com

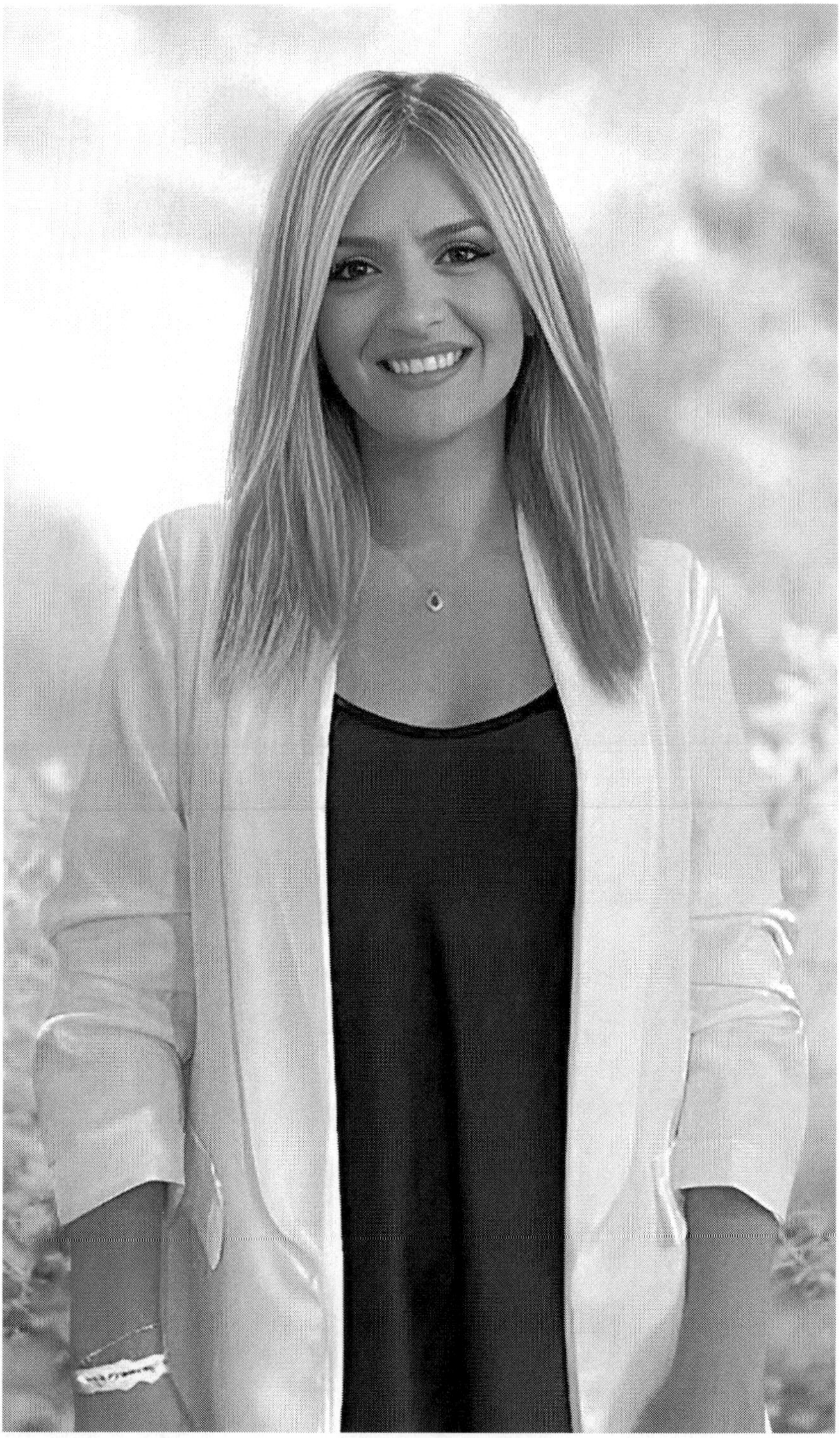

15

It's All About Discipline

7 Daily Practices That Create The Foundation For Success

Amalia Sorhent

Facebook.com/100008097781444
Instagram.com/amalia_sorhent
Tiktok.com/@amaliasorhent

It's All About Discipline

Amalia Sorhent

Hello, all you ntwrkrs! It's truly a delight to be here, sharing valuable insights with you. I am thrilled to be a part of this incredible book and to connect with amazing ladies from all corners of the world. It's a privilege to be sharing my experiences with you, and my chapter, *It's All About Discipline: 7 Daily Practices That Create the Foundation For Success*, is all about the topic of—yes, you guessed it—discipline!

If you're reading this book, it's evident that you aspire to achieve success. Perhaps, like me, you desire it to happen quickly, but it's critical that you don't achieve that success at the expense of other vital aspects of your life. My journey in Network Marketing has taught me the importance of balancing success at work with success in other key areas of life. But to do this, you must remain in control of all parts of your life, and self-discipline is the key.

Early in my career, I began watching documentary films featuring successful individuals. Their stories inspired me as I navigated the challenges of this profession! In most of these documentaries, I found that a common theme emerged: despite consistent successes or windfalls of good luck, every time a successful person abandoned self-discipline in one area, things went terribly wrong. Marriages crumbled, health deteriorated, and other challenges crept in quietly until they became catastrophic, threatening to steal all the prosperity they had built for themselves. And, as you might imagine, the opposite was also true. When they exercised discipline and focus in other areas besides their careers, their businesses grew and thrived. In this chapter, we will explore seven daily discipline practices that form the foundation for lasting success.

You might be wondering, *what does she know about discipline, anyway?* Well, four years ago, I faced one of the most challenging periods of my life. Having just completed nursing school, I learned about a job opportunity at a major hospital in Romania. Even though I already had a master's degree in European economics, I truly wanted to help people through nursing, and I found this position to be a perfect fit for my life and ambitions.

I locked myself in, studied diligently, and aced the hospital's application exam with an impressive score. I was certain the hospital position was mine, but to my dismay, they didn't offer it to me! When I inquired why I hadn't been hired, the manager told me point blank: *you're not good enough.* And even though all the evidence said otherwise, the rejection hit me hard and sent me into a deep depression. Additional job hunting in the nursing field proved fruitless. At one point, I even considered returning to my previous work in European economics.

As it turned out, life had other plans for me. I learned that it's not how far you fall, it's how high you bounce! Network Marketing entered my life, and even though I had never imagined finding career success outside a traditional full-time job, I achieved the title of manager within just one month. On top of that, I earned three times more than the hospital job would have paid me! By my third month in this new profession, I was able to bring my husband back home from his job abroad because my Network Marketing income exceeded his. I couldn't believe that in that short span of time, I went from entry-level to director! Now, after four years, I'm second in my company in Romania, leading a team of over 30,000 members.

But my journey was far from easy. I started in a state of depression, had no prior experience in Network Marketing, and I faced health challenges that left me physically exhausted and emotionally drained. Yet, through self-discipline, I achieved success! Network Marketing answered many of my prayers, but only because I learned that success should not come at the expense of other aspects of life.

We often perceive discipline of any kind as something difficult and complicated, but it's quite the opposite—it can simplify life and accelerate success. Self-discipline serves as the bridge between setting goals and achieving them. After all, in this modern life, it's difficult for anyone to stay focused and achieve results amid life's myriad challenges. Especially for women! As you read on, I want you to consider the following: *Discipline will take you where motivation alone cannot.*

My professional experiences are full of examples where the simple solution of discipline came to the rescue. In my team, I've encountered various challenges like illness, personal loss, and family issues within my community. But after I imparted the importance of discipline, they found fortitude which enabled them to maintain unwavering determination in the face of adversity.

As we journey together through these specific topics, it's important to remember a few things about self-discipline: first, that it is a continuous journey and a daily choice. It's not a one-and-done thing! Second, grace and compassion are essential. Yes, ambition is commendable, but never forget that people matter more than any achievement or accolade—and that includes you! Without self-compassion to accompany your self-discipline, you risk running yourself into the ground and you are also not able to fully enjoy your wins. And without grace for your team, you'll miss out on the loyalty that comes from showing empathy to others during difficult times.

In this chapter, we'll delve into the seven disciplines that can transform your life: physical discipline, educational discipline, spiritual discipline, communication discipline, emotional discipline, time discipline, and moral discipline.

Are you ready to dive in? Let's get started!

Physical Discipline

First, we're going to talk about taking disciplined action to protect your body. Your body is the vessel you move through life in, and keeping it strong will enable you to excel in all areas. Don't fall into the trap of being overworked and burning out! Instead, strive for a balance between work and rest.

Did you know that chaotic sleep cycles can turn an otherwise positive person into someone who sees the world through a glass-half-empty lens? I experienced this myself after the birth of my first child. At the time, I was working a full-time job. To make sure I had enough time to fit in both new motherhood and work, I neglected my own needs. I skipped meals, I didn't sleep, and I let myself become completely stressed without carving out time to take care of myself. This went on for too long, and as a result, I developed a thyroid disease.

I became depressed and unhealthy, losing weight to a dangerous point. It got so bad that I had to quit my job, and a long healing period took place afterward. I promised myself I'd never let that happen again—and if you're struggling with overloading your physical health to the point of illness or burnout, I want you to take the following action steps:

1. Find a way to reconnect with your body. Sometimes when we're stressed, we forget to check in with our bodies to truly understand how we feel. But simple exercises like deep breathing, stretching, or other slow movements can help us to notice where tensions persist or pain is trying to get our attention.

2. Prioritize your physical health as much as your business. Making sure to set aside equal amounts of time for your work and your physical health will ensure that you stay healthy and balanced. Don't just assume that you'll remember—actually schedule time in your day for it!

3. Reserve time to recover from stressful situations. No one can prevent stressful situations from happening in life. If you're alive, they're almost guaranteed! But what you *can* do is ensure that before you dive right back into your regular routines, you give yourself a time buffer to get back to baseline. Remember, no one can pour from an empty cup!

Educational Discipline

This one is very important, especially in Network Marketing. Constant learning keeps you engaged, challenges you, and expands your skillset in this ever-changing profession. I always say that anyone who gets to a certain level in Network Marketing can change careers easily—after all, they've learned so many skills that can cross over into other industries.

Remember, though, that learning requires time and patience. Just because you learn a new skill, don't expect instant results! To excel, you must practice, persist, and adapt your strategies as you learn and grow. This discipline is ultimately about adding value to yourself *first* so you can share it with others. I like to think of it like water from a fresh spring. When the water is constantly flowing, it's so refreshing to take a nice cool drink! So, keep the knowledge flowing into yourself, and then pass it on to your team.

Educational discipline can also boost your motivation and enthusiasm. I remember when I joined Instagram nearly two years after starting my career in Network Marketing. At first, it was so frustratingly hard for me to grasp that I gave up on that social media platform completely. But later, I started following other content creators and learning from them about how to use it. I started believing in myself, and soon, I was using Instagram exclusively as my recruiting tool! I even had social media influencers joining my team because they were excited about the content I was creating.

If I'd given up after my first attempt, I would never have found this kind of success, or been able to pass the information on to my team. And I've continued adding social media skills like TikTok and video editing—I'm "keeping the water fresh" for me and my team with continuous learning.

And don't forget, education without action is fruitless! I've seen people attend Zoom meetings and in-person trainings to gain education and skill, but they think it stops there and the results just automatically show up. But they never get results! I like to tell my team that leveling up is 30% education and 70% action. It's only through this action that your new skills pay off! Here are my tips to achieve educational discipline:

1. Discover what you don't know. Do a deep dive into your profession's most successful earners and identify three things they're doing to grow their business that you don't know how to do yet.

2. Find the resources, gain the skills, and jump in. Sometimes this can be as simple as watching a YouTube video, practicing the skill, and launching it out into the world! Other times, you'll find a steeper learning curve and you may need to buy a course or hire a coach. Either way, accept the challenge and persevere through the challenges and the impostor syndrome! Because education without action won't get you anywhere.

3. Share your newfound knowledge with your team. Remember, you'll empower your team to do amazing things if you directly share your knowledge and skills with them. This is how you find success at scale!

ntwrkr.com

Spiritual Discipline

This section is all about building character and empowering yourself to perform in alignment with who you really are. To succeed in Network Marketing, you must connect with people genuinely, and this requires working on your spiritual side to foster qualities like kindness, empathy, and inner peace. We have a saying in Romania, "First, be human." Success is not just about numbers or achievement; it's about caring for people. And if you can do this, people will stay with you for a lifetime.

Proverbs 19:22 says, "What is desired in a man is kindness." And I'm positive that I have earned more success, trust, and loyalty from being kind to others than anything else. To do this, however, you must be spiritually strong, and this boils down to resilience, peace, and an innate ability to reduce the "emotional size" of the situations you're thrown into with other people.

You might be wondering, how do you achieve spiritual strength? Well, just as with our bodies and nutrition, what you feed yourself spiritually influences your actions and character. Your input—thoughts, efforts, and choices—directly impacts your results! Engaging in practices like prayer and mindfulness will allow you to stay calm under pressure and maintain clarity in decision making so that you can keep people at the forefront of your business.

Alexander the Great requested that when he died, his hands were positioned to hang *outside* his coffin so that passersby could see that no matter how much success you had on earth, you couldn't take your riches with you. The good news is that you *can* leave a lasting legacy of the kind of person you were while you lived. And yes, financial success is wonderful to have, but without empathy, kindness, and genuine relationships, it's all for nothing.

I remember early in my Network Marketing career, I called up a team member who I thought could be performing better. I was very driven to achieve a new level at my company, so I didn't even ask her how she was doing before I dove into a speech to motivate her to sell and recruit.

What I didn't realize was that she had been in the hospital and was about to undergo a very invasive surgery. When I found this out, I felt terrible. I hadn't even considered her personal life; I was only worried about my own career results. Since that day, I have made it a priority to put people and their humanness first, and my business ambitions second. Spiritual discipline keeps me grounded in service to others, so here are my tips to achieve this state of mind:

1. Clarify your spiritual beliefs. You need to understand what is meaningful to you so that you can establish your spiritual practices accordingly.

2. Free yourself from the bad and be filled by the good. If your time is taken up by bad habits, gossip, and immoral behavior, there won't be room for the good things in life!

3. Remember: What goes in comes out. Keep yourself spiritually fit by putting together a routine for your spiritual practices. Make it as consistent as brushing your teeth! Choosing to put good things into your mind and spirit will result in amazing results.

Communication Discipline

Effective communication is the cornerstone of any successful business, especially in Network Marketing. And it's a dynamic skill that evolves over time—it must be worked on constantly! Communication discipline is about expressing your thoughts clearly by avoiding unnecessary details, delivering your message in a straightforward manner, and the ability to handle feedback gracefully, adjusting your tone and message based on context or audience.

Developing this discipline is important for nurturing positive relationships, avoiding misunderstandings, and of course, achieving effective collaboration in both personal or professional settings. It's also critical to use your sense of empathy to put yourself in someone else's shoes so you can understand and acknowledge their feelings, concerns, and perspectives.

It's also important that you don't sound scripted! Authentic communication is the best way to connect with people, and you can customize and compliment as needed, depending on who you're talking to. I don't mean that you should be fake or superficial—I just mean that you should be sensitive enough to know who you're talking to, and you should get a sense of what they most enjoy talking about.

In my own team, new recruits often ask me for a standard text to send to new prospects. They think that copy/pasting a text could convince someone to join their team, or that there is a magic formula that works for everyone! They hope that cold messaging a person on social media about business, without being personal first, will work. But it won't!

This is why it's so important to personalize each message. You only have one opportunity to catch that person's attention and win their trust, so remember: a follow-up message will always help your recruitment efforts. I recommend following up after two days, then two weeks, and then two months.

Once, I received a message from a man who made his money—and a lot of it—from selling an online course without investing in ads. I was so curious about his strategy, and I noticed that one of his secrets was a very good follow-up technique. I took note of this and made sure to incorporate it into my own strategy!

I'll pause here to remind you that communication discipline is also about reaching out to people *even if you're scared to.* It can certainly feel intimidating, but it's by overcoming this fear that we open the doors to new possibilities and connections. So, if you want to get better in the area of communication, here's what I suggest you do:

1. Work on yourself. Develop your listening skills, and know when and how to communicate, as well as when to refrain from communication. Practice empathy and understand different viewpoints, even in challenging situations.

2. Don't just copy/paste messages. Instead, learn how to make strong, personalized messages that speak to the human on the other end of the platform! Don't lead cold messaging with business talk—lead with personal talk. Don't think because you reach out once you are done. Follow up is key!

3. Get out of their inbox and into their life. Remember, your potential customers' inboxes are crowded! Break through the noise by

ntwrkr.com

creating personal connections outside of email.

Emotional Discipline

This discipline involves the ability to manage and control your emotions in a constructive way instead of letting them take over your life! By developing emotional discipline, you can navigate challenging situations without becoming overwhelmed by your emotions. It will also allow you to empathize with others, communicate effectively, and build positive relationships.

Remember that in Network Marketing, you'll often encounter rejection or objections from potential customers, recruits, friends, or family. These moments can be challenging, but emotional discipline helps you handle them with grace. When someone refuses to join your team or expresses negativity about Network Marketing, it's all the more important to maintain your emotional composure.

I remember a certain family member who was initially very resistant to Network Marketing. But when I heard her skepticism, instead of reacting emotionally, I remained composed and patient. Over time, her perspective shifted, and she eventually became highly successful in the business! This is a testament to the power of emotional discipline and the importance of handling objections with professionalism and understanding.

In addition, maintaining a balance between your business and personal life is essential for your emotional well-being. I've seen team members' marriages fall apart when they neglect their loved ones due to their dedication to the business. It's vital to prioritize your relationships and ensure that those you care about feel your love and attention. Remember, your loved ones can provide critical, loving support during challenging times! To master emotional discipline, I invite you to:

1. **Practice composure and consideration when you're met with criticism.** Stay graceful when others aren't and keep a smile on your face. You never know what kind of day someone else has had, or when their opinion on you or your business will change.

2. **Remember that your team members are not copies of you.** Each member of your team is a unique individual, and your team is made up of diverse personalities, situations, and communication styles.

3. **Balance your work and your relationships.** Your emotional well-being is tied to your relationships outside of work, so make sure they're getting the attention they need. Success in your business alone does not make a complete life!

Time Discipline

Time discipline is another key aspect of Network Marketing success. It involves managing and utilizing your time effectively to achieve your goals. And though it may sound simple enough, many aspiring Network Marketers come into this profession with high expectations but fail when they don't invest sufficient time in their business. They don't understand that they have to treat Network Marketing like a job, where commitment and time management are essential!

To use your time wisely, focus on activities that genuinely contribute to your business's growth. Sometimes, this means working on tasks that may not be your favorites but are necessary for success. Remember: *busy does not mean productive!*

Let's say you are spending hours a day creating makeup how-to videos for social media. You might enjoy the work, and you might even be really great at it—but if it's not getting you new recruits or driving traffic to your sales pages, then it's not a good use of your time!

And, similarly to our discussion regarding emotional discipline, it's critical to strike a balance between work and your personal relationships, it's also necessary to keep harmony between your business and personal life. Set boundaries around when you work, prioritize self-care, and allocate time for the activities you love to do. To begin practicing time discipline in your life, do the following:

1. Set realistic expectations for the time you need to invest to achieve your financial goals. If you need help, talk to your upline about how much time you should allocate based on the results you want to see!

2. Examine the results of your actions regularly. Even if you love the work you're doing, be brutally honest about how it's impacting your business. If your current approach is not yielding the desired outcomes, be willing to admit that, and then adapt and change.

3. Commit to consistently showing up for yourself. All the effort, scheduling, and software tools in the world won't make a difference if you don't actually show up and do the work. Keep your promises to yourself and your business!

Moral Discipline

Lastly, moral discipline is about adhering to a set of ethical principles and values in your thoughts, actions, and decisions. It's about consistently choosing the right path, even when it's challenging. Leaders with strong moral discipline demonstrate integrity, honesty, and a sense of responsibility in everything they do.

And while it's common to talk about doing what's right and honorable when times are challenging, it's also important to talk about remaining humble and ethical *in the wake of success*. Sometimes, you can become so successful that it's tempting to exploit people for personal gain—but focusing on helping people genuinely will attract people to you and reflect positively on your leadership.

Remember to lead with your heart in this business, with positive intentions and genuine care for people. At times, this can be difficult, especially if you've been involved in Network Marketing companies that have toxic cultures. Once, I had a woman join my team from another Network Marketing company where unhealthy competition was the way team members were motivated. Meanness, pettiness, and gossip were on the menu, it seemed, and no one was working to squash those poisonous habits.

She dove into my team believing that we were the same way, and I had to gently redirect her away from what she had known for years. Before long, though, she saw that our intentions were pure, and we ran our business with honesty and integrity. Realizing we were different made her fall in love with our team and company, and she has been a loyal member ever since.

But how do you maintain moral discipline? Part of the solution lies in staying away from those who do not have it. Choose the people you surround yourself with carefully and address any immoral behavior in your team. After all, it's easy to be morally corrupted when you're surrounded by people who are struggling with moral discipline. And upholding your morals requires constant self-reflection, understanding your values, and aligning your behavior with ethical principles. To establish and maintain moral discipline, I suggest the following:

1. Examine your motivations for everything you're currently doing. Be honest with your findings: are you exploiting people for your own personal gain? If so, shift your focus to helping and caring for others, and your success will follow.

2. Work on your own virtues every day. Find people, books, and other resources that highlight ways to develop yourself into a moral leader.

3. Be aware of temptations that come your way, and practice resisting them. Each time we resist the temptation to become morally corrupt, either through immoral people or immoral behaviors, our moral strength and fortitude increase.

So, ntwrkrs, there you have it!

Discipline is the driving force behind Network Marketing success. It takes you to places that motivation alone can't reach. By cultivating physical, educational, spiritual, communication, emotional, time, and moral discipline, you'll not only achieve success but also become an inspirational leader who positively impacts your team and the Network Marketing industry as a whole. So, stay disciplined, stay inspired, and continue your journey to success!

Watch Amalia's Video Now!
LeadingLadiesCourse.com

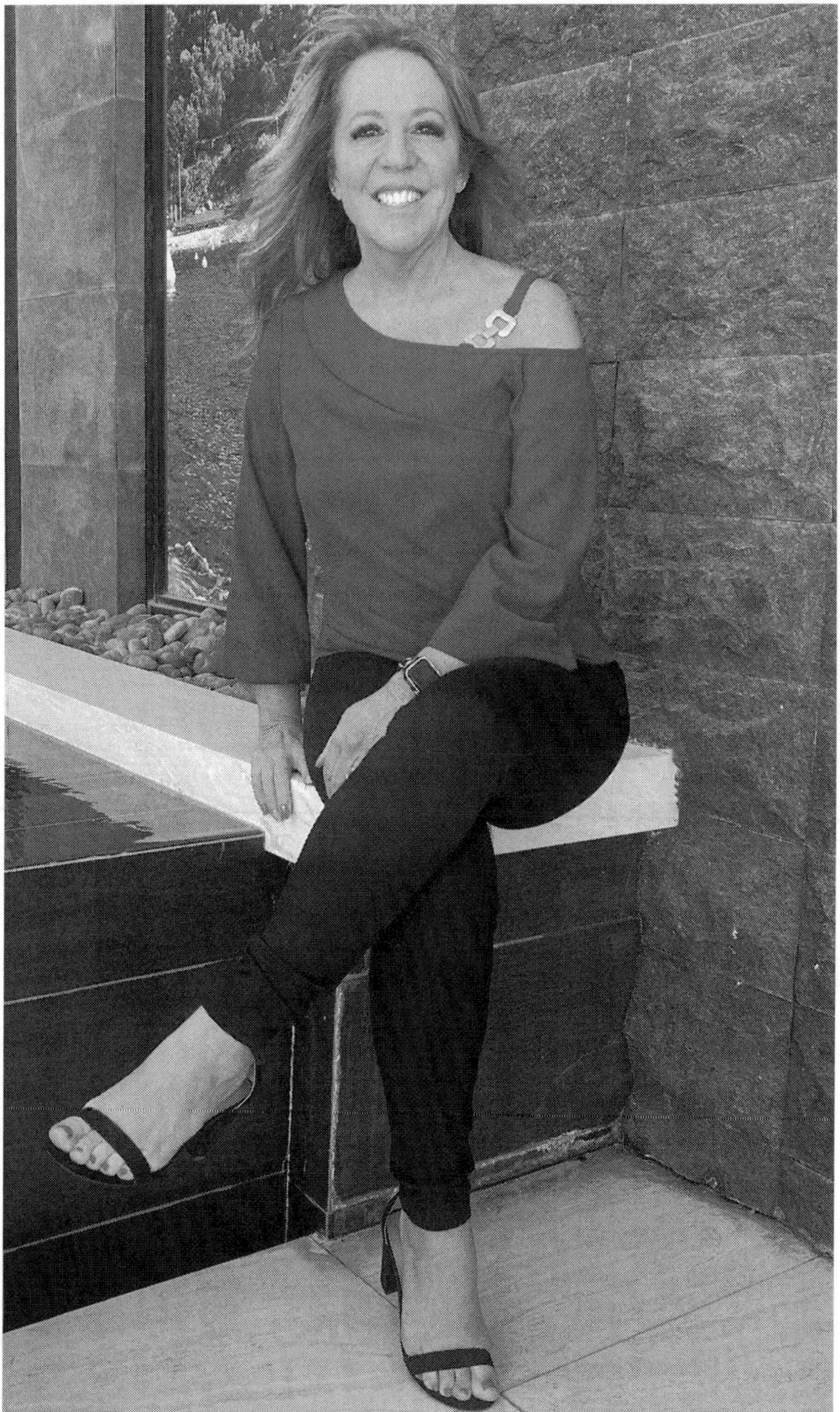

16

Don't Drop The Glass Balls

How To Identify & Prioritize The Most Important Things In Your Life

Rene Terry

🌐 TeamTerryKeto.com
f Facebook.com/teamterryketo
📷 Instagram.com/teamterryketo
♪ Tiktok.com/@teamterryketo

Don't Drop The Glass Balls

Rene Terry

Welcome, fellow ntwrkrs! I'm beyond thrilled to have you here for this chapter about safeguarding our glass balls—in other words, those critical, irreplaceable elements in our lives that demand our utmost attention and care. In this book (along with these other incredible ladies!), I aim to ensure that you walk away with every invaluable insight you came for, so let's begin!

For those of you who don't know me, here's a bit of my background. I proudly wear many hats in life: a devoted wife, a loving mom and grandma, a survivor of addiction, and a passionate entrepreneur. For the past twenty-eight years, I've taken an incredible ride alongside my life's co-navigator: my husband and business partner, Mark. He's not just my spouse but my best friend and confidant, with whom I've weathered storms and enjoyed life's triumphs.

Together, Mark and I have raised two extraordinary children and now are devoting practically all of our spare time to our granddaughter, the most recent bundle of joy in our lives! Our journey began first in corporate America, where we both honed our skills in business management at the same utility company until 2019. That year marked our leap into the world of Network Marketing—a leap I took with Mark by my side (although he might say he was more 'brought along' for the ride).

We started with a modest social circle of two hundred fifty friends on Facebook, and over time, we cultivated a digital family of over a million followers across various platforms. Now, leading a thriving organization of Network Marketers, we champion the art of blending business ambition with the joys and demands of family life. Isn't that a balance we all strive for?

Before delving deeper, let's discuss the art of juggling—a skill we, as women and mothers, have certainly mastered to perfection. From ensuring our kids' lives run smoothly to steering our businesses and finding time for self-care, it's a daily balancing act of priorities! Yet not everything we juggle bears the same weight. Some balls are rubber, bouncing back when dropped, while others are glass—delicate, invaluable, and irreplaceable, symbolizing our deepest family values and moments.

In this chapter, I'm going to guide you through seven pivotal steps: sharing your vision, identifying your glass balls, negotiating life's terms, scheduling priorities, executing with purpose, systemizing your world, and the art of continuous improvement.

Are you ready to embrace this journey? Fantastic—let's set the stage for a transformation that intertwines success with the essence of who we truly are.

Share Your Vision

Let's start at the beginning: sharing your vision. Many of my friends and teammates often confide in me about feeling adrift, sailing solo without the supportive wind of their families or partners behind them. This leads me to a pivotal question I've had to ask myself in the past and now pose to you: Have you laid out your vision and intentions to the people closest to you in life?

When I first launched my current business venture, I did it without so much as a nod to Mark. I figured I didn't need to tell him what I was doing; after all, it was so simple! I was going to host a party, invite friends, sell some products, and then close the chapter and move on with a bit of extra money. Little did I know that the small party I'd planned would lay an amazing but demanding path ahead, brimming with opportunities to build our dream lives.

As it turned out, when the business began to flourish, Mark felt completely sidelined. He longed for the shared daily moments that were now swallowed up by my new endeavor. It was after I arrived home from an event, bubbling with enthusiasm, that I finally realized I needed to take a moment to truly share my vision with him. I sat down with him, laid out the possibilities I saw before us, and invited him to be part of this journey—to share in the creation of what we could build together.

So, if you haven't shared your vision with your loved ones, or if it's time for a refresh, the action step I want you to take is to **write down your vision and share it with your family.**

Whether your vision is new or you've been after the same goal for years, take a moment and write it down on paper. Literally, write it down! Visions evolve as we progress in our business. As you articulate your vision, consider: What sparked your journey? What does success look like for you? Is it the freedom from financial worry at the grocery store, the ability to wholeheartedly say yes to your children's desires, or planning a family vacation without the constraints of a budget? Be as detailed as possible!

Once you've crystallized your vision, finalize this step by sharing it with your family. Encourage them to be part of this dream, not necessarily by contributing directly to your Network Marketing endeavors but perhaps by shouldering a bit more around the house, freeing you to focus on your goals. The end game? More quality family time, enjoyed together.

Identify Your Glass Balls

As mentioned earlier, 'glass balls' represent the essential and irreplaceable elements of our lives—family traditions, moments of joy and celebration, significant milestones, and birthdays. They require our attention and prioritization due to their profound importance, not to mention the consequences and loss we face if they are neglected. The glass balls will shift and change as you move through life's stages, making it crucial to stay attuned to new priorities and emotions as time passes!

The birth of my children introduced me to the complex dance of celebrating Mother's Day, a holiday that, for all of my life beforehand, was dedicated solely to my mom. It became challenging to bask in the love and attention of my children while also wanting to make the day special for my mom. The solution? My sister and I decided to dedicate the Saturday before Mother's Day exclusively to our mom, ensuring she felt loved through meals together, massages, and other gifts that showed her she was cherished! This adjustment allowed us to enjoy our own Mother's Days guilt-free, knowing we had fully honored our mom in a meaningful way.

This tradition is a glass ball for me; it's a treasure that I do everything in my power to protect. One year, this commitment was put to the test when Jesse Lee Ward invited me to speak at an event. I was thrilled and honored, but the date clashed with our Mother's Day tradition. With a heavy heart, I declined, explaining the significance of this glass ball in my life. It was a choice between honoring a cherished family tradition and a professional opportunity, and my family tradition won because *I had identified it as a glass ball.*

So, to help you identify your own glass balls, I want you to sit quietly, reflect on your current life situation, and **make a list of the non-negotiables.**

What are these traditions and moments that, if missed, would leave a lasting impact? There's no right or wrong number of glass balls to have, so list as many as you can think of. Recognizing these will guide you in prioritizing and safeguarding what truly matters to you and your loved ones as we go through the next steps in this process.

Negotiate Agreements

Now, let's explore the art of negotiating agreements, a key step in building a mutual understanding and a robust support system within the family. Acknowledging your family's concerns is key to preventing misunderstandings and establishing clear expectations.

In the first section, I wrote about Mark's feelings of being sidelined when my business started to take off. When I realized the importance of sharing my vision with him, I also expressed how much his support meant to me and the business. I asked him to come along and share the tasks with me, allowing us to work together *and* enjoy more quality time as a family, since now there were two people at the help instead of one.

It's vital, however, to choose tasks for others wisely, ensuring they bring joy rather than feel like a chore. This isn't about asking family members to be secretaries or janitors while you get to do all the exciting work! For example, Mark has a passion for cooking, which made him the perfect star for our cooking videos. This task naturally extended to him handling grocery shopping and organizing our video schedule, blending his interests with our business needs, as well as enabling us to cherish our moments together more deeply.

For yet another perspective on family involvement, I'll take you behind the scenes in the logistics of our trial products. While I handle the marketing and campaign visuals, Mark takes charge of website updates, inventory management, and order fulfillment. Don't worry, this strategy isn't limited to spouses; teenagers in the family can also lend a hand, providing them with valuable experience and involvement. It really can become a family affair!

So, when you decide to negotiate an agreement with your family, your actionable step is to **set aside time to discuss agreements and explain the envisioned outcome with your family**.

Understand that while your children may wish for your presence at all their games, compromises are necessary. Maybe, in service to the vision—say, earning enough money to go to Disneyland—you explain that you can attend one game a week instead of every single game. Negotiating with your family is all about setting realistic expectations and communicating openly, ensuring that no one feels overlooked or taken by surprise.

By sitting down with your loved ones to negotiate these agreements, you pave the way for a more harmonious journey, where everyone feels valued as an important part of the success story!

Prioritize & Schedule

Let's now get into the critical steps of prioritizing and scheduling. Having identified our glass balls, it's essential not to let them slip through the cracks of our busy lives! I'm a strong advocate of dedicating time each week to plan out your schedule, emphasizing the importance of self-care at the forefront. Remember, you can't effectively support others if you're running on an empty tank.

Take a moment to think about what refuels or recharges your spirit. Whether it's a date night, a workout session, or a few quiet moments with a book in a bubble bath, make sure these rejuvenating activities are scheduled into your calendar. This practice ensures that glimpses of joy are woven throughout your week, motivating you through less appealing tasks like email follow-up or expense tracking. Start with calendar blocks for your self-care and the glass balls, then organize everything else around them.

To simplify this process, consider embracing the technology most of us have at our fingertips. Our family relies on an app called Cozi that has been a game-changer! It allows each of us to maintain individual calendars while sharing a collective family calendar. This interconnectedness ensures we respect each other's commitments, like knowing not to schedule over Mark's golf days without his input. It's an excellent tool for keeping everyone's priorities in view and managing the balance between glass and rubber balls effectively.

So, if you want to master the prioritization and scheduling of family life, your action is to **dedicate time and technology to proper scheduling, beginning with yourself and the glass balls, and then filling in the rest.**

There are many apps out there available to optimize planning, and the best one is the one you and your family will actually use!

Execute With Intention

All the sharing, negotiating, agreement, and planning in the world won't matter if you can't execute with intent. Purposeful action is what truly drives progress and sets it apart from mere activity. If you're told that posting on social media can grow your business, but instead of creating strategic content to drive prospects to your website, you post a funny cat meme, then clearly, all the instruction in the world isn't going to grow your business! Executing with intention is about knowing your *purpose* and the *expected outcome* from the beginning.

Early on in my Network Marketing career, a colleague and I (both novices) heeded Jesse Lee's advice to 'go live' frequently. My friend's keto nacho recipe video unexpectedly went viral, but without a plan for harnessing its momentum, she was overwhelmed and eventually let the opportunity slip. This wasn't a failure; rather, it was a lesson in the importance of planning and intention.

Using this as a learning opportunity, she devised a strategy for future live sessions, clearly defining her intentions and follow-up actions. Her preparation paid off when another video featuring a product we sell went viral, propelling her to achieve a company rank that came with a car reward—all within two days of the video's success. The moral? Know your desired outcome before taking action. It's not about ticking boxes—it's about meaningful engagement and preparedness for what follows.

In the context of Network Marketing, the action step here is to **devise a method to capture attention and contact information and establish a solid follow-up plan.** Aim for a system so robust that anyone could step in to assist, especially when a post gains unexpected attention.

Acting with intention is a powerful declaration to the universe, setting the stage for not just good but amazing results!

Set Up Systems

In my view, setting up the proper systems is akin to practicing good form in athletics. Just as athletes recognize the significance of *form* for optimal performance, the same principle holds true for the *systems* you employ to manage your business.

A few years ago, I received a Peloton bike as a Mother's Day gift. I was eager to dive in and level up my fitness! I skipped out on the introductory videos, jumped on the bike, and did my best—only to be humbled by the superior performance of someone much older in the class. My initial lack of form not only left me trailing the group, but I was physically incapacitated for days! I spent some time recovering, returned to the bike with the proper gear, seat adjustments, and a focus on good form, which then led to an immensely rewarding workout that produced the results I was looking for after just a few sessions.

This analogy perfectly mirrors the necessity of systems in your business. Without intentionality and a systematic approach—like pedaling a bike without considering form—you're likely to find yourself exerting effort but making little progress. The goal is to ensure your business activities are as efficient and effective as possible, so you can spend as much time as possible practicing self-care, tending to your glass balls, and being with your family.

The action step I want you to take is to **scrutinize the repetitive tasks**

within your daily operations and look for places to automate the work. Are you manually responding to the same queries over and over? Could shortcuts or templates streamline these processes? If you're frequently explaining a product or program, consider whether a video could convey this information more consistently and save time.

Implementing systems and 'maintaining good form' in how you conduct your business activities will not only increase efficiency but also drive momentum and results!

Review & Improve

Once you've adopted the practices outlined above, a weekly review can be transformative—offering the chance to reflect on successes and areas for enhancement. I consistently allocate 15 minutes at the end of each week for this purpose, where I look back at the schedule and celebrate achievements like adhering to my exercise routine or making on-time appearances at my children's games. Then, I look for the places where I missed the mark or could have done better. It's not about self-criticism; rather, it's about growth opportunities!

I began using the weekly review when Mark and I were thriving in our business. Even though we had found success at work, we both sensed that there was a disconnect at home. Implementing a weekly review allowed us to pinpoint and address these feelings. For example, we realized the importance of rekindling simple rituals lost in the hustle of our business growth, such as greeting each other and spending a few minutes connecting when coming home or making sure that dinnertime wasn't interrupted. As it turned out, these moments of connection had been overshadowed by our business commitments!

By dedicating time to review our week, not only did we acknowledge what we did well, but we also were able to uncover subtle yet significant elements of our relationship that needed attention. Scheduling a regular date night made it easier to have open discussions about what we missed and how to reintegrate those aspects into our lives. Simple adjustments, like putting our phones away during dinner, significantly improved our connection as well.

Weekly reviews aren't just about business or personal productivity; they're about maintaining the quality of our relationships and ensuring we don't lose sight of what truly matters. They encourage us to make intentional changes that enhance both our personal lives and professional endeavors!

So, the simple action step here is to **schedule time each week to reflect and adjust.** It's a valuable step in fostering continuous improvement and preventing small issues from escalating!

As we wrap up this chapter, I want to reiterate the key concepts we've explored. Overall, the importance of safeguarding your glass balls cannot be overstated—those irreplaceable aspects of life that demand our attention.

The first critical step is sharing your vision with your loved ones and involving them in your journey and collective goals.

The next step is identifying what's essential to your family (while acknowledging that fulfilling everyone's desires simultaneously isn't always feasible) and setting clear expectations about your availability.

Then, it's understanding that prioritizing self-care is essential—remember, only a full cup can overflow to nourish others!

After that comes embracing technology to put the non-negotiables on your calendar while remaining flexible with less critical tasks.

Up next is executing every action, particularly in your business, with a clear intention and outcome in mind, ensuring you're prepared for any scenario (including the unexpected viral moments!).

Then comes the understanding that systems are your ally in progress, not just a means to avoid stagnation but a pathway towards your objectives.

Finally, it's dedicating time weekly to review achievements and areas for improvement, aiming for even a one-degree enhancement in your endeavors. Remember, even a slight shift could be the catalyst for achieving your goals!

It's been a privilege to share my insights on Network Marketing and the art of balancing life's priorities with you on these pages. 'The perfect balance' may be elusive, but the act of harmonizing professional aspirations with family life is absolutely achievable! I hope this guidance propels you and your family toward the success you dream of. Take care, ntwrkrs!

Watch Rene's Video Now!
LeadingLadiesCourse.com

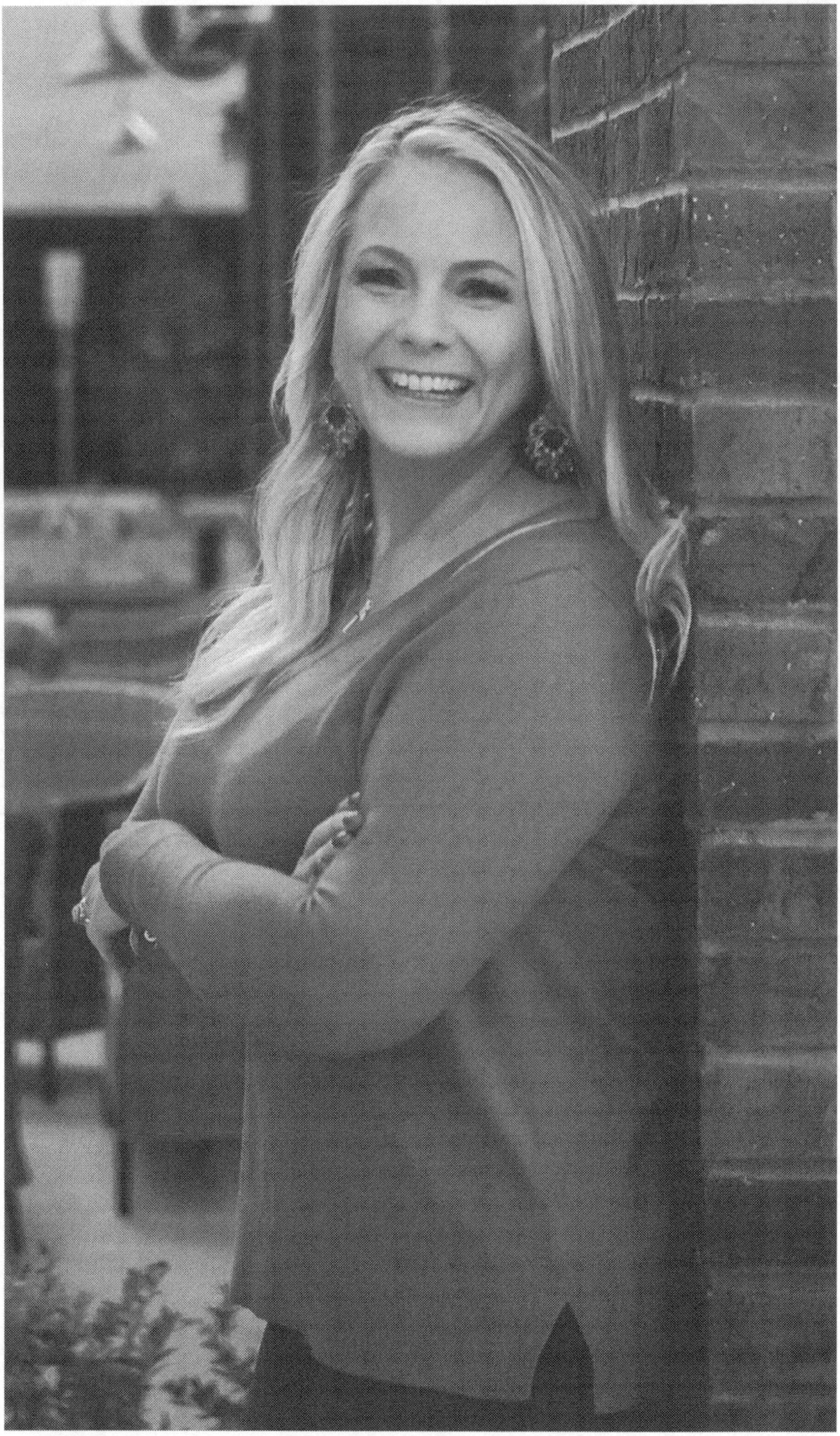

17

Just Do The Thing

How To Take Action, Get Results, & Build Confidence Each Step of Your Journey

Julie Glass

Facebook.com/julie.glass80
Instagram.com/julie.glass80
Tiktok.com/@julieglass80

Just Do The Thing

Julie Glass

Hey there, ntwrkrs! I'm absolutely thrilled to be writing this chapter in *Leading Ladies,* and I congratulate you on choosing to level up by reading these powerful stories from me and my fellow authors. We're going to embark on an empowering journey, one that's all about taking action and nurturing self-confidence at every step—and I'm here to share my story and insights with you. I titled my chapter *Just Do the Thing: How to Take Action, Get Results, & Build Confidence Each Step of Your Journey,* so let's just do this thing!

But first, I'll tell you a bit about my own journey. As a devoted mom and wife residing in beautiful North Georgia, I ventured into Network Marketing about six years ago. My background was in commercial property management, and I had absolutely no prior experience in this field. But that didn't stop me from diving into the industry head-first! This career path captivated me with its potential for ordinary people to achieve extraordinary results, and I was determined to be among them. With dedication and hard work, I saw remarkable growth: within just ten months, I had built a six-figure income, and shortly after, I quadrupled my earnings from property management, marking a significant turning point in my career.

Since 2018, I've been fully immersed in Network Marketing. However, my journey hasn't been without its challenges. Even as a top earner and leader, I've battled with self-confidence issues, which is a struggle that I believe many women face in this industry. Being part of a community filled with inspiring and powerful women can sometimes lead to self-doubt. But here's what I've learned: *it's normal to feel a mix of fear, doubt, and self-criticism.* Despite these feelings, I stand before you as proof that overcoming these obstacles and achieving great success is entirely possible!

In this chapter, I'll share the strategies I've employed from the start of my career to this day, strategies that have been instrumental in overcoming my fears and bolstering my confidence. We'll delve into concepts like becoming a 'Yes Girl,' setting and celebrating goals, transforming your self-talk, getting closer to the fire, seeking mentorship, relying on your support network, and the value of continual learning.

So, are you ready to dive in? Grab a pen and paper, take notes on what resonates with you, and let's go on this journey together!

Become A 'Yes Girl'

I'd like to introduce you to a transformative mindset: Becoming a 'Yes Girl.' This concept is simple yet profound. It's about courageously saying 'yes' to opportunities that initially seem intimidating—before fear convinces you to run and hide! It's about embracing the unknown and confronting what scares you. Remember, it's natural to feel apprehensive about uncharted territories.

Think back to when you first learned to drive a car. You didn't just read a book on how to drive! To gain confidence and skill, you had to *actually drive the car.* Similarly, in Network Marketing, it's essential to actively engage in new, and sometimes scary, experiences to build confidence.

Let me share a personal anecdote that illustrates this mindset. About eleven months into my Network Marketing journey, I received a call that tested my resolve. My upline invited me to a mastermind event in San Diego, a gathering of top performers in my company. While my heart leaped at the opportunity, my mind was clouded with doubts. *Julie, you're out of your league,* my inner critic warned. *What if you fail or embarrass yourself?*

I found myself at a crossroads, torn between my ambition and my insecurities. As I hesitated, my upline offered a piece of advice that would forever alter my path: "Julie, just say yes and figure it out later." I trusted him, took that advice, and committed to the event right then and there.

And, as you might expect, the experience was nothing short of life-changing! Being in the company of such accomplished individuals, I realized my own worth and potential. It shifted my self-perception and redefined my aspirations. It was a testament to the power of stepping out of my comfort zone.

Here are three ways you might become a 'Yes Girl':

1. Identify what intimidates you. Is it presenting your products, engaging in Facebook Live sessions, or maybe stepping into a room full of strangers? Write these down.

2. Make a commitment to yourself to confront these challenges. The only person who can make this commitment is you, so don't waste time overthinking or asking everyone you know to talk you into or out of it. Just commit.

3. Seek an accountability partner if needed. You may have made the commitment on your own, but that doesn't mean you have to go it alone. Enlist an accountability partner to remind you of why you committed and to help you stay on the right track along the way.

Don't let analysis paralysis or fear hold you back here! Take the leap and embrace being a 'Yes Girl'. This mindset isn't just about overcoming fears; rather, it's about unlocking your true potential and stepping into the person you're meant to be.

Set & Celebrate

The 'Set and Celebrate' approach is all about defining achievable goals and then honoring each milestone you reach. It's important to understand that 'achievable' doesn't mean insignificant—goals should be tailored to your personal journey and business stage.

When I think back to my early days in this profession, I remember balancing my day job in property management with my budding Network Marketing career. My family was still adapting to this new routine, especially the evenings I dedicated to my business. This period was marked by a significant goal: achieving my first leadership rank in the company. And it became a collective family effort, with each member playing a role in supporting my ambition. I even found ways to incentivize their support, so it wasn't just me who felt accomplished—it was each and every one of us!

During Christmas that year, I decided to celebrate this achievement in a unique way. My son, who was ten years old at the time and fascinated with designer sneakers, became the focus of my celebration. I surprised him with his first pair of designer shoes, a gesture that was as much about acknowledging his support as it was about my achievement. He was completely blown away! The moment of gifting, filled with tears and joy, underscored the shared nature of my success. And it cemented the tradition of setting and celebrating a goal each month.

Here are three ways you might adopt the practice of 'Setting & Celebrating':

1. Define what you want to achieve & set goals. I always think about two types of goals here: an achievable goal and a stretch goal. Both are great to have, and the stretch goal keeps me moving if I hit my achievable goal early in the month!

2. Plan your reward. What will you give yourself when you achieve your goal? This should be something that celebrates effort and success—be it for yourself or those who support you.

3. Follow through. This is the most important action step you can take here, as we often let ourselves off the hook too easily if we aren't seeing immediate results. We might even tell ourselves that we don't really want that reward, anyway. But don't give up! Instead, honor your commitment to yourself by sticking to it, even when all the evidence tells you the results aren't happening fast enough.

Remember, his process is not just about reaching a destination; it's about valuing the journey and the growth you experience along the way. So, savor every moment, every challenge, and every lesson learned as you go through this exercise month after month!

Switch Up Your Self-Talk

By now, you're probably aware of the little voice inside your head that runs constant commentary on your life, referred to as our self-talk. But did you know that a national study found that 80% of that silent commentary is negative? Transforming your self-talk is all about cultivating a more positive internal dialogue. It's about how you communicate with yourself, and it shapes your thoughts, feelings, actions, and ultimately, your results.

I vividly remember my awakening to this concept. It was during a three-hour car ride to a spa—a treat from my 'Set and Celebrate' rewards, in fact! Listening to a Zoom replay of a training on this subject, I learned how our thoughts shape our feelings, actions, and outcomes. When the recording ended, I decided to use the remainder of the drive to closely monitor my thoughts.

What I discovered was startling! In two hours, I caught myself engaging in negative self-talk seventy-two times. These thoughts ranged from doubting my abilities to being overly critical of myself and my choices. As it turned out, my negative inner dialogue was my own worst enemy! It was a profound realization that I needed to make a significant change in the way I talked to myself.

To anyone struggling with this, here are three transformative practices I've implemented to switch up my self-talk:

1. Mindful monitoring. Dedicate an hour each day to mindfully observe your thoughts. During this time, be extremely attentive to your inner dialogue, ensuring that when a negative thought arises, you consciously redirect it to a more positive perspective.

2. Positive affirmations. Speaking affirmations out loud can profoundly reinforce positive beliefs. I encourage you to choose affirmations that resonate with you and declare them confidently. Two of my favorites are, "I am deserving of success and happiness in all areas of my life," and "I am grateful for the abundance and opportunities in my life." These affirmations serve as powerful reminders of my worth and potential!

3. Practicing gratitude. Try setting your alarm 15 minutes early, and before getting out of bed, take time to think about what you're grateful for. This practice not only sets a positive tone for the day, but also shifts your mindset toward appreciation and abundance, which impacts the tone and messaging of your self-talk.

By incorporating these practices into your daily routine, you can profoundly shift your internal narrative, laying the foundation for positive outcomes in both your personal and professional life!

Getting Closer To The Fire

'Getting Closer to the Fire' is about actively engaging with your community and the activities in your business. When we're new to a team, or when we're down on our luck, it's common to feel inadequate or self-conscious, and our instinct might be to withdraw. However, I encourage you to do the exact opposite! When you feel like running away, it's quite possibly the most important time to immerse yourself deeper in your business community. Remember, we are all navigating similar paths, sharing fears, challenges, and successes. We are each other's support system, and a source of encouragement and inspiration!

There was a time when my business hit a plateau, stagnating for six months. Doubts crept in, and I began to question whether my previous success was just a stroke of luck. Coinciding with this period was a leadership development conference for my company, which I was hesitant to attend given my state of mind. Despite having invested in the ticket, travel, and accommodation, I actually considered skipping it—that's how disconnected I felt from my business.

However, after some thought and encouragement from my husband, I decided to go. That decision was pivotal. Within the first hour of being there, surrounded by my peers, everything shifted! I shared a hotel room with three other women and as I joined them in conversation, I found myself reignited by their energy and insights. It wasn't just about the new leadership techniques I learned; it was about the renewed passion and drive I felt being around my peers.

The impact was immediate and significant. Within three weeks of returning from the event, my business leaped from a standstill to the top 1% of my company. This surge wasn't due to a sudden implementation of new strategies; it was the rekindled fire from being surrounded by inspiring people!

So here are three ways you can 'Get Closer to the Fire':

1. Get closer to your business community. Remember, this is your tribe, and they're ready to help! Let their energy and passion ignite your own. Even when you feel your 'flame' waning, being around others can spark a transformation.

2. Commit to networking. This one may sound obvious, but you'd be surprised how many people let it slip without realizing it. Each month, identify one person within the industry to connect with—be it an upline, downline, sideline, or someone outside your immediate network.

3. Engage in brainstorming and sharing ideas. This practice of building connections and learning from others will not only re-energize you, but also foster growth and positive change in your business. Remember, 'together' is always better. And once you've gotten comfortable getting closer to the fire, don't forget to encourage your team members to do the same!

Find A Mentor

Finding a mentor is all about connecting with someone who possesses not only industry experience, skills, and expertise but also has the ability and willingness to transfer these assets to you. A mentor empowers you with the necessary tools to confidently navigate the industry, and their guidance goes beyond imparting knowledge. These people will offer support, encouragement, and a boost to your confidence.

I actually stumbled upon my first mentor in Network Marketing accidentally. She was a few levels above me, and every time she spoke or trained, I was captivated. Her words resonated deeply with me; she seemed to be the epitome of what I aspired to be in this industry. One day, driven by my admiration and alignment with her approach, I reached out and asked her to mentor me, and she accepted. I was elated, and I couldn't wait to learn and model my business after hers!

That partnership was instrumental to my growth. Even though she has since left the industry, her influence remains a cornerstone of my success. She played a pivotal role in shaping me into the professional I am today.

For those seeking a mentor, here are actionable steps to guide you:

1. Define your goals. Write down your goals. This clarity is paramount to identifying a mentor who aligns with your aspirations and needs.

2. Find your mentor. Look within your upline or extend your search across the network marketing community. Your ideal mentor might be closer than you think, or they might be a connection away.

3. Make the ask. Once you've identified a potential mentor, reach out to them earnestly and honestly. Be clear about why you've chosen them and what you're hoping to achieve through the mentorship.

4. Be coachable. This is key! When you find a mentor willing to invest their time and knowledge in you, show up ready to learn and implement their advice. A mentorship is a two-way street; your growth is as much about their guidance as it is about your willingness to learn and apply.

A mentor can be a catalyst for tremendous personal and professional growth. They can provide insights that reshape your approach and propel you to new heights in your career. So, take these steps, find your mentor, and open yourself to the transformative journey that mentorship can offer!

Build Your Support Systems

The importance of having a support system outside of Network Marketing cannot be overstated. This support system should consist of people who aren't involved in network marketing, and who are capable of offering you unwavering support, especially during moments when you're not feeling your best!

For me, this person is my husband. He's intimately familiar with my fears, insecurities, and journey with confidence. He serves as a sounding board for my ideas and thoughts, offering encouragement and validation. His perspective is essential, especially since he's not entrenched in the everyday details of my business. His role in my journey extends beyond being a passive supporter—he actively engages in my world. From accompanying me to events and helping me rehearse presentations to brainstorming solutions, his involvement is inherently tied to my success.

Here are three ways you can take care of those who support you:

1. Be open and honest. They can't fully support you if they don't understand your struggles! It might be difficult, but sharing your insecurities regarding confidence or feelings of inadequacy is essential for them to provide the right support.

2. Express gratitude. Acknowledge and appreciate their support. Let them know how much their assistance means to you, recognizing the efforts they make to support your journey.

3. Set realistic expectations. Understand that your supporters have their own commitments and limitations. It's important to be mindful not to overburden them with your needs. Remember, though, that balance is key. While they are there to support you, you must respect their boundaries and personal commitments.

Your support system plays a critical role in bolstering your confidence and helping you feel capable throughout your journey. Their encouragement, understanding, and outside perspective can be a tremendous source of strength and motivation!

Always Be Learning

Finally, let's dive into the principle of 'Always Be Learning.' Continuous learning and skill development are key to building confidence! It is my belief that competence inspires confidence. Years ago, I attended a workshop in one of my Network Marketing ventures where a health and fitness expert explained the science behind our products. This knowledge drastically boosted my confidence, enabling me to engage more effectively with my audience, address objections, and make informed product recommendations. This not only increased sales but also cemented my confidence, creating a virtuous cycle of success and self-assurance!

If you find yourself struggling in this area, here are three ways to make sure you're always learning:

1. Deepen your product knowledge. Understanding your products and compensation plan thoroughly can significantly boost your confidence when presenting them.

2. Stay current & informed. Attend network marketing events to keep abreast of the latest trends and practices. Staying informed contributes to competence and, subsequently, confidence.

3. Learn from successful peers. Model your approach on successful network marketers. Engaging with content like this is an excellent start!

I hope these insights have been valuable to you as you journey into the world of leadership in Network Marketing! To wrap up this chapter, I want to leave you with a few parting thoughts:

If you're struggling with doubt or fear, remember that *action is the antidote!* And the actions I've covered here in these pages are a fantastic place to start. Embrace the challenges, set and celebrate your achievements, and transform your self-talk. Recognize those who inspire you, seek mentorship, rely on your support system, and commit to lifelong learning. These practices will significantly impact your confidence as you navigate the world of network marketing.

Remember, every new level of success in business or life, demands a new version of yourself and a renewed sense of confidence. There's no ultimate finish line where you suddenly achieve perpetual confidence! It's a continuous journey, requiring you to evolve and grow at each step. And keep this in mind: you are more than capable, and more than adequate. You can achieve great things. If I can do it, so can you! It's been an honor to share these insights with you. I wish you all the best!

Watch Julie's Video Now!
LeadingLadiesCourse.com

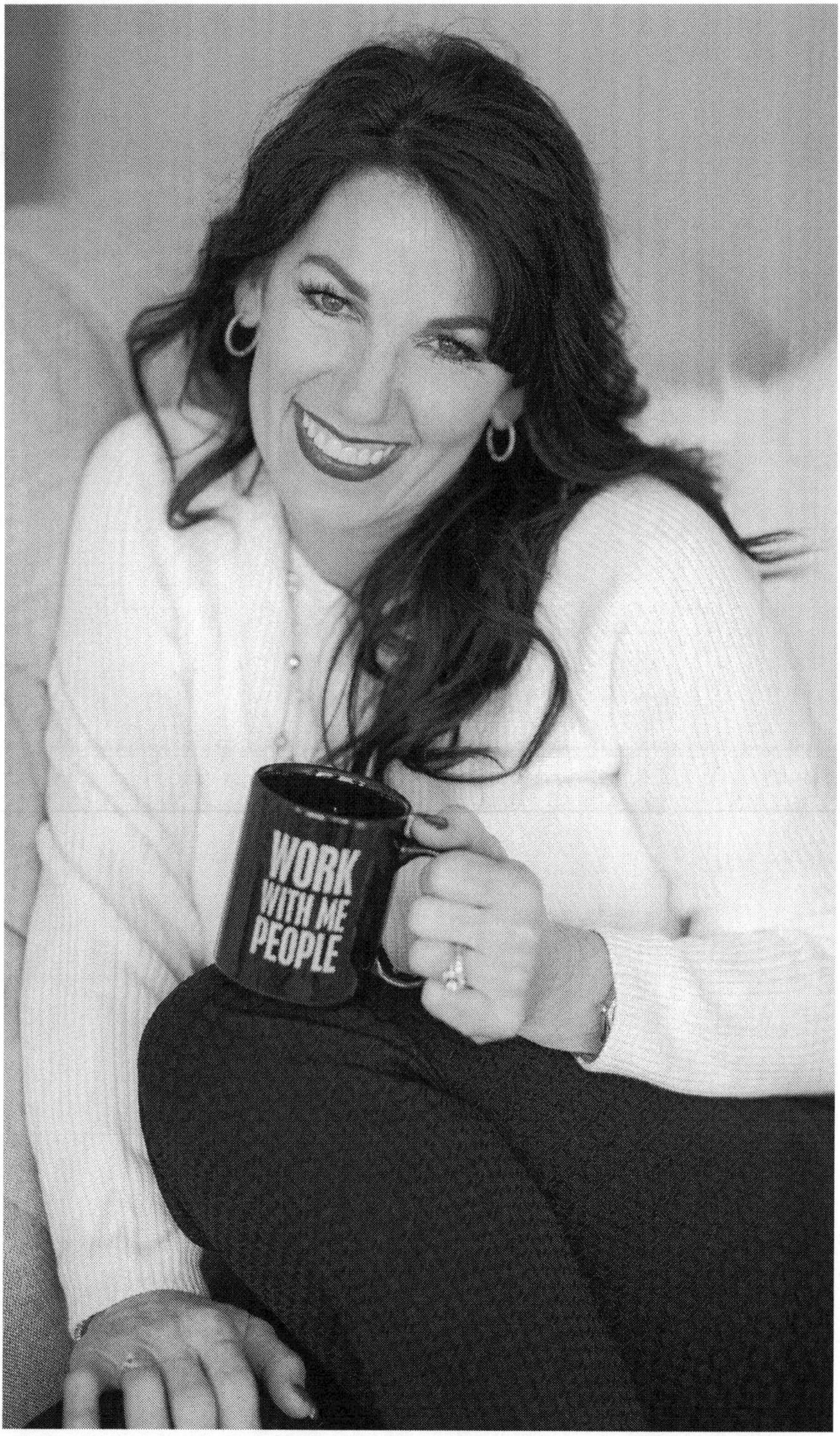
WORK
WITH ME
PEOPLE

18

The Wheel Of Success

The 4-Step Cycle That Creates Unlimited Success

Barb Pitcock

Facebook.com/barb.pitcock
Instagram.com/barbpitcock
Tiktok.com/@barb.pitcock

The Wheel Of Success

Barb Pitcock

Hey, ntwrkrs! I'm thrilled to introduce an incredible concept that has shaped my twenty-seven-year journey in Network Marketing—known as the Wheel of Success. In this chapter, I'm going to show you how to build the Wheel of Success, how to spin it, and how to get all the rewards that come from using it as you grow in this amazing career. Picture the Wheel of Success as a snowball at the peak of a hill—difficult to push into motion but once rolling, it's an unstoppable force!

Before I dive into my story, I want to emphasize the importance of two keys to success: *mentorship and coachability*. Without my mentor, the magic of the Wheel of Success would have remained elusive to me. If, in the end, I hadn't finally become coachable, I might have missed the chance to implement its valuable principles. So, as you read through this chapter, remember the significance of mentorship and coachability!

Today, as a seasoned mentor and coach with extensive experience in the industry, I've generated millions in sales and led several companies to success alongside my husband and business partner, Dave. We've dedicated nearly three decades to Network Marketing, and we've found that the Wheel of Success isn't confined to just our field; in fact, it's quite versatile. We've applied it to various ventures, from real estate to establishing a med spa and a dance school.

As we dive into our exploration of what it looks like to spin the Wheel of Success, we'll reference the acronym SCAR: Success, Confidence, Action, Results. Though the term SCAR might seem a bit jarring to some readers, it symbolizes the concept of 'failing forward,' which is a critical component of our lesson. Success breeds confidence, which in turn fuels more activity and leads to results. This cycle of success builds upon itself, creating a perpetual motion of achievement and belief. The more success you achieve, the more confident you become, spurring further action and yielding even greater results.

Warning: Once you learn to spin the Wheel of Success, there's no unlearning it. So, if you're ready to take everything you're pursuing to the next level, read on!

S For Success

First, let's dive into the initial spark that will get the wheel turning. You might be wondering, 'How can I begin if I haven't seen any success so far?' If that's you, I want to reassure you: it's not about listing achievements or bragging. After all, there was a time when I was grappling with failure after failure in multiple ventures, and I still managed to find the tiniest success to fuel the journey forward.

There was a season in my life when I had almost given up on Network Marketing, but a pivotal moment came just as I was set on quitting.

One day, my husband attended an in-person meeting for a new company, and he returned home with a revelation, exclaiming, "Honey, we're going to be rich!" I was skeptical, to say the least. We were facing daily financial struggles, with bounced checks and unpaid bills. I'm pretty sure I told him he was crazy! However, our trajectory did indeed change. When I finally got on board, we eventually made millions and became top distributors, and we were only in our twenties.

How did we accomplish this success? The game-changer was mentorship. My husband latched onto a mentor in that company who guided him, and he committed wholeheartedly to the journey. He hopped onto the Wheel of Success and got it spinning after he achieved his *first small win.*

When someone new joins the business, it's so important to secure an early win for them. Rejection is common, and doubts can quickly set in. The excitement of joining they initially felt can wane, leaving them questioning their decision. But an early victory, no matter how small, can make a significant difference.

How many of you can remember your first prospecting days where, out of all the people you approached, only a handful responded positively? Despite a greater number of rejections, that small nod of approval from a few connections likely sparked a surge of confidence, leading you to think, *maybe this can actually work.*

As I mentioned earlier, when Dave came through the door telling me about the new business he'd just invested in, the one that was going to make us rich, I didn't have any evidence it was going to work. With

ntwrkr.com

all the financial uncertainty in our lives, how was I supposed to believe that Dave's new upline was going to drive four hours to do a presentation at our house and turn our lives around?

However, Dave's new upline *did* drive four hours to do a presentation at our house. And he helped Dave sign up three people, when just a week prior, I'd invited forty-two people to a gathering in my home and not one person even showed! I remember holding the check Dave's upline gave us in my hand and preparing myself for it not to cash. But, sure enough, I took it through the drive-thru at the bank, deposited it, and the amount hit our bank account. I took one more lap around the bank, parked, and went inside. I nervously asked to withdraw the amount and took the cash back out. My jaw may as well have been on the ground! I couldn't believe it. It was a real check. Real money.

The reality of this influx of income was earth-shattering. It was as if I'd done ninety haircuts in one night, and this was all from enrolling just three people! We got everything we'd invested back that night, and much, much more. Dave was convinced, and said to me, confidently, "I'm moving forward with this, whether you believe in it or not." For some reason, I was still hesitant. But while I was harboring doubts in the face of real evidence, he was actively turning the improbable into reality.

This is the truth about embarking on any new venture: there will always be skeptics—people ready to dismiss your dreams as unattainable. But the key lies in carving out that first slice of success. If you can help someone achieve even a minor victory early on, it will significantly increase the chances of them staying the course and potentially emerging as leaders.

LEADING LADIES

This is where the concept of coachability—or teachability—comes into play. Dave was a prime example of someone who was teachable and coachable. After his initial success, he was interested in learning more, always asking, "What's the next step?" This brings us to an essential question: How high is your teachability index? If it's not high, you might struggle to grasp and implement the guidance given, which makes it more difficult to succeed.

C For Confidence

To explore how success can inspire confidence, which is the next point on the wheel, consider what happened to Dave after his first successful sign-up. He felt like Superman! So, you can imagine the boost in morale when a newcomer secures their first customer, or when someone expresses interest in a video you've shared. Each small interaction, whether it's a nod of interest or a definitive sign-up, elevates a person's feeling that they can get out there and do more! And this growing confidence breeds conviction.

When Dave and I went all in on our new venture, I had already mastered the art of dance instruction and hairstyling, and my many customers backed up the confidence I experienced in those fields. My confidence in this new field of Network Marketing, however, was minimal. I harbored doubts about whether or not I'd succeed, and I lacked the conviction I felt in other areas of my life.

Low confidence and conviction can be a major hurdle in any industry! If people sense hesitation and doubt, that often leads them to question your credibility. No one is convinced by uncertainty. So, the key to elevating confidence in your team is simple yet powerful: affirmative reinforcement. Engage with your team, recognize their efforts, and let them know they're on the brink of success.

Encourage members of your team by saying, "You're doing exceptionally well. Your victory is just around the corner, look how close you are to your goal!" Effective coaching is about instilling belief in them. Remind them of the aspirations they shared and paint a picture of their future successes—a new home, a new car. Helping them to visualize these achievements can ignite the spark of confidence they might not yet see in themselves.

This process of building confidence is similar to nurturing a plant. It requires consistent attention and reinforcement. Acknowledge their progress, with positive reinforcement such as: "You're evolving into an outstanding presenter," or "You're rapidly climbing to the top." Highlighting their presence on the leaderboard or acknowledging them as an emerging power couple within the team can do wonders. Recognition is a powerful motivator.

When you're cultivating confidence in your team, step aside and allow others to lead. Let them experience and learn from their own presentations. When someone actually does the presentation and secures a sign-up, it can dramatically boost their self-assurance, far more than if you were to handle every presentation for them.

Even during the days when our mentors were driving hours to lead meetings in our new venture, both Dave and I were somewhat reserved. And while I wouldn't have called myself shy by any means, I simply didn't feel prepared to take the lead in presentations. Instead, I'd chime in during their talks—not out of confidence but out of enthusiasm I just couldn't contain.

One day, our mentor called to inform us he couldn't make it to a significant meeting at the Elks Club Ballroom, where we were expecting a crowd of twenty-five to thirty people. He told Dave, "You'll have to run the show tonight. Someone will meet you with the slideshow." My immediate reaction was panic! I couldn't hide my worry. "If you handle it, we won't get any sign-ups!" I told Dave. Looking back, of course, I realize my comments were not exactly supportive. Maybe it would have done more for his conviction if I'd boosted his confidence by reminding him of all the wins he'd had with our mentor, but I was still navigating my way through being the spouse of a Network Marketer. I didn't yet understand the concept of the Wheel of Success.

Sure enough, despite my skepticism, when Dave took the stage, managing the slides himself, it was a moment of transformation. This was before the era of Zoom meetings and Facebook Live—a time when sharing a video meant physically bringing a TV set. Dave's performance, despite his evident nerves and a few moments of silence, was just what the audience needed. People understood his message and they signed up. Each one boosted Dave's confidence immensely! He began to think, *I can actually do this!*

Soon, we stopped waiting for our mentor to drive down from Nebraska to lead our meetings, and instead, we started hosting them ourselves, night after night. The result? A surge in confidence and a spike in activity. So, here's a key success tip: elevate your team. Celebrate them, highlight their strengths, and bring them into leadership roles. Step back and watch their confidence grow as they realize they can succeed without you.

How would your business flourish if you weren't directly involved? The ideal system should be foolproof, fear-proof, and easily duplicable, enabling everyone to participate effectively. It's about getting everyone involved in small ways, rather than relying on a few to do the heavy lifting.

***A* For Activity**

I'm passionate about this part of the Wheel of Success because I'm all about action! Still, it's important to remember that it's not just about being busy—it's about engaging in income-producing, results-driven activities. What matters is focusing your team on actions that lead to direct deposits, customer acquisitions, and transactions that result in real earnings. It's important to differentiate between mere activity and true accomplishment.

Let's explore the daily actions that contribute to your success—in other words, the activities that increase your bank account balance, expand your network, and deliver products to your customers. What's the key? It boils down to one essential activity: engaging in conversations about your opportunity or product with people who are neither current customers nor involved in the business. It's about introducing the business to newcomers and sparking their interest.

Recently, Dave and I have been heads-down with industry experts and mentors. We've spent a fortune on mentorship and coaching. We listened. We took action. We learned and we networked, and met people like Christopher Hussey—hey, he's the guy who publishes these amazing books! The consensus among these Network Marketing heavy hitters is clear: the crux of the business lies in customer acquisition and enrolling new participants. Fresh involvement is the lifeblood of any thriving business. Without growth, stagnation sets in.

Many people get comfortable in Network Marketing and fall into the trap of thinking they can get away with just coasting along. But remember, no one coasts uphill. Without consistent effort, there's only decline, leading to burnout. Instead of thinking that an overload of Zoom meetings, trainings, and seminars will bring in new prospects, focus on effective presentations that attract new customers and team members.

Too often, people experience initial success, boost their confidence, and then shift their focus to managing their existing team. Trust me, I know how easy it is to do—we were actually guilty of this when we were growing the new venture I've been writing about. Sure, we had spun the Wheel of Success. We started with just four new joiners, which grew to eight the next month, and then exponentially increased to over four hundred in just four months. We had success, built confidence, spurred activity, and reaped substantial results.

However, on the path to those results, we made some big mistakes. We elevated people in our team to leadership positions, and shortly afterward, without really even knowing it, we slipped into a management mindset. And let me promise you, this is the worst activity you can do for your business! It literally leads to reduced income for you and your whole team.

Dave and I had diverted our attention away from growing our business through recruiting and growing the number of people in our network, and instead, were focused on micro-managing the people we'd put into leadership and trying to control everything. We eventually course-corrected, but not without losing time, income, and a bit of our serenity.

This serves as a critical reminder for all of us: this business isn't about you. It's about empowering others, fostering their success, boosting their confidence, and guiding them towards effective actions. Your role is to facilitate their growth and then step aside, allowing the system and the people within the business to flourish. Leadership is about setting an example, driving results, and elevating others to your level of success.

R For Results

I'll repeat a version of what I just wrote above: The results you're looking for are *new members who can achieve the same level you've achieved*. And you can't bring others up to your level unless you show them that you aren't just standing around telling other people what to do, right? You need to show them that *you're actually doing it*. And you do this by keeping score!

I maintain a daily journal with charts and graphs to monitor where I am and where I aspire to be. I set lofty goals, which, I admit, can lead to disappointment. However, striving for excellence and failing is always better than never setting the bar high enough! So, I often ask the question: how many six-figure earners can we develop? How many individuals can we help earn a substantial monthly income? Who can we propel onto the leaderboard? And I don't hold back when I come up with the numbers.

To achieve these lofty goals, setting clear outcomes is key. Over and over again, I find that incentivizing progress and rewarding achievements in some manner creates the results I'm looking for. Every compensation plan out there is designed to reward income-producing activities! So, as a leader, remember to set a stellar example. Uphold integrity in everything you do, and don't shy away from recognizing the achievements of your team. They deserve it!

Another way I envision the path to my desired results is to keep a vision board in a prominent place, showcasing where I want my team to be, the goals I aim to achieve, and the results I'm striving for. If you do this, you can look toward these intended results and take a moment to assess your team. Consider the talents and resources at your disposal. Recognize each team member's unique abilities and think about how you can collectively reach your goals by working together. Remember, you wouldn't even start spinning the Wheel of Success if you weren't focused on a particular end goal. So, make sure the results you aspire to are staring you in the face, each and every day!

I began this chapter with a story about Dave and me as a couple, and I'll end that way, too. My husband was the embodiment of teachability, while I, on the other hand, was not. I believed I had seen it all, that I had already acquired the necessary experience and knowledge. Without Dave's willingness to learn, I would have likely floundered in our new venture. He immersed himself in learning resources, which I initially dismissed as unnecessary. I didn't even think I had time for coaching, since I was busy caring for our two children (and expecting a third), managing household chores, and taking on haircut appointments and dance classes. But in the end, I finally came to realize that to truly succeed, I needed to enhance my own teachability index.

Watching Dave—a man who, at the time, had minimal experience and talent, and an introvert who lacked the so-called 'gift of gab'—achieve remarkable success was a revelation for me. He wasn't the type to effortlessly strike up a conversation with a stranger; he was actually quite fearful of small talk with people he didn't know! Yet, he surpassed everyone in our company, and by the age of twenty-four, we ranked in the top three among one hundred and fifty thousand distributors. We lacked conventional qualifications. We had no formal education and had spent our lives leading up to that point as a bankrupt beautician and a bull rider. We seemingly had every reason to fail. But something set us apart from the rest. It was Dave's, and soon after, my own, high teachability index and an insatiable desire to learn.

As I wrap up, my overarching advice to you is simple: remain teachable and coachable. Continuously seek knowledge. Find a mentor who possesses what you aspire to achieve, and cling to them like a magnet. Maintain your teachability and coachability, and openly express your desire for mentorship.

Then, as you start accumulating successes, take a moment to recognize your own strength. Affirm to yourself, *"I am capable. I am deserving. I've achieved this."* With each small achievement, encourage yourself to strive a bit further, to stimulate more activity. As with anything in life and business, consistency is key. Evaluate your outcomes, acknowledge your accomplishments, and prepare to replicate that success time and time again. Go from the back of the room to the stage, but then stand back to applaud the others you can bring up to experience that success wheel.

In short: success breeds confidence, which in turn fuels activity, leading to results that culminate in even greater success—which spins the wheel again! It's been an honor to contribute to this book and collaborate with all of these amazing women and the team at ntwrkr. I can't wait to meet you out there at events, and I hope this chapter empowers you to reach new heights! Dream big dreams, don't be afraid to fail, and never give up!

Watch Barb's Video Now!
LeadingLadiesCourse.com

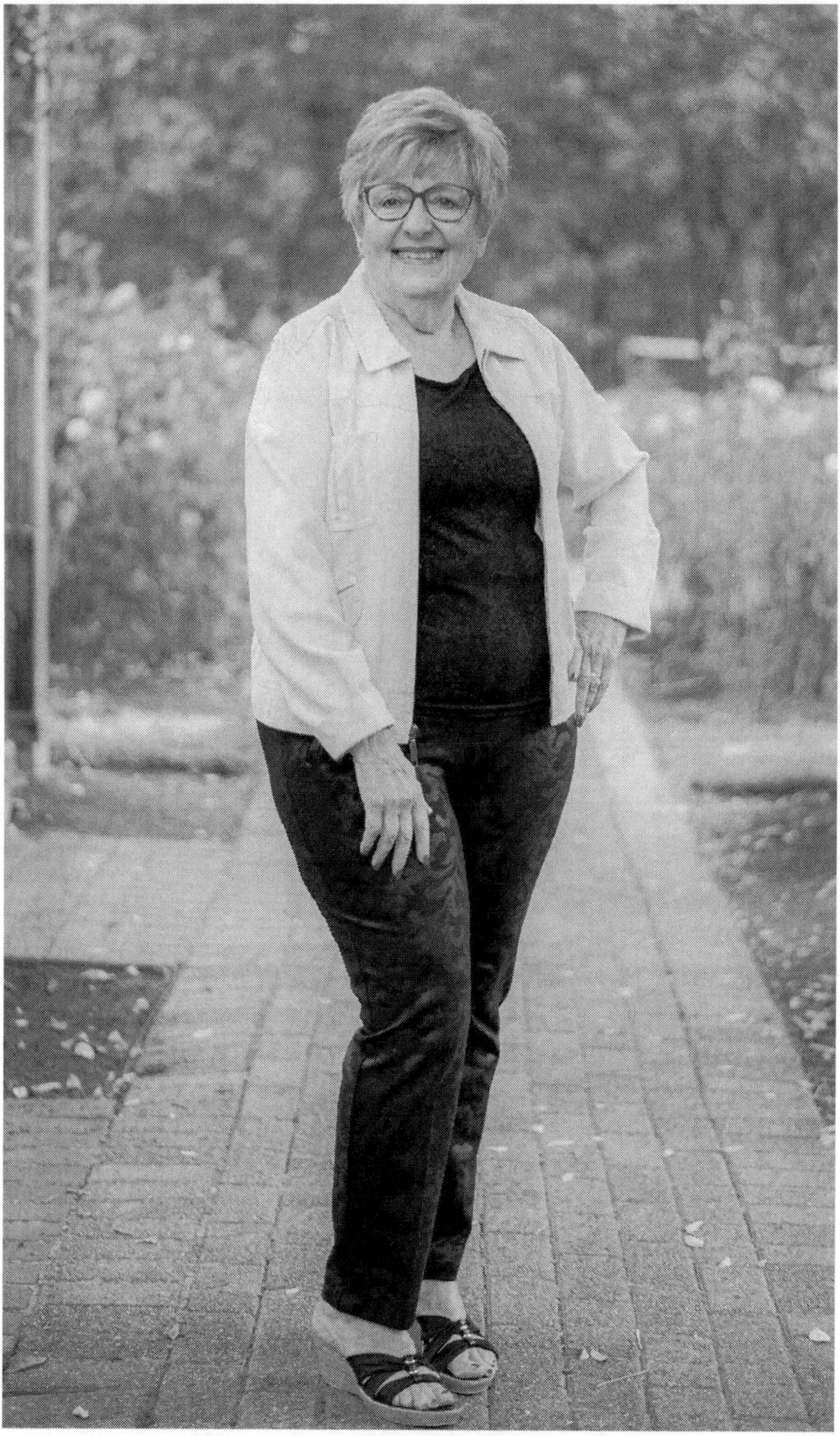

19

Knowing Is Growing

The 3 Pillars For Every Leader To
Grow Herself & Her Team

Rebecca Ferris

Facebook.com/rmferris1
Instagram.com/beccamillerferris
Tiktok.com/@beccaferris18

Knowing Is Growing

Rebecca Ferris

Hello, ntwrkrs! I'm delighted to be a part of *Leading Ladies,* and it's an absolute privilege to share my journey and insights with you through the pages of this book. My career in the Network Marketing industry spans a decade, during which I've had the honor of leading teams that have not only reached the number-one spot but also achieved the highest volume in the companies I've worked with.

My success in this field has been driven by two core passions: a relentless pursuit of knowledge alongside personal development and a deep commitment to mentoring women. I'm particularly drawn to those who feel surrounded by obstacles or challenges—those who believe that the path to success is laid with insurmountable hurdles. This chapter is dedicated to exploring the three fundamental pillars that every leader needs to cultivate growth within themselves and their team.

I firmly believe that the key to consistent growth and success lies in understanding: understanding ourselves, understanding our team members, and the mastery of a communication style that uplifts and empowers others. In this chapter, we'll be delving into three critical areas. First, we'll explore personality types, next, we'll dive into the importance of your 'what,' and finally, we'll examine the valuable nature of thoughts and how they shape outcomes. By embracing these concepts, you'll not only grow personally, but you'll also become a stronger leader, and you'll witness your team flourishing as well.

So, join me in the exploration of the intricacies of these three pillars, unraveling the ways they work on their own, and discovering how they work together to create an unstoppable force. And whatever you do, don't just read and absorb the knowledge on these pages—make sure you apply it to your life!

In my circles, I'm known as the 'knowledge person.' My commitment to this identity is so strong that I let it guide every endeavor I undertake, and this book is no different! I'm so excited about what I'm about to impart to you and how it will affect your career. So, if you're ready to transform your mindset to one of growth and empowerment, let's discover how *knowing* truly does lead to *growing!*

Pillar 1: Know Their Personality

The first step on our journey is to understand the diverse personalities that make up your team. The world of personality frameworks is vast, and it's key to explore and choose one that resonates with your team's dynamics. This understanding is not just about putting labels on people; rather, it's about appreciating the unique perspectives and approaches each person brings to the table.

Your team is a vibrant tapestry of personalities, each member bringing their own unique blend of traits and qualities. Recognizing and appreciating these differences is *essential* for nurturing effective communication and creating a peaceful work environment. Remember: when someone behaves in a certain way that you might perceive as negative, it's often a reflection of their personality, not a personal attack on you!

So, let's dive into four basic personality types that I've commonly encountered within my teams:

The Go-Getter: This person is a dynamo of action. They're always ready to jump in and tackle goals, even if it means making a few mistakes along the way. Their energy is infectious, and they often serve as the driving force behind the team's momentum.

The Nurturer: With a heart as big as the sky, the nurturer thrives on emotional connections and is driven by a desire to make a positive impact on others' lives. They are the glue that holds the team together, providing support and encouragement when needed.

The Knowledge Seeker: Knowledge seekers are the ones who need to understand every detail, who crave the 'why' and 'how' before taking any steps forward. Like me, their analytical approach ensures that the team's decisions are well-informed and thought-out.

The Planner: Methodical and strategic, planners need a clear roadmap. They won't take the first step until they can see the entire path laid out before them. Their foresight and organization are invaluable in guiding the team's efforts towards long-term goals.

By identifying these personality types within your team, you can leverage each individual's strengths to build a stronger, more cohesive unit. Encourage each team member to take a personality test, and use the insights gained to tailor your leadership approach and communication style. This personalized approach not only boosts team morale but also enhances productivity and efficiency.

I'd be leaving out a critical part of this pillar if I didn't mention the negative and stagnating effects of not knowing your or your team's personality type. For years, I found myself comparing my own personality to others. I felt out of place among the charismatic stage presenters or the life-of-the-party types. It took coaching and a journey of self-reflection to finally embrace my nature as a knowledge seeker and recognize the value it brings to my team. I encourage you to appreciate your unique personality and help your team members do the same. Celebrating diversity in personalities enables a culture of inclusivity and mutual respect, where every team member feels valued and understood!

To ensure that personality type is a factor in the way you run your team, take the following action steps:

1. **Read *How To Know A Person* by David Brooks.** This book is a treasure trove of insights into building deeper connections, a crucial skill for team building. Brooks poses thought-provoking questions that can lead to meaningful conversations and personal growth. The book offers a fresh perspective on understanding the complexities of human behavior and the importance of empathy in leadership.

2. **Explore personality tests.** Dive into the world of personality assessments. Believe me, there are many to choose from! I did a quick

Google search and found thirty-one, so find one that suits your team's needs and implement it. Understanding the diverse strengths and communication styles within your team can lead to more effective collaboration and a stronger team dynamic. Consider using tools like the Myers-Briggs Type Indicator (MBTI), the DiSC Assessment, or the Enneagram to gain deeper insights into your team's personality profiles.

By embracing the unique personalities within your team and leveraging their strengths, you create an environment where everyone can thrive! This approach not only enhances team performance but also fosters a sense of belonging and purpose among team members. So, take the time to explore the rich tapestry of personalities in your team, and then watch as it transforms your leadership and your team's success!

Pillar 2: Know Their 'What'

This next concept is all about the personal aspirations and desires of your team members. Traditional approaches often emphasize discovering one's 'why,' but I've found that diving into the 'what' can be more tangible and accessible for many people! Asking "What do you want?" cuts straight to the heart of their aspirations, yielding more concrete and personal responses.

The spectrum of answers can be as vast as a world tour or as focused as enhancing personal health or achieving financial stability. The magic lies in the follow-up questions: "Why do you want that?" and "What impact will achieving this have on your life?" These questions will help peel back the layers of motivation and reveal the true significance of their goals.

Make sure you're capturing their answer by writing it down. After all, reminding your team members of their 'what' will serve as a potent reminder and motivator, particularly when the going gets tough. And encourage them to do the same—except they should have it somewhere visible, so they can see it every day.

In my team, cultivating an awareness of each other's 'what' is a top priority. This shared understanding creates a supportive atmosphere where everyone is aligned toward not only individual objectives but also collective achievements.

Once, a woman on my team struggled with going live on Facebook. She was terrified of what people would say about her broadcasting skills and felt quite unconfident about the whole thing. But—she had a monumental 'what.' She was determined to bring herself and her family out of financial peril through Network Marketing and give them the life they deserved.

So, she confronted her fears and persevered through initial hurdles and criticism. She went live day after day after day, and guess what? It paid off! Her unwavering dedication to her 'what' fueled her journey to success. She had been apprehensive about going live, but she embraced the challenge, honed her skills over time, garnered a following, and ultimately ascended to the pinnacle of her game.

To truly flourish, it is imperative to not only recognize your own 'what' but also to grasp the 'whats' of your team members. Allow this understanding to inspire and drive you to surmount challenges and fulfill your aspirations!

To cultivate an environment where everyone's 'what' is known and nurtured, try out the following action steps:

1. Read *The Obstacle Is The Way* by Ryan Holiday. This enlightening book presents a novel perspective on tackling challenges and transforming them into stepping stones for success. It's an invaluable resource for anyone eager to explore and achieve their 'what.'

2. Clarify your 'what'. Dedicate time to define your aspirations. Keep this vision prominently in your mind every day. Allow it to guide and inspire you to realize your life's ambitions and craft the life you envision.

3. Engage with your team members. Initiate meaningful conversations with your team members about their 'what.' Understanding the significance of their goals can create a deeper sense of purpose and motivation within the team.

By embracing and championing each other's objectives, you create a dynamic synergy that propels the entire team toward collective and individual success. Reflect on your 'what,' share it with your team, and let it illuminate the path on your journey to greatness!

Pillar 3: Know Their Thoughts

This final component is crucial in shaping the path to success. Thoughts are the origin of results—they are the 'architects' of our reality, if you will! While it's tempting to attribute success solely to actions and behaviors, the roots of these actions lie in our thoughts. Thoughts give rise to feelings, feelings lead to actions, and actions result in outcomes.

Understanding the thoughts of your team members, especially during challenging times, is essential in guiding them toward more constructive attitudes. Thoughts like, "I'm a failure," or "This will never work out for me," will only lead to negative results! Shifting the negative mindset of those in your community can transform negative emotions and behaviors into positive results, promoting growth and success for both the team members and the organization.

Earlier in my career, a close friend of mine and a prominent leader in the profession faced an unexpected challenge when her top team member suddenly resigned. Initially, her mind was filled with anxiety and doubt about her ability to connect with the newly promoted team members. Would they like her? Would she be able to lead them effectively? She was paralyzed by these fears and felt like she might not survive the restructuring of her team.

However, she tapped into the power of positive thinking and refocused on her strengths as a leader. She looked back on all of her success as a leader and applied all of that previous confidence to her new relationships. This change in mindset not only helped her overcome her fears but also enabled her to effectively inspire and guide her new team members.

To help positively shape the thoughts of yourself and your team, take these action steps:

1. Read *Choose Your Story, Change Your Life* by Kendra Hall. This insightful book is a valuable resource for understanding how your internal narrative shapes your life. Hall provides practical strategies for recontouring your story to achieve positive outcomes, highlighting the transformative power of thought in creating our experiences.

2. Reflect on your thoughts. Make it a regular habit to reflect on your thoughts and their impact on your achievements. Consider whether a shift in mindset is necessary to achieve the desired results. Cultivating self-awareness and mindfulness is the key to identifying and changing unproductive thought patterns.

3. Empower your team. Create a supportive environment where your team feels comfortable when expressing their thoughts. Help them understand how their mindset affects their emotions, actions, and ultimately, their results. Encourage open communication and promote a culture of positive thinking, fostering a collective mindset oriented toward success.

By exploring and managing your thoughts and those of your team, you open the door to positive change and growth! Remember, knowledge is the precursor to growth, and by nurturing a positive mindset, you will lay the foundation for success. Embrace the power of thought as a catalyst for change and watch as it propels you and your team to new heights of achievement!

As we wrap up this chapter, let's recap what we've learned together. We've explored the three fundamental pillars of growth and success when it comes to your team: understanding their personality, uncovering their 'what,' and guiding their thoughts. These pillars aren't just theoretical concepts; rather, they're practical tools that, when applied with dedication, can transform your team's dynamics and lead you to both personal and professional fulfillment.

Knowing each team member's pillar involves recognizing the unique traits and characteristics each team member contributes. It's about acknowledging that diversity in personalities is a strength, not a challenge. By comprehending the individual personalities within your team, you can customize your leadership approach to resonate with each member, fostering a more inclusive and harmonious environment.

The second pillar, understanding the 'what' of each team member, dives deeper than surface-level interactions. It's about connecting with your team members on a more profound level, understanding their aspirations, and aligning their goals with the team's objectives. This alignment creates a sense of purpose and drives motivation, pushing the team towards collective success.

The third pillar, knowing their thoughts, is perhaps the most introspective. It's about recognizing the power of mindset in shaping our reality. By promoting a positive thought process within your team, you can cultivate a culture of optimism and resilience, essential for overcoming the challenges that are inherent in any endeavor.

As you incorporate these principles into every aspect of your life, you'll notice a shift in how you lead and interact with your team. The path to success, once clouded by uncertainties and obstacles, will become clearer and more attainable. The journey doesn't end here—in fact, it's an ongoing process of learning, growing, and evolving. I am grateful that you took the time to read this chapter, and I hope the insights and strategies shared here have sparked a desire within you to unlock your full potential!

As we part ways on these pages, I leave you with these final words of gratitude and encouragement: *Go out and make your mark on the world.* Create the life you've always envisioned, a life full of love, success, and fulfillment. You deserve all the happiness and success that comes your way. Remember, ntwrkrs, the journey to greatness begins with a single step, and that step starts with *you*!

Watch Rebecca's Video Now!
LeadingLadiesCourse.com

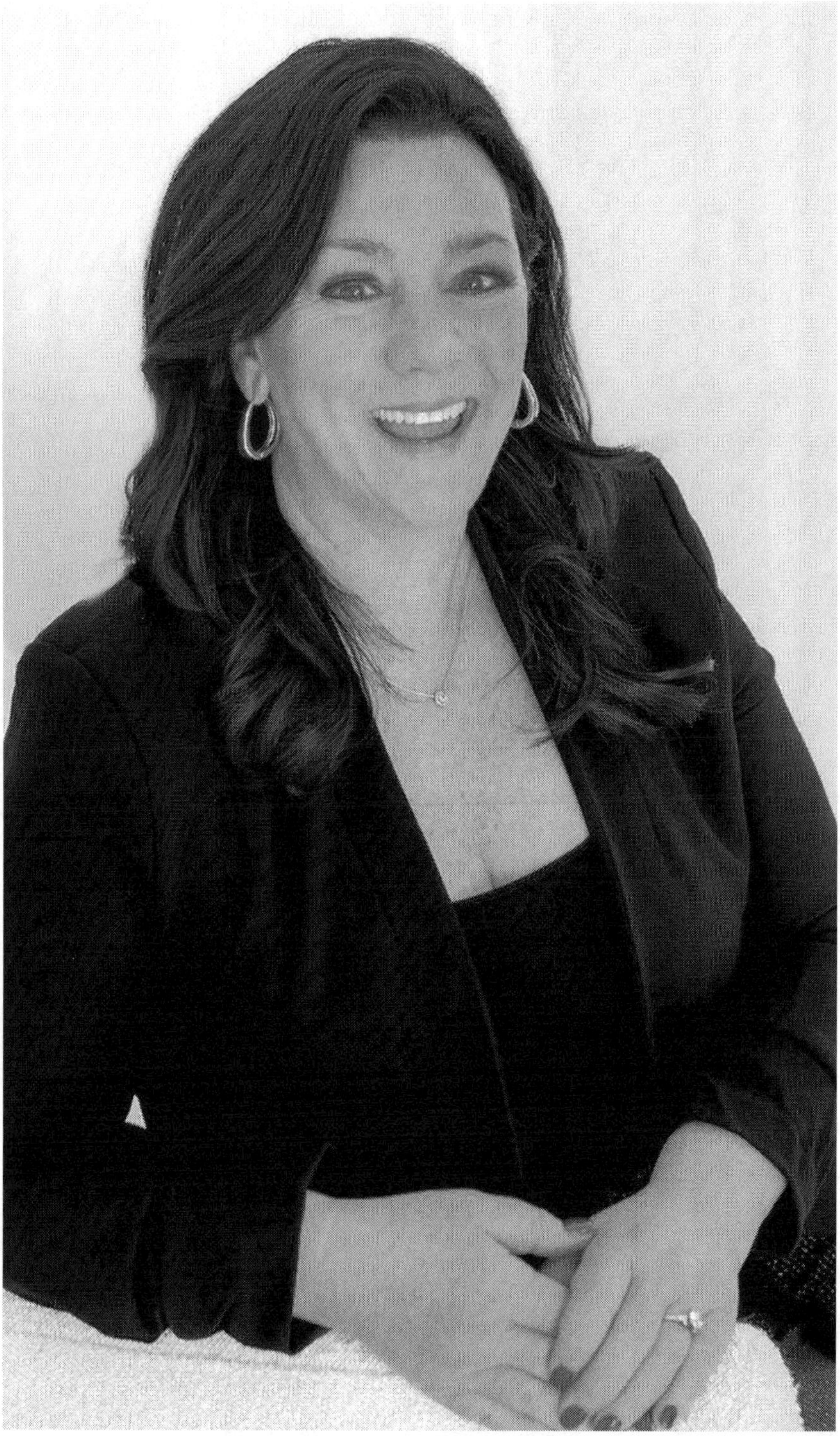

20

You Can Have It All

Motherhood, Career, And Success In The Network Marketing Profession

Lori Hart

🌐 TheKetoLadyLori.com
[f] Facebook.com/theketoladylorihart
[◎] Instagram.com/the.ketolady
♪ Tiktok.com/@theketolady

You Can Have It All

Lori Hart

Hey, ntwrkrs! I'm excited to be here with you in this book! We're going to have fun together on these pages as we explore a topic that resonates with many of us women: the art of juggling motherhood, career, and achieving success. Specifically, we will dive into the ways that Network Marketing can help us do that! I'm thrilled to be able to share my own personal experiences and insights with you, in hopes that you walk away with the understanding that yes, *you really can have it all.*

Looking at where I stand today, I can confidently say that Network Marketing has been instrumental in helping me achieve my dreams. I had a previous career as a hairstylist, but I've since built a thriving business in this profession that surpassed my former income by ten times! I'm the proud mother of two beautiful, independent, adult daughters, and I just became a grandmother. I found my success—the dream life I wanted—by envisioning what I desired, taking action, and adjusting my direction as needed during different chapters of my life. So, I'm going to walk you through the ways I balanced motherhood, career, and success, and provide you with the actionable steps so you can do the same!

Maybe by this point, you're wondering 'who is Lori Hart to tell me I can have it all?' Well, I've lived it! Motherhood has been the cornerstone of my life, filled with boundless responsibilities, deep love, and cherished connections. My two daughters (and now my baby grandson) have filled my days with joy in ways that I could have never imagined. They also *challenged* and *strengthened* me in ways that I never dreamed of! The desire to be able to experience that full range of emotions, be present for all the pivotal moments, and create long-lasting memories for my family led me to Network Marketing.

My journey into motherhood coincided with my career as a hairstylist, a role I enjoyed and excelled in for three decades. During those years, my life was a whirlwind of clients, haircuts, and color appointments, interspersed with the precious moments of raising my daughters. This dual role was my first venture into the world of multitasking—a skill that would become invaluable when I transitioned to Network Marketing.

Initially, in the early years, the demands of motherhood were largely tactical or nurturing: changing diapers, preparing bottles, and soothing through sleepless nights. However, as my daughters grew, these responsibilities evolved. The after-school pickups, homework sessions, and bedtime routines filled my evenings. And amidst all this, I wished for a career that could accommodate my role as a mother without forcing me to choose between professional aspirations and family life.

This longing led me to Network Marketing—a profession that promised flexibility and empowerment! Unlike the rigid schedules of corporate jobs or the unpredictable demands of being a hairstylist, Network Marketing offered me control over my time. It allowed me to be there for the school plays, the doctor's appointments, and the unexpected sick days—all without the guilt of letting down a boss or big clients.

In this new profession, I discovered that motherhood and career building were not mutually exclusive. Network Marketing gave me the space to flourish as a professional while being an ever-present figure in my children's lives. It was a revelation, and I continued down the path that defied the traditional trade-offs between work and family.

Network Marketing has not only allowed me to be a present mother, but it has also become a legacy that I've been able to pass down to my daughters as I enjoy more of a 'consulting' role rather than a 'managerial' role in their adult lives. I see the seeds of this profession sprouting in their lives, offering them the same opportunities for balance and success that it offered me! So, now that I've shared the details of my own path, let's explore the ways Network Marketing can help you have it all. Let's go!

Motherhood

Being a mother is a continuous, sometimes chaotic journey of love, sacrifice, and growth. In Network Marketing, this journey is not a barrier to success but a catalyst for it! Countless numbers of women have proven, day after day, that it's possible to nurture a family and a flourishing career simultaneously, without compromising values. So, we're going to dive into flexibility, meaningful connections, and positive influences on family.

One of the most compelling aspects of Network Marketing is the flexibility it affords, especially for mothers. Take, for instance, a recent winter day when my grandson fell ill with RSV. In such moments, the ability to be present for my family, without the stress of seeking permission from a boss or worrying about work commitments, is priceless. Network marketing empowers you with control over your time, a luxury that's not available in most traditional careers.

And it's not just the flexibility that offers help in the midst of motherhood! The opportunity to make meaningful connections to others when your days are filled with toys, toddlers' games, and *Sesame Street*. In this profession, the relationships you develop go beyond mere acquaintances. I've been blessed to meet and bond with other women who share similar aspirations—women who seek more than the routine of daily chores, who strive for a balance between nurturing their families and nurturing their own dreams. These relationships aren't just about business, they're a support system, a space where we share ideas, challenges, and victories, both as mothers and entrepreneurs.

This network of professional growth, personal development, and friendship extends its influence to our families as well. My daughters, for example, have been inspired by the practices they've seen me learn and embody. From embracing the concept of manifestation to adopting productive habits, they are learning life's lessons not just from my words but from my actions. These moments of influence, where career and motherhood intertwine to set a positive example, are among the most gratifying experiences of my journey.

And I have to make a special mention of the fact that Network Marketing plays an immense role in empowering single mothers! I've encountered numerous single moms who have turned to this profession not just out of financial necessity but because it allows them the freedom to be both the caregiver and the breadwinner without leaving their homes. This aspect of Network Marketing holds a special place in my heart, as it underscores the profession's potential to be a lifeline for those in challenging circumstances.

One of my favorite memories of being a mother in Network Marketing when my daughter was about ten years old. She was having a tough year in the fifth grade and was being bullied by her peers. I was so grateful that I could be home with her after school so that we could talk the day out, and I could have her friends come over to play while their moms were still at work.

At one point that year, she was part of her school's on-stage version of *American Idol*. She was so excited to perform, and I remember exactly how lucky I felt to be in that audience at two o'clock in the afternoon. I looked around for the other moms in the audience but didn't see many—most were at work. My daughter got up on stage in her ankle boots and braided hair, smiling in front of the glittering backdrop, and belted out Adele's *When We Were Young.*

I cried the entire three minutes or so, in awe of her bravery and her beauty, feeling immense gratitude for a career that allowed me to see her in that moment. These precious times when you can witness them growing up, help them through problems at school, or nurture them when they're sick, make Network Marketing the perfect profession for mothers!

Career

Beyond the financial rewards and flexibility that Network Marketing offers, it's also a journey of personal growth and development. This profession equips individuals with valuable skills that not only enhance their business acumen but also enrich their personal lives. Leadership, time management, and self-belief are just a few of the many attributes nurtured in this field. These skills have a ripple effect, influencing not just our professional endeavors, but also our roles as mothers, friends, and community members.

My own venture into Network Marketing began in the unlikeliest of places: a hair salon! As a stylist, I loved the creative essence of my job, but I also recognized the limitations of a career that required me to be in a fixed location (the salon) and a fixed, four-days-per-week schedule. My introduction to the world of Network Marketing came from a salon client whose simple suggestion to meet his wife opened the doors to a new world of possibilities. It was an opportunity to dream bigger, to envision a career that wasn't confined to the walls of a building.

"We've got three-year-old twins," he mentioned as I cut his hair. "My wife does Network Marketing so she's able to stay home with them."

"Network Marketing?" I asked. "What's that?"

"I don't really know," he admitted, laughing. "But with your personality, I think you'd be really good at it. You should come over sometime and talk to her about it."

I was intrigued—especially the part about being able to be home with my then three-year-old daughter, since I was having to hire babysitters to watch her while I worked at the salon. So, a week later, I went over to their house and talked to his wife for three hours about how she had transitioned from a traditional career into Network Marketing.

She introduced me to concepts I'd never heard of before: not trading time for money, residual income that kept coming in long after she'd made a sale, and the personal development that was helping her become a better businesswoman, wife, and mother. I continued to go back to her house to learn more about the profession. I viewed income and career through a new lens, and gradually, I knew that Network Marketing was a better fit for my long-term goals than hairstyling.

This transition wasn't just about seeking better income; it was about redefining what a career could be. It was a realization that my professional identity could extend beyond being a hairstylist to that of an entrepreneur, a leader, and a mentor. In Network Marketing, I found a career that harmonized with my life as a mother, offering me the flexibility to be present for my family while leveling up professionally.

Success

True success transcends financial gains, flexibility, and rank advancement—that is to say, it's about more than just the professional aspects of success. It's about the overall sense of fulfillment that comes from balancing a thriving career with a fulfilling family life! This definition of success is deeply personal—It can be the freedom to dictate your own schedule, to be there for your family's significant moments, or to build a life not constrained by traditional work boundaries.

For me, success in this career has also been marked by tangible rewards! I'm the proud owner of a white Range Rover, complete with extra-long sunroof and leather interior. I love my car. She's beautiful, and I feel safe and confident and powerful driving her. Earning my dream car through my company's reward program was not just a personal achievement, but a symbol of the collective success of helping *others reach their goals!* It's a reminder that in this profession, success is often a shared journey, where your accomplishments uplift those around you.

It takes work to get the perfect blend of family and professional life, to get the cars and the trips and the other amazing rewards this career has to offer. I showed up consistently. I did the work every day. I figured out how to believe in myself. I went all in on my company, its products, and my upline and leadership. And when I did all those things, I became this unstoppable superwoman who could be everything I sought out to be: a mom, daughter, aunt, friend, and successful career woman. I can assure you, you have the power to embark on a similar journey and emerge as your own version of that superwoman.

Now, let's delve into the actionable steps that will propel you toward achieving your own vision of success!

1. Execute Clear, Realistic Goals

Sounds simple enough, right? But navigating multiple roles as a mom, a wife, a friend, and more can indeed be challenging. The first step in this process is setting boundaries. This may involve telling your children, "Hey guys, mommy has to work for an hour first, but then we'll go see a movie, okay?" or telling your friends, "I need to work until three o'clock, but after that, I'd love to go for a run." Get silent, get by yourself, and set the expectations for those around you.

Once you've set your boundaries, it's important to make sure your goals are realistic. This means that you should consider whether your financial goals align with how much time you have to work on them. To say, "I want to make a million dollars this year," but only set aside two hours a day to work on your business, is unrealistic, and setting these types of goals will only disappoint and discourage you. Ask a mentor or your upline to give you a reality check if you need to—just make sure that you're honest with yourself about whether your goals match your bandwidth to work.

Now that you have defined your goals and allocated time to work towards them, it's essential to make sure you know what the critical path to success looks like. What is your company's comp plan? How do rewards and incentives work? Exactly what will you need to do, and in what order, to achieve the goal you've set for yourself? Without knowing this, you'll be walking through a maze of possibilities—so gather all of the information before you set out on your path.

And finally, you need to employ some sort of time management system. Don't leave it up to your memory—our brains were never designed to be alarm clocks! Instead, use a physical planner, an online calendar, or another software tool that will help you organize the way your day flows. Trust me on this, it's essential to have this in place before you get going!

With a clear path to a realistic and scalable goal, and the time and space to work, as well as a time-management system, you're ready to execute!

2. Know That You're The Boss

This one is a double-edged sword, my friends. When you're the boss, it's easy *to do* and it's just as easy *not to do.* When you have your own business, it can be tempting to not take yourself or your work too seriously—but this is not your hobby, it's your career. If you treat it like your hobby, well, you'll get hobby-sized results. If you treat it like your career, you'll get career-sized results.

And since your boss is you in this career, it's your responsibility to ensure you don't burn out. It's essential that you make time to practice self-care, stay healthy, and be with your tribe—in other words, those who support you and can recharge your batteries. Get out of bed in the morning and put on your makeup and blow out your hair if that's what makes you feel confident. It's easy in this profession to get so focused on work that you lose yourself in the process!

It's a huge responsibility to manage yourself in this way. if you're not showing up for yourself as a great boss, it will impact everything you do. If you're too relaxed, then as a result, productivity will suffer, leading to unmet goals. If you're too hard on yourself and your health and energy suffer, then the people you meet will feel like something's off, and they'll look for someone else to work with. Remember, energy is everything! Make sure you're treating yourself like someone who deserves a great boss.

3. Don't Be Afraid To Pivot

If you find that something you're doing in your business isn't yielding the desired results, don't hesitate to redirect some of your time, energy, and resources to another target. You don't have to quit the company you're with, but you also shouldn't beat something over its head if it's not giving you the results you want. Instead, put some effort into trying something new, then evaluating if it's working. If it is, well, keep going! And if it's not, it may be time to pivot once more.

It's not uncommon for many women to pride themselves on their ability to stick with people, jobs, and situations that span a spectrum of dissatisfaction, from the mildly unfulfilling to the downright toxic and dangerous. *Do not fall into this trap.* This is your one and only life, after all! There is no reason to invest your time, energy, and resources into people or endeavors that aren't going to get you closer to having it all. Hold your head up high, and be willing to pivot when necessary.

Network Marketing is not just a career choice; it's a lifestyle choice. It offers a unique blend of flexibility, personal growth, and the opportunity to build meaningful connections. It's a profession that understands and accommodates the complexities of motherhood, empowering women to pursue their dreams and aspirations without sacrificing their family life.

ntwrkr.com

As we conclude this chapter, I hope you feel empowered and assured that you can indeed have it all. Motherhood, a fulfilling career, and success in Network Marketing are not only achievable but can complement and enhance each other beautifully! You possess the power to be your own superhero—flourishing as a mother, thriving in your career, and achieving success beyond your dreams.

So, to my fellow ntwrkrs, embark on this journey with confidence and enthusiasm. Remember, you are capable of incredible feats! Embrace your journey with determination and joy, and watch as you transform into the embodiment of success, balance, and fulfillment. You've got this. Step forward with determination, crush your goals, and join the many women who prove that in the dynamic, supportive, and growth-oriented world of Network Marketing, you can truly have it all!

Watch Lori's Video Now!
LeadingLadiesCourse.com

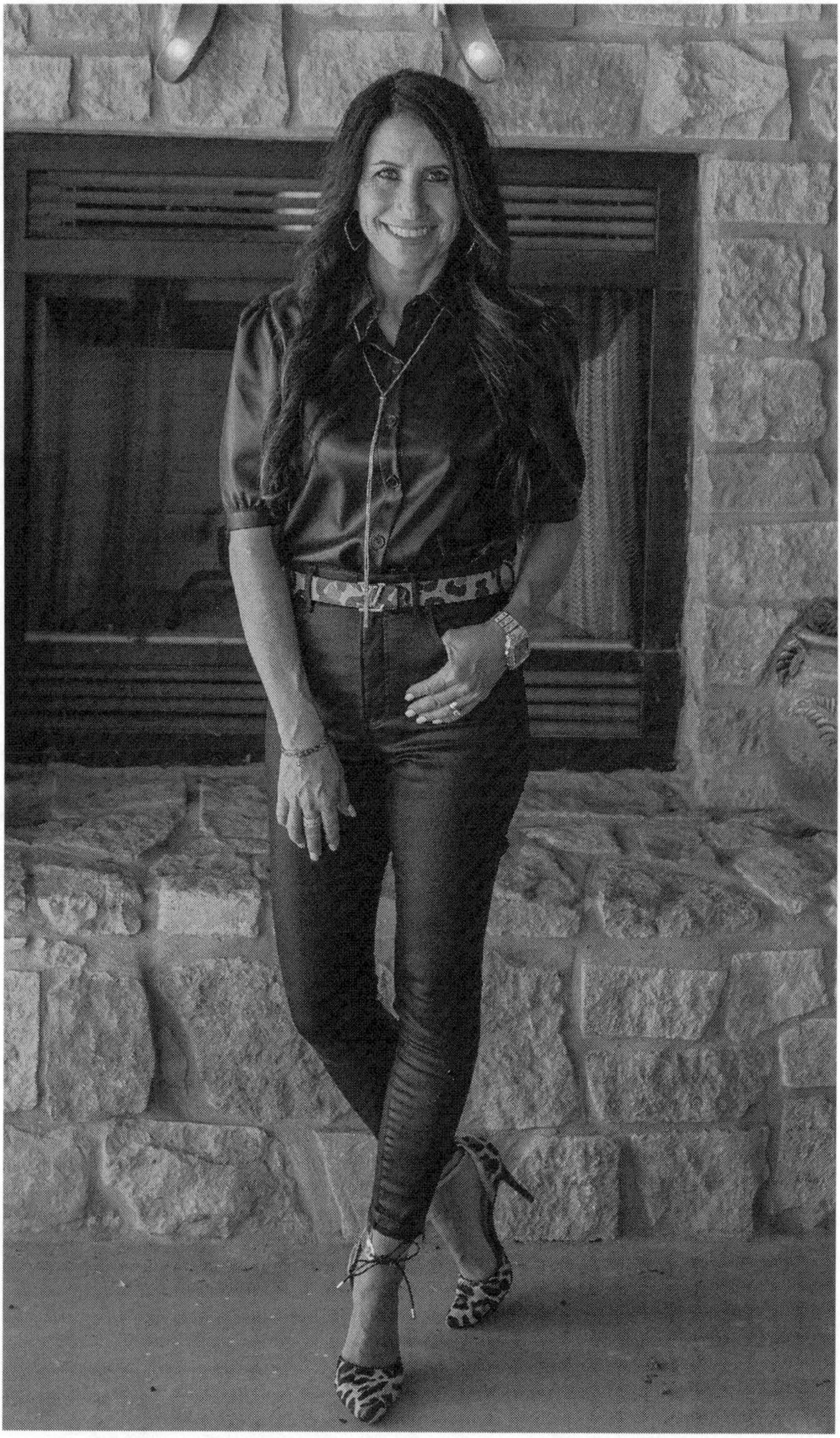

21

Not Everyone's Going To Make It

The 5 Survival Skills Every Network Marketer Needs To Know

Ursula Myers

Facebook.com/ursula.v.myers
Instagram.com/ursulastrailofturquoise
Tiktok.com/@ursmyers

Not Everyone's Going To Make It

Ursula Myers

Hello, ntwrkrs! It's great to be here with you in this book, and I'm excited to share some of my top tips with you on how I've achieved success in our amazing profession. My career in Network Marketing spans over eight-and-a-half-years, and my path has not only been rewarding but it has also shaped me into a serial entrepreneur and a mentor to many. This chapter is titled "Not Everyone's Going to Make It," but don't you worry—I've got the five survival skills every Network Marketer needs to create a thriving business, and I'm going to walk you through them on these pages.

Before we jump in, I'll tell you a bit about me: I started my entrepreneurial journey as a boutique owner but became interested in Network Marketing once I saw the time freedom it allowed. Compared to my brick-and-mortar business, this new profession promised low overhead, flexibility, and the opportunity to take my business as far as I wanted, without being tied down to one location or traditional business hours. Just like that, I jumped in, waved the world of physical retail behind, and built a seven-figure business that, to date, has paid me over seven million dollars. So, I hope my story gives you a bit of insight into what I'm going to teach you in this chapter!

When I teach these skills to my team and community, they get the results they desire. They become focused, they stay on track, and they keep their heads in the game like never before. They realize that Network Marketing is not one constant volume of business but an ebb-and-flow type dance that requires commitment, determination, and perseverance. And if they can stay on track this way to get everything they want out of this business, so can you—with the help of these five survival skills.

Stick with me in this chapter and you'll learn how to build your own momentum, be your own cheerleader, ride the rollercoaster of Network Marketing, embrace the change that inevitably comes with this profession, and ensure that you never give up. After all, *quitting* shouldn't even be in your vocabulary! My goal is to help you see the potential within yourself to build a thriving business and to stay on track, just as I have done and continue to do with my teams and community.

So, are you ready to transform your business and build the life you've dreamed of? If so, then let's get to it!

Create Your Own Momentum

When I started my career in Network Marketing, I quickly realized a fundamental truth: momentum—the force that propels us toward our goals—cannot be borrowed or gifted; rather, it must be generated from within. This realization came to me not through easy wins but through understanding the essence of perseverance. It dawned on me that waiting for external triggers like a company promotion or a training session to spark action was nothing but misplaced hope. True momentum is self-created and self-sustained!

Whether you're leading a team of many or you're just focusing on yourself, this principle applies. In fact, if you're a team of one, then creating your own momentum will attract a team to you quickly! And even if you have a team already, you must learn to lead yourself first—and that means you can't be waiting around for something external to motivate you into action.

Creating your own momentum means cultivating an inner drive that pushes you toward your goals, regardless of external circumstances. It's about making a promise to yourself—a promise that holds more weight than any other commitment. This personal pledge is what keeps you showing up every day, taking steps that inch you closer to your dreams. It's important to realize that to achieve the extraordinary, you have to be extraordinary in your daily actions.

I learned this firsthand on New Year's Eve in the year 2015. It was on the last day of December, the last day of 2015, that I found myself looking at sales numbers that fell short of my goals. My team and I had only managed to sell twenty-six kits that month, and this simply wasn't going to get me to the goal I'd set to hit by June of the next year: my one-year anniversary of being in Network Marketing.

However, out of those twenty-six kits, eighteen consisted of my personal sales. It was sobering to realize that all the festivities of the holiday season had lulled my team into complacency, and essentially, everyone besides me had taken the month off from work. Although it was all of our first years in Network Marketing, I realized that if I wanted to hit my goals, I was going to have to build a team made of people who were willing to work as hard as I was.

And so, that's just what I did. I went out and found people who were self-motivated to hit goals, and who wouldn't slow down because external motivations waned during the holiday season. This might sound a bit harsh, but it's 100% true. Not everyone on the team you have right now is going to get you to your goals. Will some of them? Sure! But not all. And that's why you never, ever slow down your own action waiting for someone else to decide they're going to work.

My best advice is to lead from the front, motivate yourself, and choose team members who will do the same. When I finally did this in January 2016, our sales were huge. In February, we surpassed that. And by the end of April, two months before my one-year anniversary in Network Marketing, we crushed the goal I'd set for June. Fourteen months later, I broke every company record, and I had built the fastest-growing team in company history.

So, start with yourself: build the momentum inside of you, independent of what you're experiencing around you, and it will be ready for the team that's coming. Because when you do, the right people will enter your life. Here are some action steps to ensure your motivation comes from inside you:

1. No matter what your team is doing, never fall out of recruitment mode. If everyone around you is taking the summer months lightly in their business or falling away during the holidays, don't fall to their level of engagement! Instead, double or triple your efforts. When you do, you'll attract team members who want to do the same.

LEADING LADIES

2. No matter how big your team gets, never slip into management mode. Even though it's tempting to take a break from active recruiting, it's never the time to sit back and supervise! Always be enrolling, even if your team is crushing recruitment goals.

Creating your own momentum is an empowering process. It's about taking control of your journey, setting the pace, and maintaining it against all odds. For me, it was not just about reaching a goal but about transforming myself into someone capable of overcoming *any* challenge. In my experience, transformation became the catalyst for not only my success but also the success of my team! As you walk farther down the path of your Network Marketing career, remember that the power to create momentum lies within you. It starts with a promise to yourself—a promise that you are worth the effort, every single day.

Become Your Own Cheerleader

In my relentless pursuit of success within Network Marketing, I've encountered countless challenges and moments of self-doubt. Yet, one of the most transformative lessons I've learned is the vital importance of being your own biggest, loudest cheerleader. This concept might seem simple and straightforward, but its implications are far-reaching. In an industry where external validation can be hard to come by, the ability to self-motivate and celebrate one's achievements becomes indispensable.

Being your own cheerleader means cultivating a mindset of self-support and recognition—understanding that while accolades from others are gratifying, they should not be relied upon as the fuel that drives lasting success. This mindset is crucial because, let's face it, Network Marketing is tough! It demands resilience, persistence, and an unwavering belief in oneself. I've learned that success in this business is not just about achieving goals, but about overcoming the mental and emotional hurdles that accompany the journey.

Your upline may not be the most supportive—believe me, I've been in that situation before, and that's okay! Understand that not everyone is going to be supportive or cheer you on, so you *must* be that person for yourself. Early on, I learned how to support and cheer for myself, and it changed the way I approached my business.

Instead of dampening my spirits, being my own cheerleader ignited a fire within me. It propelled me to work harder and prove to myself that I could exceed my personal expectations. I became my loudest advocate, celebrating every win, no matter how small. This self-support was not just about self-congratulation; it was a statement of self-belief and resilience. So, how can you become your own cheerleader? Well, you can start by taking these steps:

1. Celebrate your wins. Start by acknowledging every success, big or small. Did you reach a new milestone? Celebrate it. Did you outperform your personal best? Give yourself a pat on the back! It's important to recognize your efforts and achievements because this recognition will fuel your motivation and ambition.

2. Create visible reminders of your success. Whether it's a printed picture celebrating a trip you earned or a post on social media sharing your latest achievement, make your successes visible! These reminders are not just for others; rather, they are for you, so you will remember your capabilities and accomplishments.

3. Use lack of support as fuel. Instead of being disheartened by a lack of support, let the lack of support motivate you to push harder. Prove to yourself (and, by extension, to others) that you have what it takes to succeed. This mindset transforms potential negativity into a powerful driver of personal growth and achievement.

Network Marketing is as much about personal development as it is about business success. Learning to be your own cheerleader is a key part of this journey. It teaches you to rely on your inner strength and to find motivation within yourself, even when external support is lacking. This self-reliance not only drives your business forward, but it will also foster a deeper sense of self-worth and confidence. Remember, your journey is unique, and your achievements are worth celebrating—*by you, for you.* Let your voice be the loudest in the room, cheering you on to greater heights!

Ride The Rollercoaster

What comes to mind when you read the word *rollercoaster?* If you're thinking of a slow climb to exhilarating highs, then a terrifying race to daunting lows, then back up again, well—the metaphor fits! This journey of ups and downs describes the path of Network Marketers as well, where embracing the inherent ups and downs becomes not just a strategy but a necessity for survival and success. If my years of experience have taught me anything, it's that the true measure of our resilience and potential for growth lies not in how we revel in our victories but in how we navigate our valleys.

So, riding the rollercoaster in Network Marketing means acknowledging and preparing for the inevitable fluctuations in business. It's about understanding that no journey is a straight line to the top! Every leader in this industry, myself included, has faced their share of peaks and valleys. However, it's in the valleys, which represent the toughest times, where the most critical work is done. This work isn't just about pushing through; it's about becoming the person who can not only reach but also sustain those peaks.

For me and many others, the year 2020 was a sobering example of this rollercoaster. My former company experienced unprecedented growth, and we reached a sales peak that seemed insurmountable. Yet, as with all highs, a decline followed that was not just a challenge, but a test for leadership. Make sure you're doing the necessary personal work during your ascent to handle the inevitable decline with grace.

My journey through this period reinforced an important lesson: the importance of continuously working on oneself, especially during the lows. It's this personal growth that equips you to handle the highs *and the lows* and maintain your success. So, if you're ready to navigate the rollercoaster with confidence, here are three action steps:

1. Lead from the front, especially in the lows. Your team looks to you for guidance. In the valleys, your leadership is more critical than ever. Continue reaching out, following up, and demonstrating through your actions that the path forward is through persistent, consistent effort.

3. Prepare for the inevitable declines. Understand that business cycles are a part of the journey. By anticipating the valleys, you can prepare yourself and your team for them, ensuring that when they arrive, you're not caught off guard but ready to use them as opportunities for growth.

4. Embrace personal development in the valleys. Use the challenging times for deep personal growth. Ask yourself: who do I need to become to overcome this? Engage in activities that build your resilience, expand your skills, and strengthen your vision for the future.

The rollercoaster of Network Marketing is not just a test of endurance, it's a testament to our ability to grow, adapt, and lead. It teaches us that success is not only about enjoying the highs, but also about using the lows as a foundation for growth and learning. By embracing the entirety of this journey, we prepare ourselves for temporary achievements and fleeting celebrations as well as sustained success and leadership in the industry.

Remember, it's the work you do in the valleys that propels you to the next peak! Let this understanding guide you and your team through the ebbs and flows, and together, you'll emerge stronger, more resilient, and more successful!

Embrace The Change

In the dynamic world of Network Marketing, one of the most crucial skills for success is the ability to embrace change. Change can be scary for many people—it brings with it uncertainty and the need to adapt.

However, those who welcome change with open arms are the ones who continue to grow and flourish in their careers. On the other hand, those who resist change and quickly resort to negativity often find themselves left behind, struggling to keep up with the evolving landscape of the profession.

Change in our business can come in various forms, such as updates to your company's product line, modifications to the compensation plan, shifts in corporate leadership, or even changes in what your customer base desires! It's important not to get bogged down by these changes but to view them as opportunities for growth and improvement.

I recently experienced a significant change in my career. After eight-and-a-half years with my previous company, I made the bold decision to move to a new company. This transition was not easy; it was a leap of faith that required me to step out of my comfort zone and embrace the unknown. The change was challenging, filled with uncertainties and adjustments; however, it was also invigorating and empowering! It reaffirmed my belief in my potential and my commitment to personal and professional growth. It reminded me that embracing change is about trusting the journey and believing in one's ability to adapt and thrive in new environments.

When facing change, it's important to remember that you are not defined by the company you work for. You are an individual with a unique brand and value. It's easy to get caught up in company loyalty, but it's essential to maintain a sense of independence and be open to exploring new opportunities that align with your goals and values. Embracing change means being ready to adapt and evolve, even if it means finding a new table to sit at!

LEADING LADIES

To successfully navigate change, here are a few action steps to consider:

1. Accept change and assess your attitude. Recognize that change is a part of the journey and come to terms with it. This might take some time. While you're getting used to the idea, work on the understanding that your attitude towards change can significantly impact your experience—so choose to view it as an opportunity for growth and development rather than a setback.

2. Prepare for transition. Anticipate changes that are coming down the pipeline and think about ways you can adapt to them. Whether it's learning new skills, expanding your network, or adjusting your business strategies, being proactive can help you navigate change more effectively.

3. Stay true to your brand. Remember that you are your own brand, regardless of the company you represent. Continue to build and nurture your personal brand, as it will remain constant even when other aspects of your business change.

4. Seek support. Change can be challenging, so don't hesitate to seek support from mentors, peers, or even professional coaches. Having a support system can provide guidance, encouragement, and different perspectives as you navigate change.

In short, change is an integral part of the Network Marketing industry! By embracing change, you open yourself up to new possibilities and opportunities for growth. It's about betting on yourself, trusting your abilities, and moving forward with confidence. Change can indeed be a breath of fresh air, bringing with it a renewed sense of purpose and direction. So, as you face changes in your business and personal life, remember to approach them fearlessly and with an open heart. Your ability to adapt and embrace change will be a key factor in your continued success and fulfillment in this ever-evolving profession.

Don't You Dare Quit

Friends, even in my less-than-a-decade Network Marketing career, I've encountered countless junctures where the path forked, presenting me with a choice: perseverance or surrender. Yet, here I stand, urging you with every fiber of my being: *don't you dare quit!* This isn't merely my slogan; rather, it's a personal and professional lifeline that has anchored me through storms and propelled me to places I once thought were unreachable. Abandoning the journey—quitting—is a tempting option we all face, but it's one I've learned to push away through unwavering determination and unbreakable resolve.

I took the word *quitting* out of my vocabulary, and I want you to do that, too—in all shapes and forms. Commit to never, ever, again say things like, "I'm going to quit," or, "I guess I could quit," or, "I could always just quit, right?" Because if you entertain those thoughts, they linger in the back of your mind like a permanent plan "B," taking your focus off of your goals.

And before we go further, I'm not talking about stopping the pursuit of something that no longer serves you; this is about refusing to give up on your dreams, your potential, and the essence of who you are and who you're meant to be. I'm also not telling you to avoid a strategic pivot—because while quitting on yourself is a surrender, pivoting is an informed choice to embrace change. Do you see the differences?

While we're clarifying the definition further, I want to focus on a form of quitting I call *micro-quitting:* the tiny quits you commit to yourself or your business that add up to a major quit in the end. This one is sneaky, something that creeps up on you over a period of time and blindsides you in the end.

In fact, maybe you've experienced it before: It's Saturday afternoon and you need to make a follow-up call to someone really interested in your business, but there's also that new Netflix series you've been wanting to binge-watch. So maybe you push the call and spend your day on the couch. Or perhaps it's a training your upline told you about that was scheduled for a Sunday night. Sunday? *Nah.* So you just didn't show up.

Maybe over the next thirty days, you micro-quit every other day by not showing up or not prioritizing your business. Well—in thirty days or less, you'll likely look back and wonder, "Where did my team go? What happened to my business? What happened to my *paycheck?*"

Don't let this happen to you. Take quitting off the table as an option. Even though you'll see those around you quit for any number of reasons—they don't like the industry, the product, or maybe they don't like *you*—whatever the reason, let them go. Wish them well. Understand that this profession is not for everyone and commit to being a great leader who doesn't badmouth others just because it wasn't a good fit. It doesn't matter that they quit, it only matters that *you don't quit.* So, here are some action steps you can take to make sure you stay in the game:

1. Make a list of attributes for your 'dream distributor.' What are they like? What qualities do they have? How would they show up on social media? How often would they show up to team trainings? How would they recruit? List out all the details.

2. Step up to the mirror. This is one of the hardest steps for people to take, but you must assess yourself *honestly* and decide whether or not you embody and display the qualities of the person you just described in the previous step. Where are you showing up, and where are you lacking?

3. Become that ideal distributor. Now, it's time to do the things necessary to become the person you described. When you start doing the things you wish your dream person would do, you'll attract *multiple people* who match the description. It's truly amazing!

This survival skill of never quitting isn't just about not stopping, it's about pursuing the highest standard you can imagine for yourself and your team. Yes, the introspection and critique of oneself can be difficult, but it will be worth it in the end, when you've persevered and manifested a team of high achievers! You'll grow and change and be stretched during this process, and you'll have to sift through a ton of people to find your team. But if you do it, and if you stick with it, you're going to see life-changing results.

Now that I've shared with you five pivotal strategies that have not only fueled my growth but have also become the cornerstone of my teachings to my team, let's recap. We explored creating your own momentum, being your own cheerleader, riding the rollercoaster through its highs and lows, embracing change, and refusing to quit—even if everyone around you is leaving the profession.

This industry is difficult. Not everyone's going to make it. So, the question I have for you now is: are you going to make it? Will you do the work to make sure you're prepared for both the triumphs and the pitfalls? Beyond the strategies and insights, I offer you a piece of advice that transcends the practicalities of business, and that is to take God with you wherever you go.

If you don't have God by your side through all of this, you're never going to make it. And if you do by chance get to the top without God, you're not going to stay there! Make sure that you are *working for it* as hard as you are *praying for it*. Ask God to give you strength, the right people, and to the ability to do the work necessary to achieve your goals.

And while God has instilled greatness in every single one of us, it's going to be up to *you* to find that greatness within yourself. If you take the steps I outlined above, you'll get there. It might sting a little to do the internal work required, but it is only because you care about the truth. It matters to you, and it demands your attention. And it might just be the very thing that can change the legacy of your business.

I want you to think *big*. I don't just want you to become a leader in this profession, I want you to become a top leader in your company and in the world. There is so much potential out there for you! And there are so many people wanting to join us. Never in the history of Network Marketing has there been a better time for us to be loud about who we are, what the opportunities are, and how we can help anyone and everyone make an income from home—from their phone!

My biggest hope is that this chapter has helped you in some way. I'm all about building people up and helping them become their best selves, and I'm not afraid to give hard-hitting tips that will compel you to do the things you need to do personally to achieve the huge goals you say you want to reach. I'm cheering you on from afar, and don't ever forget that! Good luck and God bless, ntwrkrs!

Watch Ursula's Video Now!
LeadingLadiesCourse.com

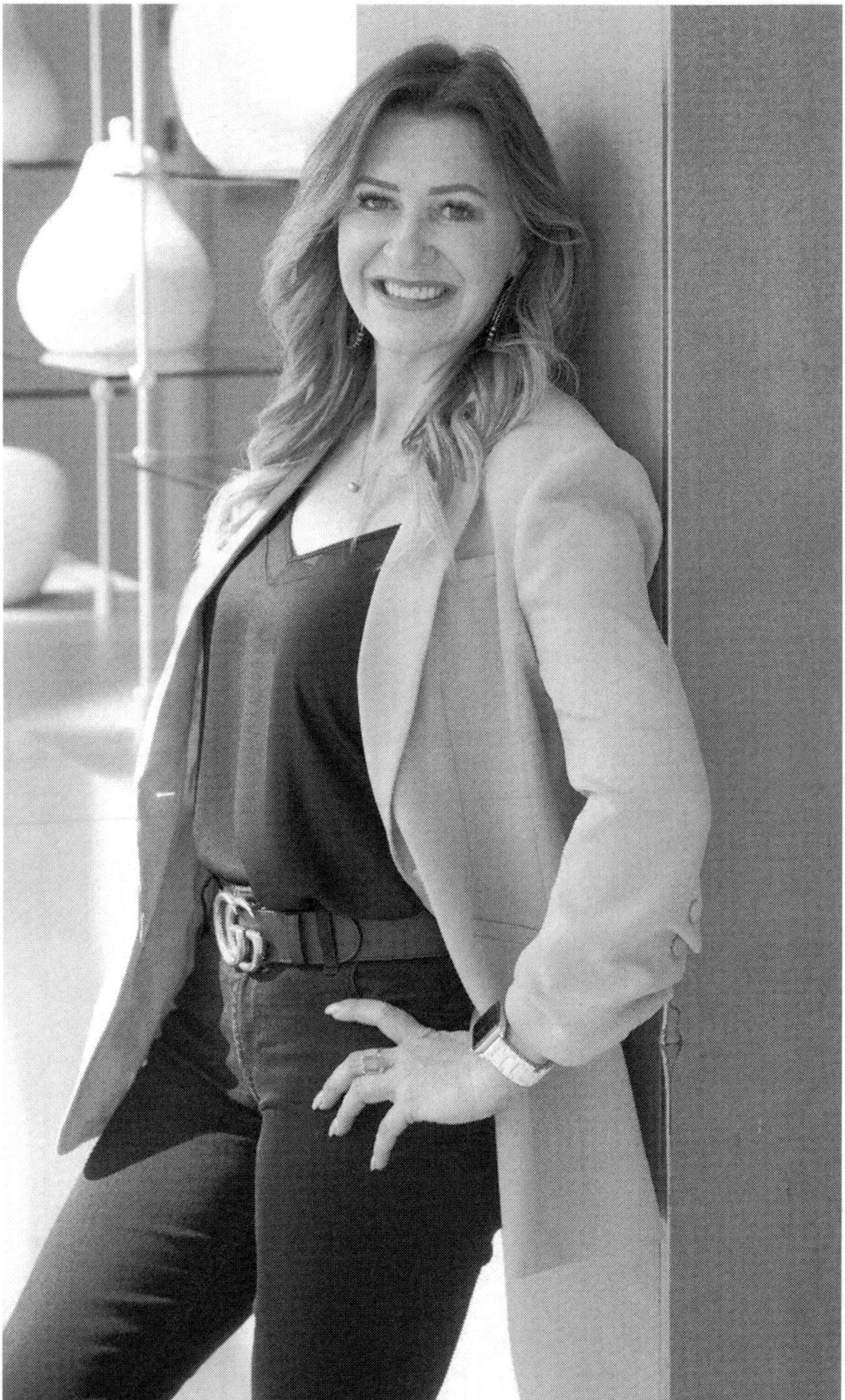

22

Never Ever Quit

Why Grit & Determination Are The True Keys To Success

Jennifer Piper

Facebook.com/ItsJenniferPiper
Instagram.com/itsjenniferpiper
Tiktok.com/@itsjenniferpiper

Never Ever Quit

Jennifer Piper

Hi there, ntwrkrs! Greetings from the beautiful city of Kamloops in British Columbia, Canada, where the rivers and mountains meet! I'm absolutely thrilled to have you with me on these pages, because my heart beats to empower women entrepreneurs. The opportunity to be in this book is one I don't take lightly, and I'm going all in to impart to you the best ways to cultivate joyful, supportive communities and craft a life-by-design that you *adore*, all through the power of culture and connection.

But first, a bit about me! My journey into entrepreneurship through Network Marketing was anything but ordinary. Picture this: a bustling business woman with not one, not two, but *three* traditional storefront businesses. Yes, you heard that right—I was the proud owner of a Sears store, a clothing boutique, and a grocery store alongside my ex-husband. Running retail businesses wasn't just a job for me; it was a passion, and taught me a ton about entrepreneurship.

However, the joy of motherhood brought curveballs and complexity into my life, as it often does. With three boys arriving within five years, the joy of new parenthood brought with it a new longing—I didn't want a daycare to raise my boys, or to miss all the important moments in their lives. They say you only have eighteen summers with your kids, and that weighed on me! After all, rushing out the door every morning and dropping my boys off with someone else wasn't what I pictured when I became a mom.

It was during one such morning, amidst the chaos of untied shoelaces and running-out-the-door breakfasts, that I found myself at a crossroads. I'd dropped the boys off at school and daycare and called a friend to commiserate on the craziness of working mom life, but she wasn't in so much of a commiserating mood. Instead, she was having coffee in her bathrobe with her husband, out on their deck. *At 10am on a weekday!*

She'd gotten into Network Marketing about a year earlier, and there she had mentioned it to me several times as a possible solution to my work/life balance woes. But I'd always shot it down, thinking that Network Marketing was below me. However, the contrast between her leisurely morning and my frenzied start to the day was stark, and there was no denying that she had it made, and had a better work/family balance, too. It was then that I realized there had to be another way.

And so, my transformation from traditional, brick-and-mortar retail entrepreneur to Network Marketer began. Within six months, I was financially able to go all in, making enough money in my Network Marketing business to hire a store manager. This leap of faith wasn't just about changing careers; it was about reshaping my entire life.

The results? Astonishing. I soared to the top of the company my friend brought me into, bid farewell to my traditional business roles, and embarked on a path of designing a life filled with love, passion, and purpose. Since that pivotal day in 2008, my journey has been nothing short of a rollercoaster—complete with dizzying highs, challenging lows, and invaluable lessons learned along the way. From speaking on international stages to co-authoring books and achieving a seven-figure income, the adventures have been endless, and I can't wait to see what's next.

But why share this story with you? Because being a Network Marketer is a test of wills; a battle fought with grit and determination. In this chapter, I'll share more of my experiences as I lean into the concept of resilience: never, ever quitting, even when those around you are falling down like dominoes.

You'll discover that unwavering determination is not just a surface trait, but the foundation of success. Refusing to quit, especially on yourself, is the transformative force that will drive you towards your dreams and make you unstoppable. Together, we'll explore the profound impact of grit in shaping our destinies, and how to design a life of intention and fulfillment. Remember: the only surefire way to fail is to give up! So, if you're ready to redefine what your life is all about, let's dive into the heart of what it means to 'never, ever give up," even when the going gets tough!

Don't Quit When Your Family Quits

It's not uncommon for Network Marketers to share the same story when it comes to the beginning of their journey in this profession: they got excited about starting in this business, bought their starter kits, and shared the news with their families, expecting those closest to them to be their biggest supporters. I, too, believed this as I launched my business, envisioning a rush of excitement coursing through my inner circle.

Yet, reality painted a different picture, for me and so many others. As it turned out, the most negative voices often came from friends and family. I still hear stories of this today, whether it be a well-meaning family member trying to talk a new recruit out of Network Marketing as a profession, a breakdown in a marriage due to career choices, or friends saying unkind or judgmental things about the industry you've chosen.

As I mentioned earlier, my own journey in Network Marketing started in 2007, as a way to retire myself from my brick-and-mortar businesses to be home with my children. During that first year, I worked at the retail shops all day long and then attended parties or meetings at night, sometimes driving an hour each way to get there. My then-husband was supportive because he was excited for the potential benefits of this new business as well.

But as my commitment to the business deepend, so did the rifts in our partnership. My days were a marathon—getting kids ready and off to school in the morning, managing stores during daylight, rushing off to host parties in the evenings, and then coming home to do it all over again the next day. The support I desperately needed from my husband waned, giving way to resentment and a tension that could be felt throughout our home.

Finally, in that weakened state of partnership, my husband chose to step outside our marriage—with a woman who had been a close friend of mine. And just like that, the marriage broke down completely. I was devastated, to say the least. The person I once shared everything with became a stranger, and the life we'd built together unraveled.

The soul-sucking divorce that followed crushed my confidence and left me feeling like I wasn't good enough, smart enough, pretty enough, or successful enough. I fell into the trap of constant comparison, and before long, I began to believe those things about myself. But after I fell down that rabbit hole, so to speak, I learned that it's the most difficult times in our lives that mold us into the incredible, strong women we were meant to be. I realized that the breakdown of my marriage wasn't about me or my ambitions—it was about him, and his choices. And I taught myself resilience, self-love, and the spirit of independence.

This period of my life underscored a vital lesson: the actions and choices of others are reflections of their own journeys, not a verdict on our worth or capabilities. It's easy to internalize the lack of support or the end of a relationship as personal failures. However, the truth is, our paths are our own, and we must tread them with conviction, regardless of approval or understanding from those we hold dear.

I also learned to face some of my deepest fears. Transitioning to a single mother did not, in fact, add insurmountable burdens to my shoulders. Instead, I found that the skills, and determination I honed in Network Marketing were powerful allies in my personal life. Through this profession, I achieved true financial independence and raised three boys without a dime of support from my ex-husband. And I don't say this to brag—it's simply a testament to what we can achieve when we refuse to let external circumstances or opinions dictate our worth or potential.

So, to anyone facing doubts from those supposed to be their bedrock of support, remember this: your journey is uniquely yours. Don't let the absence of understanding or the presence of skepticism deter you from your path and your dreams! Hold fast to your vision, because it's the act of persevering that allows us to uncover our true potential. Forge ahead with the knowledge that you are capable, you are worthy, and above all, you are unstoppable!

Don't Quit When Your Company Quits

In the world of Network Marketing, aligning with the company of your choice feels like stepping into a dream—the dream of entrepreneurship with the perks of low overhead, marketable products, and comprehensive support. Yet, this dream carries a hidden caveat: the lack of control over the company's decisions and directions.

Imagine dedicating years to building a business, nurturing relationships, and cultivating a brand, only to have the rug pulled out from under you by the very company you partnered with! Changes in product lines, compensation plans, or even the sudden closure of the company can feel like betrayal, leaving you questioning the foundation you've built your dreams upon.

In 2017, I faced such a turning point. After a decade of commitment, with recognition for being in the number one spot, my company shuttered its doors with little more than a phone call from a lawyer to deliver the news. The devastation was real and it hit my family hard.

As a single mother with three boys, a mortgage, and no outside support, the closure wasn't just a professional setback; it was a personal crisis.

The temptation to succumb to despair was strong. Doubts about the profession and my future within it clouded my thoughts—yet, it was in this moment of uncertainty that the true essence of entrepreneurship shone through: resilience. I told myself I had to pick myself up *now*, and faced the reality head-on, determined to not only survive but thrive.

I had to remember that even though the company I worked for provided the products and the support, I was my brand. I built that trust and loyalty. I had been in those relationships for ten years! I believed my customers would still choose me, and trust in my choice of a new company. Within days, I was charting a new course and partnering with a new company. This quick pivot wasn't just about salvaging a career; it was a testament to the power of personal branding and the unbreakable bonds formed through genuine connections.

The journey taught me invaluable lessons about the nature of Network Marketing and the persistent spirit required to navigate its ups and downs:

1. You are your brand. The essence of your success isn't tied to a company; it's rooted in the value you bring to the table. Your personal brand is your most significant asset, carrying weight and influence that transcends company affiliations.

ntwrkr.com

2. Resilience is key. The ability to bounce back, to start from scratch, and to achieve success in the face of adversity underscores the importance of resilience. It's not just about recovering from setbacks; it's about emerging stronger and more focused.

3. The power of relationships. The real currency in Network Marketing isn't the product you sell; it's the relationships you build. These connections become your lifeline, especially when transitioning between opportunities. They trust you, your judgment, and your recommendations, illustrating the profound impact of personal trust and loyalty.

4. Always be evolving. The closure of my initial company was a dramatic catalyst for change, but it also highlighted the importance of continuously seeking growth and development. By nurturing new relationships and constantly reevaluating your approach, you ensure that you're always moving forward, regardless of the challenges you face.

The transition from one company to another wasn't just about finding a new source of income; it was about reaffirming my identity as an entrepreneur. It reinforced the belief that while companies might quit, my vision, my determination, and my brand would carry me through.

So, to anyone facing the daunting prospect of a company "quitting" on them, remember: your journey doesn't end with the company. It continues with the strength of your character, the resilience of your spirit, and the depth of your connections. You are not defined by the company you represent but by the impact you make on those around you!

Don't Quit When Your Upline Quits

Just like life, Network Marketing is filled with unexpected turns and shifts in the tide. Among these, the departure of your upline—the person who sponsored you, and a person often seen as a beacon of guidance and support—can feel particularly destabilizing. Yet, it's in these moments that the essence of true leadership and self-reliance emerges.

When your upline decides to leave the company, it's not just a challenge; it's an opportunity to redefine the shape of your own leadership and courage. It's here, when you're standing alone, that you'll realize the value you bring to the table and the vision you have for your business. You'll be called to trust your inner strength and stand your ground, rather than being swayed by the actions of others.

Imagine this: You're six months into a new Network Marketing company, giving it your all, and reaching the highest rank in just under a month. You're excited, you've got tons of momentum, and you feel like you're on top of the world! Now—imagine that you wake up the next day and find out that six people in your upline have decided to quit, and they disappear almost instantly. *Six people!*

Well, friends, this actually happened to me. And when it did, the temptation was to drop the success I had built under their guidance, and fall back into beginner mode. Doubt and fear crept in, and my unanswered questions and massive amounts of uncertainty weighed heavy on my heart. Paranoia followed, filling my inner dialogue with unnerving thoughts like, *what do they know that I don't? Is this venture fundamentally flawed?* In these moments, my resolve and my belief in myself were being tested.

I had a decision to make—a choice between leaning in or retreating like so many others on the team. And instead of focusing on the fear, I chose to focus on my passion for the work, the people I'd met and bonded with, and the potential of what I was building. It was a conscious choice to move toward my dreams, my aspirations, and the unique vision I had for my business, independent of anyone else's trajectory.

This experience showed me a pivotal truth: Your dreams are uniquely yours. They cannot, and should not, be contingent on the presence or absence of any person, no matter their role in your journey. The departure of an upline, while initially disappointing and concerning, does not diminish the value of your dreams or the potential of your hard work. If they leave, that's *their* choice—it doesn't have to be yours.

In fact, the wide open spaces left by departing uplines became fertile ground for my new growth. It prompted me to reach out and make new connections, expanding my network and exposing me to perspectives and possibilities I hadn't seen before. Instead of being a setback, this upheaval ended up being a stepping stone, an invitation to evolve and adapt!

Sometimes, growth requires us to step out of the shadows and into the spotlight, to embrace our potential fully and lead from the front. In hindsight, what seemed like a loss was, in fact, one of the most empowering developments of my career. It taught me the importance of self-reliance, the value of personal leadership, and the irreplaceable strength found in fostering direct connections with my team and network.

So, to anyone facing the prospect of an upline departing: See it not as a sign to quit but as a call to action. Embrace the opportunity to define your leadership, to solidify your vision, and to reaffirm your commitment to your dreams. Your path is yours to shape, informed by your values, your goals, and the unique brand of leadership only you can bring to the world.

Don't Quit When Your Team Quits

You may have heard the statistics, but at the time of this writing, over 75% of Network Marketers are women. And as women, we often build relationships with our team members that transcend mere business transactions. Instead, they become friends, almost like a sister! This intertwining of professional and personal bonds is one of the unique aspects of this industry, but it also presents its own set of challenges, particularly when a team member decides to leave.

It's the nature of our business that, when someone joins our team, we invest not just time and effort but also a part of ourselves in their success. We see potential in them—we have more belief in them in the beginning than they do in themselves! So, when someone decides to leave, it's not just a professional loss; it feels deeply personal. It can lead to self-doubt, questioning our abilities as leaders, and internalizing their departure as a failure on our part.

This has happened to me multiple times in my career, and even though it's part of the business, it can hurt deeply. Once, an extremely close friend—I'm talking borderline family—who was integral to my team, chose to leave the business without much warning. Her departure hit me hard, because our families were deeply intertwined. I couldn't help but take it as a personal failure, wondering what I could have done differently to prevent her exit.

But the pain didn't stop there. In my defeated state, I became aware of the fact that she was openly speaking negatively about me and the products we once championed together. It was a harsh reality to face—I had lost a team member, a close friend, and maybe even part of my reputation because of the way my business and personal lives were woven together.

Through this experience, though, I learned some hard but valuable lessons:

1. Divergence of dreams. Your dreams and goals may not always align with those of your team members. Your belief in them does not necessarily equate to their belief in themselves or the business.

2. People are just people. Everyone has their own battles and external influences. Decisions to leave are often more about their journey and less about your leadership or the quality of your relationship.

3. Accepting change with grace. Not all relationships can withstand the changes in professional paths. While some friendships may endure, others may not, and that's okay. It's vital to accept these changes gracefully, recognizing that each person's path is their own.

4. Reflecting on your role. When someone leaves, it's an opportunity to reflect. Have you done all you could? If the answer is yes, then it's time to let go with grace, understanding that their departure is a part of their journey, not a reflection of your worth or abilities.

5. Embracing the future. Losses are inevitable, but they also open doors to new opportunities and relationships. Embracing the future with optimism is crucial. Your team's composition may change, but your vision and mission can remain steadfast.

It's essential to realize that in Network Marketing, as in life, people come and go. Their presence in your business, no matter how impactful, is not permanent. The true test of leadership is how you respond to these departures—do you wallow in your own self-doubt and feelings of rejection and loss, or do you forge ahead with renewed determination?

The departure of team members, even those closest to you, is not an endpoint. Just like when an upline quits, it's a juncture that tests your resilience, your ability to adapt, and your commitment to your own dreams. Embrace it as an opportunity to grow, to strengthen your leadership, and to continue on your path with courage and conviction. Don't allow anyone else to determine your dreams!

What To Do When You Want To Quit On Yourself

So far in this chapter, we've talked about what to do when *other people* quit on you, but we've saved the most complex topic for last: quitting on yourself. We all know that life and business will be challenging. Setbacks will be inevitable, people will leave, and circumstances will most certainly change. You can't control the situation, but you *can* control your reaction to the situation.

It's tempting to blame external events, the actions of others, or corporate decisions as the underlying factors when you want to quit. So I want to arm you with universal action steps to help you stay focused, resilient, and on track toward your goals, no matter the obstacles or negative self-talk you face.

1. Always remember your 'why'. Your 'why' is the anchor that keeps you grounded in the face of adversity. It's the reason you started on this journey, and it should be a constant reminder of your goals and aspirations. Make it a daily practice to reflect on why you are grateful and why you are doing this. Keep your 'why' visible and central in your life, so it continues to inspire and motivate you every day. There are times when you may need to redefine your 'why,' as it changes with time.

2. Remember who you are. Often, we get so caught up in our challenges that we forget our strengths and achievements. Take time to write down all your accomplishments, big and small. Reflect on your growth in various aspects of your life and career. Regularly reviewing this list will reinforce your self-worth and remind you of how far you've come. This practice is especially crucial for women in leadership, as it helps maintain confidence and perspective. Don't forget who you are!

3. Celebrate your wins. Celebrating your wins, no matter how big or small, is essential. It could be through a small gift to yourself, sharing the news with your family, or posting about it on social media. The act of celebrating not only boosts your morale but also reinforces your success mindset. It's equally important to celebrate the achievements of your team, fostering a culture of recognition and positivity.

4. Keep developing your grit. Grit is like a muscle that needs constant exercise. Surround yourself with people who uplift and inspire you. Engage in regular personal development activities to strengthen your resilience. Develop non-negotiable daily habits that contribute to your growth and push you out of your comfort zone. By consistently working on these habits, they become a natural part of your daily routine, seamlessly integrated into your life.

By implementing these strategies, you ensure that no matter what happens, no matter who quits or what changes, you remain steadfast in your pursuit of success and fulfillment. Remember, the path to success is not linear; it's a journey of learning, growing, and becoming unstoppable in the face of any challenge.

So, as we wrap up this chapter, I want to distill my message back down to its most basic call to action: *Never, ever quit.* Whether it's you contemplating quitting on yourself, or your company, upline, team, or even your family giving up, the resilience and strategies discussed here are your armor against these challenges. By embracing these principles, you not only become unstoppable in your business but also transform into a force of inspiration and strength!

Other people are going to do what they're going to do, and there's nothing you can do to stop them. Your job is to ensure that your daily actions and your mindset are intact. Wake up each day with a purpose, engage in personal development, and continuously work on habits that cultivate grit. Step out of your comfort zone as a rule, not an exception, and watch as you rise above the noise and drama that slow other people down.

I want you to realize that, as women, we hold the unique power to alter generational patterns—to set new standards and paths not just for ourselves, but for our children, grandchildren, and beyond. Embracing leadership roles in our businesses and lives allows us to be the change makers, the trailblazers who reshape the future for generations to come!

Imagine being remembered as the woman who changed the course of her family's history—a woman whose grit, determination, and unwavering spirit became the foundation of a new legacy. *This is the potential that lies within you!* By refusing to quit, by holding on to your dreams and aspirations, and by continually pursuing a life crafted by your design, you become a beacon of hope and strength.

The journey to success is peppered with challenges, but it's your relentless spirit and determination that will carve out a path of fulfillment and achievement. By being gritty and never stopping, you have the power to create a life you love, a life-by-design, not just for yourself but for those who look up to you. I believe in you, and I wish you the best as you go forward in strength, resilience, and unwavering determination. See you out there, ntwrkrs!

Watch Jennifer's Video Now!
LeadingLadiesCourse.com

Made in the USA
Columbia, SC
02 July 2024